BRECK

MY LIFE IN FOOTBALL

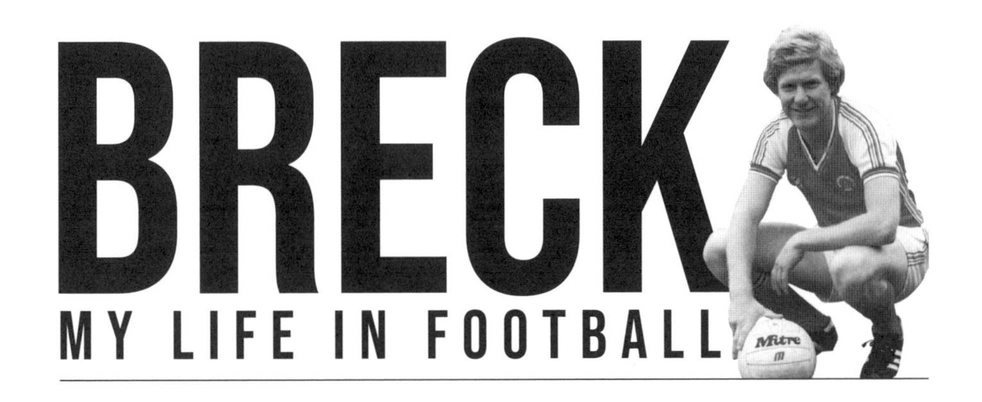

JOHN BRECKIN
WITH LES PAYNE

Best Wishes

VERTICAL
editions

First published in the United Kingdom in 2021 by Vertical Editions, Unit 41 Regency Court, Sheffield, S35 9ZQ

www.verticaleditions.com

Follow us on Twitter:
@VerticalEds
@JohnBreckin

ISBN 978-1-908847-23-2

A CIP catalogue record for this book is available from the British Library

Printed and bound by Jellyfish Print Solutions, Swanmore, Hants

For Mum
and Dad.

CONTENTS

FOREWORD

First impressions so often count and I can still recall the first time I met John Breckin. He was uber-friendly and I guess everybody who has met him for the first time, before or since, had a similar experience. It came about after Rotherham had seen me play, and score, against them for Wigan in a cup game a couple of weeks beforehand. The Wigan assistant manager called me to say Rotherham wanted to take a look at me and he advised me to go.

I didn't exactly jump at the chance. I didn't even know where Rotherham was and life was pretty calm at Wigan. I was in the squad and a bit comfy really, but maybe in football you should be a bit uncomfortable if you want to improve. To be honest I didn't want to go, but I knew it made sense because I knew I would be a better player if I did. I was a bit nervous really, but John's greeting really helped.

He was really honest and candid, humble and hard working – and all those friends and people I surround myself with have those attributes. I liked him straightaway. Ronnie Moore, the manager, was good, but a bit more aloof. Breck had a different role and just made me feel at home straightaway really. Over the years there are loads of great memories of Breck. He's the first person I've ever seen in professional football take a training session and do the demonstration, such as bounce on one leg. We had to copy him, a bit like Simon says but with a group of professional footballers. It always amazed me that he had the confidence to do it because it was just so cringeworthy. But the lads loved it – even though none of them would admit it. It's a bit like no one would admit to loving Wham! on the radio. You'd say you want to turn it off, but deep down you'd want to keep it on!

He has always had the ability to sense when you needed picking up, a really good human skill that he has even to this day. That's why I brought him back into the fold when taking over in 2016. I knew that John Breckin would be supportive of me. He has always made players feel good. You knew that he did it to every player, but I would walk into a room with, say, Alan Lee and Breck would pipe up: "Here they are, the two best players in the club." Alan knew he was one of the best, but I would always look behind me for someone else! Then, when we were just out of earshot, he'd say it to the next two who came in.

If you were down about your game or something else, he had this ability to know, to sense, and he'd come and have a chat to you on the team bus on the way home or the next time you walked on to the training pitch. Those are little things, but also the things that make him great and also the things that people don't see. They see managers run up and down the side of the pitch, throwing their arms in the air, or talking in a Press conference afterwards. But just like a marriage whereby behind every good man is a good woman, it is a bit like that with a really good assistant. And John was definitely that.

He is synonymous with Rotherham United. That's because he has the ethos of the club and all the attributes you associate with it – he's hard working, honest, friendly and he knows who he is. I just think that his qualities sum up our football club. He has been given the honour of Honorary Life President, and rightfully so – he is the heart and soul of this football club, to be honest. Players come and go, managers come and go – but people such as John Breckin are made of stone. I often joke, tongue in cheek, I should have a statue, but I sincerely think John should have one.

There is no greater time in my day than having time with him; chewing the fat, enjoying his company. He's a really good football bloke and, even if he's giving you bad news, he manages to put enough sugar on it so that you can swallow it, but still get an after-taste of the bad news. That is a real good skill to have. The human touch. No one likes receiving bad news and no one likes giving it, but it is the way it is delivered. I have leaned on John no end of times about how to deliver this or that. Whether he tells me the right thing or not, he fills me with confidence.

I am glad to involve him still. Perhaps we could say he's a consultant – although I'm not sure we've yet got round to the door with "John Breckin – consultancy" embossed on the glass. But he has certainly acted like one and, particularly in the first few months when I became manager, he was a rock for me. He was invaluable. Even now, after home games when he's done his bit up in the lounge, he'll normally pop and see me and have a drink in my office. He knows what it's like and he'll often say: "Don't beat yourself up on that; it's not your fault they got a penalty in the last minute" and find words of encouragement and reason.

When I first did the job, he was kind and wise enough to make me breathe before I did a Press conference. You never want to criticise players publicly, but, if you've lost and you're really low and still emotional after you've spoken to the players and walk straight to the Press room, you need that pause. It was such a good learning curve for me at that time and even to this day I remember John's advice and have a couple of minutes to myself. As he pointed out, the owner is listening, players may be listening and fans will be listening. He has stopped me from saying something that I might regret.

If I have a squad of 22, then it means 11 aren't going to like me on a match day. But John puts it in context really. He'll ask why I picked this team and why I did this or that. I explain and he'll say: "Yeah, I can see that." By the time the conversation has ended I'll know I've done it for the right reasons and have confidence in the decisions. He listens to me ranting on, listens to my reasons with another good skill he has – listening. People want to be giving you advice and ram it down your throat.

It's a lonely place being a football manager without a shadow of a doubt and John is well aware of that. After a defeat I have to try to keep upbeat; for the staff, for the players, for the chairman, for the fans. When everyone leaves the office, you are on your own. Who picks you up? Having good people at a football club is essential and invaluable. John Breckin most definitely fits into those categories.

I wish him all the best with his book and hope it proves a success. In view of all his many stories and anecdotes I'm sure it will be a great read for the fans. Did you ever hear the one about his wonder goal against Exeter? What was it ... 35 yards? Because there's no TV footage – it might even have been before colour television – we'll all have to take his word for it...!

- Paul Warne, Rotherham, 2021

PROLOGUE

It was bedlam. Pure bedlam. As fans ran on to the pitch and then back off again, the referee bent over the ball just outside our penalty area at the Tivoli End, having given us a free kick. I stood next to him to ask if we'd finished and he just said: "When I pick this ball up, run like hell for the tunnel." He picked it up and I just sprinted towards the other end, hoping I'd get through in one piece and wouldn't be mobbed as hundreds of Millers fans, realising it was all over, surged on to Millmoor's hallowed turf.

Some players didn't make it. The King – aka Ronnie Moore – was hoisted on to fans' shoulders as they chaired him off. The fans stripped him for souvenirs and took everything; his shirt, shorts, socks and even shinpads. I remember him coming down the tunnel in a ripped T-shirt and his jock strap. At least they'd not taken that! I managed to emerge unscathed, but the fans were coming from all sides, so you had to run the gauntlet anyway.

They simply wanted to share the great moment with their heroes. What better feeling for them and, if I'm honest, for us Rotherham United players, too? By the time we'd got up to the directors' box to survey the scene there were hundreds – nay, thousands – of jubilant fans on the pitch, dancing, singing and hugging each other. It was quite a sight as they stood packed together, scarves stretched over their heads, bellowing out football's anthem: *You'll Never Walk Alone.*

That moment, with so many happy faces, captured what success means to football fans and particularly when their team, their club, win a league title. Rotherham United – my beloved Rotherham United – had just clinched the old Division Three championship crown on an unforgettable, sunny afternoon in May 1981. Promotion to what we now call the Championship had been clinched four games earlier with a 1-0 win at Carlisle and we had gone into this final game against Plymouth Argyle, knowing that a point would be enough to make us champions, regardless of what our only rivals Barnsley did.

But we wanted to sign off in style and finish with a win in our final match in front of our own supporters. Ten minutes from time that's what we got, courtesy of a goal all Millers fans in the 11,500 crowd that day will always remember, scored by that finisher supreme Rod Fern for the 2-1 win. I shouldn't imagine too many remember who played the ball through for him, helped by a deflection off an opponent. They're tagged as an "assist" these days. But there might just be those who relive it on YouTube and who might note it was a certain blond-haired left back! As a Rotherham lad through and through, as a supporter from the age of five who not only dreamt of it, but forever had lived for the day when I might wear the famous red shirt with white sleeves, it was an unforgettable day. And an emotional one, too.

Yes, I'd proudly been in the promotion team of six years earlier under Jim McGuigan, but actually to finish as champions was very special indeed, coming as it did exactly 30 years after the club's first ever title in the 1950/51 season. But it wasn't just because I had become a title winner that I sat and reflected, amid the boozy haze of a great night of celebrations, on how life really had never been better. I had just come to the end of what had been, and remains, the greatest 12 months of my football life.

It had all begun with happiness off the field the previous spring in 1980 when I married my first wife Elaine. We were extremely happy – and have always remained very good friends even though we eventually split up – as young newlyweds are when they set off on their own "honeymoon" period of the first months of wedded bliss. On the field I was to become a part of what I regard as the best team I ever played in. But it wasn't just that we had some very good players in that 1980/81 promotion side or that we were superbly led and organised by an excellent young manager in Ian Porterfield.

It was that we all just gelled and got on so well with each other as people. We were all friends; no cliques, no outsiders and everybody pulling in the same direction and supporting each other. I so much looked forward to going to work that I used to get in an hour early before training because it was so enjoyable being with my teammates – what with the banter and the humour and the fact we all really liked each other, all so enjoyed each other's company.

We were mates and, yes, really were like a family. When there was a night out arranged or a function to attend, everybody who was able to go, supported it and went. Training was great, we had characters, there was humour and, to top it all, success on the pitch, which is what it's all about. It was unbelievable.

In that 12 months I was also fortunate enough to meet the bloke who was to become my best mate in football. Ronnie Moore and me hit it off from the moment we first met when he arrived just before the start of that same 1980/81 season and it developed into an amazing friendship that lasts to this day. Perhaps we should have had a drink last summer, 2020, to celebrate our 40th anniversary! We're more like brothers and we have enjoyed some wonderful times together. Those great memories will last us until we head off to that great football pitch in the sky.

Of course, the promotion success meant I couldn't have been happier and there was even a nice twist to that as well. As club captain – Jimmy Mullen was the on-field skipper – I did a lot of things around the town and in the community; going to functions, making presentations, etc. I was asked if I could pop across the road just before the first game of the season at home to Fulham and officially open Ladbrokes' new betting shop opposite Millmoor. Well, the timetable was too tight so I asked one of the players not involved that day, Ken Tiler, if he'd do the honours instead. So Ken went across and, because I'd been offered a free £25 bet, he could pop it on anything. He noted the tasty odds of 66-1 for us to win the division – yes, we were big outsiders – so stuck it on us for the title.

He came back to the dressing room with the betting slip and gave it to me. I said to all the lads that, if it came up, I was going to divide it up among all the squad. I put the betting slip in a drawer at home and forgot all about it. I never looked at it again until just before the Plymouth game. Anyway we ended up with more than £1,650 to come back which, in 1981 terms, was worth quite a bit more than it might seem today. It meant about £80 each for the squad, even if they played only once or a handful of times as some did, which was roughly half the weekly wage for some of us – for context, a pint of beer back then was only about 50p!

On the playing front there was the satisfaction of being an ever-present, playing all 46 league games plus the four cup ties that season, with the honour of being selected in the PFA Division Three Team of the Year at left back – my third such accolade to follow on selection by my fellow professionals in season 1974/75 and 1978/79. Must have been those overlapping, attacking runs which kept taking the eye!

There was one more reason for reckoning it was the greatest 12 months in my life in football. I had been granted a testimonial by the club in recognition of 10 years' service and my game against Bolton Wanderers was to be at Millmoor, two days after we'd won the title on the Monday night. It was perfect timing. The Football League came to present the Division Three championship trophy and more than 6,000 loyal fans turned up to see that historic moment and to show their support for me, for which I was really grateful.

Overall there were so, so many happy memories from that year and I just hope I carried out a favourite saying of mine which was passed on to me – and one which I urge all football fans to follow whenever they or their team have success. Because there are many more downs in football than ups, when those rarer successes do come along I say this ... Make sure you smell the flowers as you pass them by!

1

THE OPENING MINUTES OF THE GAME OF MY LIFE

I may as well start with a surprise. Many an article I've seen describes me as "Rotherham-born John Breckin." Here's the surprise. That was wrong! I was born – whisper it – in Sheffield! Here's why. Jim Breckin, from Rotherham, and Vera Hague, from Sheffield, were newlyweds in the late 1940s in a post-war Britain still awash with austerity and rationing. Despite Jim doing everything to find a house in Rotherham, their search for a place to rent ended at Janson Street, Attercliffe – more or less opposite where Sheffield Arena stands nowadays.

They soon had their first child, Brian, and I've to thank him for my name. Young Brian, only four, suggested the new baby be called John. My mum hadn't decided on a name because she was hoping for a girl! So, that was me, John Breckin, born July 27th, 1953, in Attercliffe, Sheffield. But my stay in the terraced house on Janson Street was short-lived. I was just two when I toddled down that cobbled street for the last time and got whisked off to start my life in Rotherham – my home town really. Here's how it happened.

My dad was born at 7 Clough Road at Masbrough. One of 10, he was only three when his dad died, leaving his mum to bring up nine children alone – one daughter died very young – in a two-bedroomed terraced house. How she possibly managed it, I don't know. When his mum died suddenly, my dad – within hours – went to see the landlord to secure the Clough Road property in his name. That might sound mercenary, but rented properties were in high demand and Jim knew he'd have to move fast if he was to leave Attercliffe for a place back in his home town. He got it. Like many houses then, it didn't even have the basics. No hot water, no bathroom, no central heating – just a coal fire – and an outside toilet in the backyard. You had to be desperate to go in the winter!

Friday night was bath night – in a tin one in front of a roaring fire. Not joking. Perfectly true. It was fetched from the coal shed, where it hung on a nail. It was rinsed out and Dad went first, then Mum, then Brian, then me. Both of us were shouted in if playing outside, as we usually were. Me and Brian shared a bedroom and one of my earliest memories is the two of us scraping ice from inside the window in winter so we could see out. How Grandma Breckin brought up four brothers and five sisters in that little home is amazing. There were others like her and medals have been handed out for less.

But for Jim the move was worth it. My dad was back in Rotherham and my destiny was pointed in a different direction. What I couldn't possibly know then was that my first connection with Rotherham United was closer than I could have imagined. I got packed off to Thornhill Junior and Infants' School, very close by Clough Road, and, when I switched schools five years later, it was just up the road to Park Street School.

Of course, Park Street didn't just have a school. It had a football ground – the Red House Ground, named after the Red House Inn on the corner. In 1882 it was the original home of Thornhill United, the football club formed five years earlier who were to change their name to Rotherham County in 1905 and therefore is the unbreakable link with the Rotherham United of today. The 1925 merger of County with Rotherham Town to become United was with the "second" Rotherham Town club after the first one went defunct.

I actually played on that Park Street ground of the original Rotherham United club for both Thornhill School and Park Street School – although it was the "illegality" of doing so at other times that I remember most. Me, my brother Brian and our mates would climb the wall to go and play on the pitch, but then if we saw the caretaker – Old Man Taylor we called him – we'd scarper. Then we'd watch and, when the coast was clear, climb back over the wall. If you drive round the roundabout next to Aldi at Masbrough – and the supermarket is actually on Park Street – then you more or less know where the pitch was. It may have been the sloping old Red House Ground, but it was Wembley to me as a kid. Little did I know that that football pitch would be my first link with the club that was to shape my life.

***

We all probably have at least one teacher we remember more fondly than the rest. For me he was a great guy called Alan Archer. His influence on me at Wingfield School would prove to be life changing. In fact, life had started to change anyway. I was 10 when we had to leave Clough Road, just three houses up from the now-demolished Butcher's Arms on the corner. Between us and the pub were two of my dad's sisters, my Auntie Mona at No. 3 and my Auntie Hilda at No. 5. As with some other houses Rotherham Borough Council made a detailed inspection of ours at No. 7, condemned it as unfit to live in and we moved to the new council house development that had sprung up at Wingfield and Kimberworth Park in the early 1960s.

It was only about three miles away, but was a different world. It was a modern, three-bedroomed house and meant the sort of home comforts we have all long taken for granted – hot water, inside toilet, a bathroom, a gas fire and even a garden, which meant I could practise my keepy-uppys on grass! There was still no central heating at that time, but what luxuries indeed after those days of scraping ice off the inside of my bedroom window and bath nights in a tub in front of the fire. We were part of an entirely new community, including new schools, and it was all very exciting.

I still travelled back to Park Street School for another few months before moving up to the "big school," the new Wingfield Comprehensive. My school football really started at Wingfield and at the start of my second year Alan Archer had a big effect on my young life. His first job was at Park Street School and, like the rest of us, he had moved to Wingfield, initially as a maths teacher. But he taught PE, too, and the whole attitude to sport at the school changed dramatically when Alan took charge at the start of my second year. After a year when no one seemed particularly interested in organising school football, Alan was like a breath of fresh air. Suddenly we had a teacher who was interested, enthusiastic and committed. It was just what the football-mad John Breckin needed. In fact, it was all football for me. I had no real interest in the academic side of things. I liked art, metalwork, and woodwork. But as for the rest? I got by, we shall say.

By the time I was 13 Alan Archer had got me involved and interested in most sports – football, cricket, swimming and basketball. Here was a proper sports teacher who clearly loved his job and it rubbed off on me. It all spurred me on and it was about this time, at 13, that I was convinced I was going to be a footballer. I know all kids have that dream, but I just *knew* that I would be – and badly wanted my dream to come true.

As well as playing for the school team – and often for the age group above – I started to play for Rotherham Boys, the town's under-15 representative schools' side. I also got selected for Yorkshire Boys. One midweek evening I had played for Yorkshire Boys at Hartlepool, which meant arriving back late and getting to bed after midnight. So I was given permission to be at school mid-morning the next day. I got my attendance mark, but then Alan Archer sent me straight back home to get some rest and said that I should be back when school finished – because he needed me to play basketball for the school at Dinnington that evening.

At the time I didn't realise it, but it was brilliant "man management" and also he was ensuring that after a tough game, a long journey and a very late night, I would be in the best condition to play and represent the school again the next day. I look back now and realise what an influence he had on the very young me. He spent hours nurturing and developing the school football teams and it was nothing short of a revelation. He was someone who cared about sport – as well as, it must be said, the academic bedrock of English and maths – but he also prompted my interest in other sports and I remain grateful for that, too. As an under-12s' player I was doing okay, but, with Alan's added support and encouragement, I started to develop both as an individual and as a team player.

Looking back, I realise Alan had not only spotted my potential, but also did something about it, including often playing me a year above my age group. I often wonder how things might have turned out otherwise. He was also a huge Millers fan and I remember one day after school in 1968 he put me and a couple of other football-mad lads in his Vauxhall Viva and drove us to Leicester for Rotherham's FA Cup fifth round replay one Wednesday night. I remember standing crammed together in a packed, swaying crowd that felt both exhilarating and dangerous. Then getting dropped off at home in the dark about midnight. It couldn't happen today, could it? But that was an indication of the keenness and enthusiasm he had.

In later years he became a great friend and I was saddened by his death in 2009 at the relatively young age of 65. I saw him in Rotherham Hospice not long before he died and gave him a big hug. I was told that, one night when he was asleep, he had been unknowingly calling out "Breck, Breck" and I am sure I'm not the only student who remembers Alan Archer fondly.

***

As you might expect, Alan wasn't the only influential figure on my burgeoning schoolboy career. Other mentors kept appearing, too, including Ken Knowles – a no-nonsense giant of a man and school headmaster who helped to oversee Rotherham Boys as their chairman – and another PE teacher many will remember with fondness, Bob Earnshaw, of Kimberworth School. Ken was a big character, passionate about his role in schoolboy football and even did his own scouting. If you played for Rotherham Boys and showed real promise, then you can be sure Rotherham United would know about you and, if you were to progress, then it was highly likely you would end up signing for the club.

My first Millmoor experience came with that Rotherham Boys squad, drawn from schools across the district, because we would meet and train at the big, new, state-of-the-art gym at the ground. It had been funded by the big money sales of two of Rotherham United's young stars of the mid-1960s – notably Ken Houghton and Ian Butler who had joined Hull City for a combined total of £90,000. It was a massive sum at the start of 1965 and equivalent to millions of pounds today.

Bob Earnshaw was our coach and his will be a name familiar to older supporters as a flying winger for Barnsley in the late 1960s and early 1970s. He played as a part-time professional because of his job as PE teacher at Kimberworth School, a situation pretty common many years ago, but which couldn't continue as football progressed and everyone became full time professionals. Bob took me under his wing and was a great help and influence in those formative years. He even came round to my house one Sunday morning to tell me I had been picked for Yorkshire Boys, the county's schools' representative under-15 side. Although he was a Barnsley player, Bob never tried to persuade me to join the Reds.

But he did get me to play for a school other than Wingfield! Just the once, but a memorable one it was. I had been to play in Belgium with Wingfield School at Easter and Bob got in touch and asked if I fancied going to play in Germany with Kimberworth School on a summer trip there. My parents had stumped up for the Easter one so I wasn't sure if they'd be able to afford for me to go on another so soon afterwards.

When I told them about the Germany one, my mum and dad didn't hesitate despite the extra cost they could never have bargained for. "Yeah," they said. "You can go on it." So a short time later they walked with me to Kimberworth School to meet Bob's party for another footballing trip to Europe. When you think about it now, I was a "ringer" on that trip! I didn't know the term at the time and wasn't bothered anyway. For me it was just a chance to play more football.

2

A SURPRISE VISITOR AND THE DREAM IS COMING TRUE

The journey to Rotherham United began with my dad planting a seed inside the mind of the five-year-old John Breckin. He was a big Millers fan and it was inevitable I'd be taken to Millmoor one day. I can remember the first time he did so. Vividly. The pattern of that day would become a familiar match day routine. My first inkling it was match day would be the stream of cars coming on to our street at Clough Road to park, including outside our house. It wasn't far to Millmoor and we'd walk across the bridge over the railway line, past Masbrough railway station; I was wearing the red and white scarf my mum had knitted.

Our Brian had a big wooden rattle as many kids had back then. You held the handle and swung it round to make a massive clicking sound. If he left it, then I'd pick it up and take it. I was always happy when he left it. They went out of fashion a long time ago; they'd be viewed as weapons by police and stewards today and you would never get into a ground with one now! I recall my dad sneaking an even more potent potential weapon into the ground, though. On cold days he'd wear his big coat which conveniently included a large poacher's pocket. Opposite Masbrough station we would detour through an alleyway between the Pentecostal church and the Tivoli cinema, which always had a lot of loose bricks for whatever reason.

My dad would put a brick, or most of one, in his poacher's pocket before we queued at the turnstile, he paid and then lifted me over for free. It was a sort of unwritten rule, it seemed, for those aged five and under. We stood on the wooden railway sleepers that made up the terracing on the Millmoor Lane side of the ground – they weren't replaced with concrete until 1960 – and this is where the brick came in handy. As with most kids, I preferred to stand at the perimeter wall to get a close up view of the action. But there was a problem – I was too small to see over the wall. The solution was to stand on Dad's brick!

But those early memories of being pitchside also included something else other than football. Teenagers were employed to patrol the pitch perimeter, wearing a white coat and carrying a tray secured by a strap round their neck. The pull for me was in the contents of those trays, filled with a tempting selection of sweets and chocolate bars. No matter what was happening on the pitch, my mind would move on to chocolate when those lads came walking slowly round.

***

It was actually a very serious accident to my dad at work that sort of helped to push me – even at the age of only seven – towards wanting to be a footballer. And most definitely not wanting to work in the steelworks. Dad had been a steelworker all his life, working at Steel, Peech and Tozer, which stood on the site where Magna is now at Templeborough and later became British Steel Corporation. He was a fettler, working in the soakers' section, an area around the blast furnaces and a hot, dirty and dangerous environment.

The blast furnaces, huge things, produced industrial metals by smelting, i.e. heating, metal to a very high temperature to ensure the correct composition before the metal was sent to the rolling mill and shaped into bars to become the finished product. This unbelievably hot metal would be "soaked" close to the base of the furnace so as to get the correct temperature for rolling. In such extreme conditions accidents were pretty common. Most were minor or not too serious, but in 1960 there was an incident which was to have a massive effect on the Breckin family.

My dad worked with Tommy Bullass and they were great mates. They would go out and have a drink together. Their job included getting rid of the spilled slag from beneath and around the furnace and they would share the load – one of them would drive the dumper truck one day while the other shovelled and the next day they would swap roles. I can still remember what I was doing when the knock came at the door one night. We were watching *Take Your Pick* with Michael Miles – remember him, *your quiz inquisitor?* My mum went to the door, two officials from the steelworks were there and she suddenly burst into tears.

There had been an explosion in the soakers at Steel, Peech and Tozer – in fact, the huge noise from the explosion a couple of miles away had been clearly heard on Clough Road. Dad was badly burned, but alive. Sadly, Tommy was killed. Tommy had been driving the dumper truck and had no chance when it toppled over on an unsafe part of the floor. My dad had started to run for it, but was sent flying by the blast. Of course, had it been his day to drive the dumper truck ...

For the next six months Mum had to look after me and Brian, then 11, on her own and I remember all three of us making countless journeys to hospital to visit Dad. He went through the slow, painful process of skin grafts and was lucky to be alive. The memory of that accident actually galvanised my desire to become a footballer. Obviously at seven years of age I had no idea if I would be any good and I wasn't showing any particular potential then, but it made me want to go for something I wanted to do – and certainly not to Steelos!

***

People ask if I can remember when I first kicked a ball. No, I can't. But I know when and where it was – if that doesn't sound too contradictory! When me and Brian were little, a trip out in the summer would involve walking up to Clifton Park with Mum and Dad, egg sandwiches on the grass and plenty of room up there to play, run about and things for kids to do. My dad remembered the moment very well indeed. I was three years old. It was the first time he had rolled a ball towards me and I kicked it back with my left foot. He rolled it again and I still kicked it left-footed. Just to make sure, he rolled the next one towards my right foot, but I moved round it so I could kick with my left.

"Eyup, Vera," he said to my mum. "We've got a left clogger in the family. Watch this." Again the left foot was used after he rolled another one to me. Next day, apparently, he couldn't wait to get me in the back yard with a ball. Where that left-footedness comes from further back down the line I don't know unfortunately. Neither Mum nor Dad were left-footed and our Brian isn't either. My uncle Eddie – my dad's brother – was a footballer and had one game for Rotherham County in 1922, but that was at right half, so we can assume he wasn't a natural left-footer.

So, unfortunately I don't know who handed down that particular gene. But I'm always grateful. It's a good job that school didn't take the same approach with my left-footed skills as they did with my writing abilities. I was left-handed, but made to switch and learn to write with my right hand, a fairly common trait at some schools in the late 1950s.

I realised my own playing skills were starting to develop when I was eight and at that time I would go with my brother and his pals on to the fields. They reluctantly let me take part in their game although I was a lot younger – by at least three or four years and therefore much smaller, too. I was always the last to be picked after the two "captains" had had their alternate pick of the lads – best always first, leaving the worst, fattest, smallest or weakest until the end. I didn't look as pathetic as Billy Casper in *Kes*, but I regularly knew how he must have felt! But those experiences helped and, as I grew stronger and taller in the ensuing years, things changed. I found not only did I enjoy playing against the older lads but also competed comfortably with them. Although I also remember taking lots of kicks, too! I'm sure it all helped when I got to Wingfield Comp and was regularly drafted into the teams a year, or even two, above me.

Soon after I first got into the Rotherham Boys' side, the under-15s, we played a friendly at Wickersley School and I had the job of marking a lad called Dennis Fairhurst. He was a big lad, a hard player and had the reputation of being a bit of a nutcase. But I stood my ground and had a good game against him. I had no idea that Fred Green, the assistant manager at Rotherham United, was watching on. Later that week he got in touch with my parents and invited me to Millmoor to have a look around. In hindsight it was a very subtle move, inviting a football-obsessed schoolboy for a personal, behind-the-scenes view of his local professional club. Just think what that was like for a mad-keen Millers fan – I felt like a kid in a sweet shop who'd just been given his pocket money.

A week later I made my way home from Wingfield School. It wasn't unusual for me to get home via the back garden because it was a short cut. What was unusual was that my dad was in the garden to meet me. Now if I had returned home the conventional way – by the front – then I might have been curious as to why a Rover 2000 was parked right outside my house. Not too many people in Wingfield had cars then and certainly not a Rover 2000.

I walked in from the back garden with my dad, who clearly had something on his mind, and, as we got to the kitchen door, he said: "If you were to become a professional footballer, who would you want to play for?" It took me by surprise, but I didn't hesitate with my reply: "Rotherham United." "Well," he said, "you'd better come in here then," and took me in the front room. Sitting there was Jack Mansell, the manager of Rotherham United, talking to my mum.

A highly-respected coach, Jack had taken the Rotherham job after coaching in Holland and during his brief few years with the Millers was responsible for some of the most attractive and entertaining football ever produced by any side in the club's history. I had enjoyed that Mansell style of football because I began seriously watching the Millers in the mid-1960s – Jack became manager in August 1965 – with players such as Barry Lyons, Ken Houghton, Ian Butler, Frank Casper, Brian Tiler, Chris Rabjohn, Colin Clish and a couple who were genuine heroes – Peter Madden, a giant of a centre half and my personal favourite, and speedy, goalscoring striker Albert Bennett, who left to join Newcastle United just before Mansell arrived.

Now here in my front room was the same Jack Mansell, visiting the parents of a promising youngster who was only 12 at the time. No wonder I was a bit overawed. He spent a couple of hours with us, chatting about all the footballing possibilities. He had been very professional in his approach as well, asking Wingfield School for permission to speak to me, and the afternoon culminated in me signing the blue associate schoolboy forms that initially tied you to a particular club. Taking that first step towards becoming a professional footballer should have been top billing for me, of course, but a part of the deal that appealed to me most was the players' pass I'd get. This would enable me to watch all Rotherham United's home games for free. *Wow.* I certainly was in the sweet shop now and didn't even need any money!

3

THE SWEET TALK SWUNG IT

So I was on my way. The precious blue form had my signature. I was going to play for Rotherham United one day. The club I supported. Well, when I went to bed that night and couldn't sleep, that's what I was thinking. But it might have been different. Scouts from other clubs were making noises with invites to go to Sheffield United and Sheffield Wednesday, while there was great interest from West Bromwich Albion where a very fine young player from Maltby, Chris Baker, had been taken on. But one thing above all else stopped me from going elsewhere and ensured I stayed in my home town.

It was the persuasive tongue and the calculated reasoning of Jack Mansell when he came to my house to ensure I signed. In his pitch the Millers manager talked about the club and the local lads getting a chance to play in the first team if they worked hard. He was more or less impressing all this on me and my dad. Then he turned towards my mum and looked her straight in the eye – me and my dad may as well not have been there!

"I know that he's got other clubs looking at him, Mrs Breckin, and there's even one from Birmingham showing an interest," he said. "But you don't want your son – when he's only 15 – living away from home in a big city or town. As a mum, you want to know about his wellbeing; that he's getting good food at the right time, that he's in bed early and in his own bed here at home, so giving him the best chance to become a footballer."

The words had the desired effect. They hit home instantly. My mum reacted the moment Mr Mansell stopped talking. "Get those forms signed, John," she said. I've never forgotten that moment; nor did I forget the manager's method and his words. I often used the same persuasive words many years later when I was a youth coach and trying to convince the parents of youngsters that their son should join Rotherham United. Dad and I had discussed other clubs, as you would. Wednesday, a big club, were in the top flight at the time. I asked him about the invitation to go and look round there and I almost laugh out loud to this day when I recall his answer. "I don't know really," he said. "It's three buses."

Believe me, that was a big consideration in the 1960s. It would have been a bus to Rotherham, the 69 to Sheffield city centre then a bus out to Hillsborough. Incidentally Jack Mansell wasn't just smart with my mother. He acted smartly all round. Boys could sign only a "blue" form committing you to a club when they had turned 13. Mr Mansell was at my house when I was still only 12; a couple of weeks before my 13th birthday, in fact. He knew what a clamour there would be from clubs when a promising boy got to his 13th birthday. There were stories of scouts camped outside the house of the most talented boys just waiting for a youngster to come home from school on his 13th birthday.

But the Millers manager wasn't taking any chances. He was in first and had the simplest and most obvious way around the fact that the blond-haired kid from Wingfield couldn't actually sign a "blue" form because he was only 12. "Sign it," he said, "but don't date it today. Instead put down July 27th." That was my 13th birthday! In my mind I was going to be a footballer and play for Rotherham United.

Yes, I still had two more years to do at Wingfield School and I enjoyed it there. But my involvement in and obsession with football in particular – and love of sport in general – may have held me back and I didn't excel academically. It wasn't a lack of intelligence, just that I had other things on my mind. I certainly had no interest in continuing my education and can still remember the excitement of receiving the official letter from Rotherham, asking me to report for training on July 22nd, 1968.

When I left Wingfield School it was eight days before my 15th birthday. So three days after leaving, I was off on the bus with my dad and heading to Millmoor to start my first job, still only 14, by signing a three-year contract as an apprentice professional. The manager who greeted me and watched me sign those forms was Tommy Docherty, a really big name in the game who had stunned football when he turned up at Rotherham eight months earlier after leaving Chelsea. Can you imagine if Jose Mourinho had done the same when he was there? This was the 1960s' equivalent!

Tommy was a big character. In fact, one newspaper report at the time described him as "by far the most controversial figure in British football who'd had several brushes with authority." He had inspired a young Chelsea side to finish second in the top flight and the previous season had led them to Wembley, where they lost the 1967 FA Cup final to Spurs.

He'd had a fall-out at Chelsea and no one in football could believe it when he abandoned the bright lights of London and arrived in much dimmer Rotherham in November 1967 to try to rescue a side struggling badly in Division Two. While eager to do so, actually going to Millmoor and signing for my home-town club was daunting enough without doing so in front of such a big character in the game at that time. In his long career he was never anything less than that. That signing got me my first mention in the *Rotherham Advertiser* as a Millers player. It came out on Saturdays back then and my name was in the edition of Saturday, July 27th, 1968 – a nice surprise on my 15th birthday!

Noting that Herringthorpe was the new training base, the article added: "Before training commenced, the Doc was busy completing the signing of full back John Breckin, the Wingfield schoolboy who last season played for Rotherham and District Boys." It went on: "John, who also played for Yorkshire Boys, agreed to come to Millmoor some time ago, but had to wait until he left school before joining the ground staff as an apprentice professional."

That first mention was cut out by my mum and put in a scrapbook. She appears to have saved every mention I ever got! However, when a photo of the entire squad, including all the apprentices, appeared in a future edition of *The Advertiser,* missing from it was one person. John Breckin. We had booked a week's holiday for the family in Blackpool. My dad mentioned this to Tommy Docherty: "Go and get off and enjoy your holiday," he said, "and we'll see him next week."

I wasn't the only apprentice to start that summer, but some first-year newcomers were already there having left school at Easter, as you could do back then. Among them were three players with whom I was to enjoy many years of fun, companionship and, yes, success. They were goalkeeper Jim "Seamus" McDonagh, Mick Leng, who played midfield or in defence, and Trevor Phillips, who came from Barnsley and was a striker with a frightening turn of pace. I never did find out who was responsible – perhaps they all were – for my "initiation ceremony." All new apprentices would have to go through it at some point – it was part of arriving at a club – although you couldn't actually do it now in the 21st century. I was jumped on by the rest, who stripped me and covered me with black boot polish – including in all the sensitive areas that you'd normally keep covered up. Welcome to Millmoor, Breck!

Of course, we weren't just there for the football and to learn the game. Oh, no. Clubs had other uses for us eager young kids and there were plenty of jobs to be done around the ground, particularly during the close season in the summer. Painting turnstiles and the crush barriers on the terraces plus a job to really look forward to – coating the men's and women's urinals with black bitumen! For the clubs their young apprentices were a way of keeping down the maintenance cost. Like many old grounds back then, Millmoor needed sprucing up ready for the new season and, if it didn't move, you painted it or tidied it up.

I well recall that when the season started, me and Trev Phillips helped groundsman Albert "Sheeny" Wilson when he was preparing the pitch for a match day. No fancy white-line machine either. Me and Trev were on our hands and knees with a brush, painting whitewash on the touchlines. Not quite what I'd envisaged as a dreamy schoolboy, but that's how it was.

Another Friday job was putting toilet rolls in the toilets. Only one in the away end because fans would throw them towards the pitch and they'd get tangled in the goal nets. On Monday, after a home game, it was the apprentices' job to clear all the rubbish from the terraces but if it was windy and had blown all over, we might have to finish next day. Then we'd wheel it all to an incinerator down Millmoor Lane.

Only after we'd got it all sorted would we train with "Sheeny" – a former Millers player after the war. That was an extra job for him because we actually didn't have a youth coach on a day-to-day basis. But it was just one of the roles Albert did in his time because he'd been the trainer, running on with his magic sponge in an old caseball bladder to "treat" an injured player. Trainers are now called the physios, and they're fully qualified. Albert was not!

Really, apprentices were like cheap labour. But everybody had to muck in and I'm sure it helped to forge a bond with your fellow apprentices. We had some enjoyable times. It amounted to lots of hard work during that three-year apprenticeship, but it was an unbelievable experience and a learning one, too. And it made you appreciate the amount of clearing up and the work associated around a football match at your ground.

Not only that, you cleaned the boots of the senior players as well. I well remember being Neil Warnock's boot boy the following year after he'd arrived at the club. And just think, we thought we were there to learn the arts of the game, to practise our skills. Yes, other things did intervene on those vital aspects!

Of course, it was all about when I would pull on that coveted Rotherham United shirt for the first time – No.3, of course: what else? – and I did so at Millmoor against Barnsley in the Northern Intermediate League for the under-19s on the Saturday afternoon that the 1968/69 season opened. It ended 1-1 but just a few weeks later when I proudly made my debut for the reserves, it was a winning start. It was against Chesterfield at Saltergate and we won 4-2 in the North Midlands League Cup. I was just 15 and my direct opponent on the Spireites' right wing that night was Neil Warnock! Also in the Millers side were Roy Tunks in goal, Chris Hudson in central defence and Trev Womble up front. I was to play first team football many times with all three.

My mum would have stuck that in the scrapbook, too, but I'm not sure she'd have done the same after my first Millmoor game for the reserves a week after that Chesterfield one. We played Barnsley reserves and the report in *The Advertiser* was written by Martyn Sharpe – later to be a top news reporter with *The Sun* – who is still a Millers season-ticket holder and sits only a few seats away from the Press area in the New York Stadium. Barnsley got a late winner and Martyn wrote: "Defensive covering was weak, at times virtually non-existent, particularly on the flanks where full backs Peter Atkinson and John Breckin had a night to forget." That would have been a painful read for a 15-year-old.

A further example of how tough professional football was going to be was brought home to me not long afterwards when – still aged only

15 and a few weeks, remember – I played for the reserves at Doncaster Rovers. It was also my first example of how a manager can "lift" a young player. I'd had little contact with Tommy Docherty in my opening few weeks at the club, which was understandable. But he was there when I ran out at Belle Vue for the reserves in a night match very early that first season. I had the job of marking Brian Usher, a flying winger and quite a "speed merchant," as we call them, and obviously out to make an impression because he'd just signed from Sheffield Wednesday and had been playing in the top flight.

The first time I easily caught up with him. Trouble was, he was already on his way back from delivering the cross having skinned me. It was a harsh lesson because he murdered me, as we say. I ran as fast as I could, but could barely get close enough to him to say: "Hello," let alone get a challenge in. I was dreading the team talk in the dressing room at half-time. And so I did what all good professionals would do at that point ... sat on the bench, kept my head down, fiddled with my boots and my socks. Anything but look up. When I did look up, Tommy Docherty was standing there and looking me straight in the eye. My stomach tensed and my heart started racing. I was certain what would be coming my way!

"Hey, you," said the Doc. "Well done, son. Don't you worry about him beating you for pace. He's played at a high level and he's been doing that to defenders up there. When you get another year on your back, you'll still be three or four yards behind him. When you've two years under your belt, you'll be just about level with him and in three or four years you'll be two yards in front of him. So don't worry, son. Well done. You've stuck at it and you keep doing that." He made me feel 10 feet tall.

I thought I was in for a bollocking, but my spirits were lifted by the manager's words and I went out a different player in the second half. I was still miles behind Usher, but I felt more relaxed and confident. It was a good lesson and one to absorb for future reference.

The Doc also gave me a pat on the back following an incident when I thought I might be in trouble, but it was actually the moment I realised that professional football is a tough sport and you have to stand up for yourself. It was in that first season so I was still only 15. I got smashed into the gym wall by a full back called Mick Harrity, who had already played about 30 first team games and was about five years older than me.

Angry, I instantly reacted and jumped up to confront him and some of the others had to step in.

I didn't regret it because I reckoned you had to stand up and be counted. But I did wonder if I might be in a spot of bother. Later on the assistant manager Jim McAnearney pulled me aside. "The gaffer liked your response when you got smashed into the wall," he said. That was a boost for me and just confirmed my reaction at the time. It was a very early realisation that in this game you have to grow up quickly and stand up for yourself.

4

AND BRECKIN SCORES ... AT OLD TRAFFORD!

As a footballer, you never stop learning and are never too old to learn. As a young apprentice, you certainly take new things on board every day and also start to appreciate how invaluable advice can be from those more experienced who have been there, seen it and done it. Naturally it was exciting to be part of the football club, but disappointment hit me like a thump in the chest as I eagerly anticipated the team selection for the juniors' next game in the Northern Intermediate League.

Back then the teamsheets for the forthcoming games would be pinned on a notice board in the dressing room. That was the only way you found out if you were playing; teamsheets for the first team, reserves and juniors all went up at the same time, adjacent to each other. Even at 15 I had become a regular in the juniors, but one Friday morning I checked the notice board and I wasn't in the team. My stomach churned. I couldn't believe it. A mistake, surely. I went down the team again. And again. Just to make sure I hadn't somehow missed my name. I didn't think I'd been playing too badly the previous few games and I stood staring at it in disbelief. It must have shown on my face. One of the professionals came up and asked what was wrong. I told him.

"A word of advice, son," he said. "Always check the first team, then the reserves and then the juniors, in that order. Then, if you're not in any of them, that's when you knock on the manager's door and ask for an explanation." It was sound advice. I checked the others and, to my great surprise and delight, there my name was – I had been picked for the reserves. At such a young age, and still being a boy, it was a struggle playing against men, but it did me a lot of good. I learned a lot and got used to playing against physically bigger opponents. All of it helped me to mature a bit earlier as well.

Back then several of your teammates in the second team would have played in the first team a lot and you were up against players who had experience of the Football League. It was quite a grounding for young lads still wet behind the ears. It was a privilege to play for the reserves, but I really loved it with my fellow apprentices in the juniors. Perhaps because you were with lads your age, you were "growing up" together at the club; all striving to make it, all enjoying the fun and the scrapes together.

There were local lads you knew from playing against them for your school or even with Rotherham Boys, a good source of young talent for the club. There were no academies at clubs then and Schools of Excellence came in a bit later. Lads such as Jim McDonagh, Alan Crawford, Mick Leng and Trevor Phillips all came through the ranks and eventually became regulars with me in the first team. Tony Henderson and Freddie Robinson had brief first team careers and others such as Dave Abrahams, Les Saxton, Bernard Coop and Kevin Ball, who is sadly dead, were close, but didn't quite make it.

They were a great set of lads and an indication of how good is reflected in the club's record during two seasons in the FA Youth Cup, including a goal I could never forget! We set off in the 1969/70 season with most of the side a year under age for the under-18 competition which meant we had at least two seasons in it. It went well. We beat Mansfield 3-0, Scunthorpe 6-0, Hull City 4-1 and Bolton Wanderers 1-0 to earn a real dream draw in the quarter-final – away to Manchester United at Old Trafford.

So here we were, starry-eyed, budding young footballers getting the chance to play at probably the country's most famous stadium – excluding Wembley, of course – which something many an experienced professional never gets the chance to do all his career. An exciting time. Every Manchester United side was expected to do well in this competition which they had dominated in its opening years, winning it the first five years. During that incredible run they played a fourth round tie at Millmoor in 1954 with a talented side including Bobby Charlton and the great Duncan Edwards. It ended goalless and Man United won the replay 4-1. We so nearly avenged that defeat and how close we came is one of two memories from the game which will stay with me forever.

Wilf McGuinness, who played in the 1954 game, was appointed Manchester United manager in the summer of 1969 after Sir Matt Busby had stepped down and the pair were at Old Trafford that night in February 1970 to see their youngsters take a 1-0 lead. But Trev Phillips – whose electric speed and sharpness caused massive problems for any defender he came up against – equalised to keep up his record of scoring in every round. Then in the 58th minute came my memorable moment. A left wing corner and a run across the penalty spot towards the near post before glancing a header into the far side of the net. Cue mad celebrations with my teammates. We were 2-1 up and I'd scored at Old Trafford – and at the Stretford End, too. I'll have that for a happy goalscoring memory, for sure. As the game wore on, I remember thinking: "We're going to win this and I'll have got the winner at Old Trafford."

They didn't call stoppage time "Fergie time" back then, of course, but whatever they called it, we were well into it with the referee seemingly playing forever. Then – and I can still see it unfolding now – our red-haired right winger Paul Short broke away. All he had to do, and I've said it so many times in all the years since whenever I've talked about this game, was to keep going towards the corner flag. Keep it there and eat up a bit of time, perhaps win a throw-in or a corner. But no. With the sort of naive innocence you get at that age, Shorty thought he would try to set up the third goal.

It was a commendable, positive idea, but unfortunately the wrong decision. His cross was caught by the goalkeeper who launched a giant clearance downfield. Inside about 30 seconds the ball was in our net. No sooner had we kicked off than the final whistle went and we were left with that horrible feeling of having a win snatched away after being so close ... and thinking: "Why did Shorty cross that ball!?"

But a 2-2 draw was still a great result and meant a replay at Millmoor, which certainly caught the imagination of the Rotherham public who were enjoying the exploits of the first team after an 18-match unbeaten run in Division Three. A crowd of 8,633 turned up for the replay – higher than all but a handful of our Football League gates that season – and they saw the teams draw again – 0-0 after extra time. That's when a bit of luck broke my way! In the tunnel the referee called for the two captains. We tossed for choice of venue for the second replay. I called heads, which it was. And it can't be often that footballers are happy not going to play at Old Trafford!

So on to a third game and more than 5,000 were at Millmoor this time to see a controversial turning point surrounding a dreadful decision that was wrong, wrong, wrong and still rankles to this day. I know because I was the one on the receiving end of the most blatant foul possible, but one which, for some unfathomable reason, didn't get punished. We'd gone into extra-time, having finished 1-1, Bernard Coop scoring an early penalty for us and Man United equalising before half-time through Tony Young, who at that time was part of their first team squad.

In the first minute of the extra half-hour I was in charge of the situation and set to knock the ball back to the 'keeper Seamus McDonagh when Man United's striker, an Irish youth international called James Hall, challenged me from behind, blatantly pushed me in the back and barged me to the ground. He ran on to the ball and, with McDonagh having his arm up appealing for the clear foul, Hall put the ball in the net. The whistle went. I knew it was a free kick to us and you could tell by the reaction of the Manchester United players that they expected a foul to be awarded. Instead, to everyone's astonishment, the goal was given.

It was clear to everyone in the ground that I had been fouled. The referee was a very experienced Football League referee, Kevin Howley, from Middlesbrough. I don't want this to sound like sour grapes, but the decision was in keeping with his officiating in all three games. He always appeared to favour the big club and a lot of decisions did seem to go their way. It put them 2-1 up and definitely had an effect on us, not least the controversial manner of it. After all the fight we had put up in the Millmoor mud, we now felt we had been cheated. We couldn't recover and ended up losing 4-1, a scoreline most definitely undeserved after three great battles. We were all gutted in the dressing room afterwards and I was in tears in the bath.

Incidentally I shouldn't imagine too many Millers fans, knowing my career, can guess what position I played in the first round in that FA Youth Cup competition when we beat Mansfield. I actually played at right back that night, obviously because we were short of one due to injury. I don't think I would have done too much overlapping down that side and, if I did, would have crossed it only after dragging the ball back on to my left foot!

We were a young side and eight or nine of us were still eligible for the FA Youth Cup the following season when we again got to the quarter-finals in 1971. We beat Sheffield United 1-0 at Bramall Lane, Middlesbrough 1-0 after extra time in a replay and edged a 2-1 thriller against Doncaster Rovers at Millmoor before losing 3-0 at home to Cardiff City, who finished runners-up to Arsenal that year.

It is the furthest the club have ever gone in the competition and it was obvious some of the young players had a chance of making it. There was an end-of-season honour for me and Seamus when we were chosen for the Northern Intermediate League representative side to play Middlesbrough in the annual Champions versus the League XI game. It was at their old Ayresome Park ground and we all got a commemorative medal.

Holland, where we went for youth tournaments, was certainly a touch "exotic" for lads from Rotherham back then. When a group of us went on holiday together, it wasn't abroad, but to Skegness with eight of us in a six-berth caravan! Alan Crawford's auntie had the caravan and me, Crawf, Seamus, Lengy, Phillipsy, Dave Abrahams, Les Saxton and Freddie Robinson treated ourselves to a week in Skeggy. I did say "treated" which may be slightly exaggerating because we slept three in a bed – in the two double beds – with the other two sharing a single bed. Yeah, we were really close, we apprentices!

I managed to get by with only £6 in my pocket and I wasn't the only one. The caravan was right next to Butlin's holiday camp. Families staying there had a pass to walk straight in and we would all split up individually and just tag on to a family to get in for nowt. It then meant we had free swimming, all the rides and everything, for free. We also hid a bar of soap, "borrowed" a towel or two off somebody's washing line so we could get a shower and then put the towel back on the line. Then at night we got dressed up, got back into the camp again on someone else's pass and enjoyed ourselves at the disco to the sound of Tamla Motown and what have you.

One night we met these Cockney lads who were the same age as us, about 16, 17, 18, and they fancied themselves at football. We actually didn't let on who we were and they challenged us to a game, eight against eight. We arranged to play them the next day. Even though they weren't bad, we battered them and scored 10 or 11. One of their lads said: "We think we're good, but you lads are miles better than we are." If they'd only known! Yes, great holiday memories. And all for £6.

All those apprentices from the Youth Cup squad mixed well and I'd like to think our singing helped the Millers to get into Europe. Although having heard some of the lads sing, I'm not sure we should take much credit! The BBC organised a Kop choir competition in 1970 with Football League clubs invited to enter with the prize a trip to the European Cup final in Milan. The Beeb were to film at the grounds and the best singing crowd would get the chance to send a group of fans to Italy. One Tuesday night home game the other apprentices and I finished our pre-match duties and decided we wanted to be on the Tivoli End where a lot of fans were crammed in because the cameras were going to film the crowd behind the goal.

So we got in there and sang our hearts out as loud as we could with the rest of the Millers fans on the Tivoli. After we'd completed our post-match duties, clearing away and tidying up, some of us went to the fish and chip shop across from Millmoor. The TV was on and the votes for the competition were coming in. We all assumed Liverpool would win easily and were gobsmacked when it was announced Rotherham United had won. It was the only thing those apprentices could have ever won for their singing – except me, of course, because it is widely known I am a wonderful singer!

It meant that a dozen or so Millers fans got an all-expenses paid trip to Italy to the European Cup final a couple of months later when Celtic lost to Feyenoord. The following day at Milan airport they saw the Feyenoord squad on their way home and actually got the chance to touch the European Cup. I guess it's the closest any Millers fans will ever get to that famous trophy!

5

A PAINFUL WELCOME TO THE REAL WORLD

It's exciting to think about playing for the first team one day when you are a young lad working through your three-year apprenticeship, but you are also nervous at the same time, particularly coming towards the end of your apprenticeship. The questions nag away. Am I good enough? Can I do any more? Will I get taken on as a full time professional? What if they kick me out, what will I do then? I was all too aware that many young professionals make it this far, but then get released.

I was just short of my 18th birthday when the big day arrived, a day destined to map out my future. I was taken on as a full time professional and proudly walked into Millmoor on Monday, July 12th, 1971, now on the princely sum of £12 a week! However, there was an issue that I had to confront. I found out I was getting LESS than my young fellow professionals who had just signed on as well, so I went to see the manager, Jim McAnearney. It was a rather nervy prospect for a young lad, but I was standing up for my rights. Or, as I saw it, I wanted a wrong righting. I knocked on his door, went in and said I wasn't happy. Perhaps a strange sentiment, considering I was delighted to have been taken on.

I said the other lads were on £14 a week, but I was only on £12. What actually gave me extra confidence was that Sheffield Wednesday had actually tapped me up. A scout there, former league referee George McCabe, had pulled me one day and said that, if it didn't work out at Rotherham, then I should give him a ring. So that gave me a bit of clout if Rotherham happened to be awkward about the matter. McAnearney acted swiftly, spoke to the directors and the next day he took me aside. "You were being penalised because of your age," he said. "You're only 17:

the others are already 18. But it's your birthday in a couple of weeks and you'll get the £14 a week straightaway."

Although I had signed as a full time professional, I hadn't signed the forms enabling me to play in the Football League. Basically I wasn't registered so couldn't play for the first team. Actually it was a crafty, money-saving ruse by the club. When you signed those forms, the club were committed to paying £250 to the Football League and £250 to the player – a tidy sum when my weekly wage was only £14. So the club obviously decided it would be cheaper not to register their young, first-time professionals straightaway. The line of thinking was: "Register them if we need them or when the time comes when we think they're worth their chance." That day arrived sooner than expected for this eager young left back.

There was an injury crisis in the opening months of the season. In November 1971 there is an entry in the club's minute book – the official record of the meetings of the club's board of directors. "Approval to sign John Breckin" is written neatly in blue ink in one of those old-style, lined ledgers. This was the board acceding to the manager's request for me to sign the Football League forms because I just might be needed at some stage as the injuries began to bite.

So I rubbed my hands together in anticipation of my little £250 windfall. A princely sum for a young 18-year-old then and you don't need to be much of a mathematician to work out what that might be approximately worth in today's terms considering it was about 18 times the weekly wage back then. But even so I didn't get it all! The Purshouse family in charge, chairman Eric and son Lewis, were shrewd businessmen and, even though they ran things frugally, they were sensible in their financial dealings.

So you didn't get your £250 all at once. It was £125 now and the next £125 a year later. So who was benefiting for 12 months from the second £125? Not me for sure! The contract was only for a year with a year's option. But that option was totally at the club's discretion. If they wanted to keep you on, they could, but you couldn't exercise your option by staying on if they didn't want you. And it wasn't just at Rotherham where it applied. Either way it meant I was now available for the first team should the injury situation get worse. I was playing regularly for the reserves and had enjoyed success just a few months earlier in 1971 when the Millers reserves won the North Midlands League Cup, winning at Sunderland after drawing the first leg of the final at Millmoor.

My first taste of the Millers match day experience was only a month or so after becoming eligible. It was the longest trip of the season, to Torquay, on the Saturday before Christmas in 1971 and I was the substitute – only one then. Be under no illusion, it was only due to a horrendous injury list that weekend with four more regulars unavailable that I was called up. We were struggling for numbers. Fellow youngster Mick Leng made only his second appearance. Trev Womble and Eddie Ferguson hadn't even played in the first team all season but had to start. In "Willie" Womble's case it was his first senior outing for seven months. It was a makeshift line-up all right, but, as so often in football, adversity can pull you together even more and we won 1-0. But what I recall more so than the match from this initial first team "experience" is breakfast in bed at the hotel!

I thought I was in the Ritz because I'd been used to only a poky little boarding house on a back street in Blackpool. I always remember that place in Torquay, the Livermead Cliff Hotel. It even had towels with the hotel's name on them. I roomed with my big mate Seamus McDonagh, the back up goalkeeper, and for a lad from Masbrough and one from Canklow, we thought it was the height of luxury. But my actual first team debut wasn't far away at all, just two weeks later on New Year's Day, 1972. There were actually six players missing on that day, which may not seem over the top. But consider that only 14 senior players had been used during that first half of the season and one of those, Neil Hague, had been sold to Plymouth Argyle. Underneath the figure of 14 you started with lads still in their teens.

I was told the day before the game I would be playing although I suspected I might be because of the horrendous situation. All three senior full backs were out, including regular left back Dennis Leigh. There was talk that players not 100 per cent fit would have to turn out and a suggestion the club might not be able to field a team. We even sought to get a postponement from the Football League, but had to get on with it. Hardly ideal circumstances then to be making my debut – and Bradford City certainly had no sympathy and no lack of sarcasm when we turned up at Valley Parade.

I well remember getting to the dressing room and there was a notice on the door from the Bradford chairman Stafford Heginbotham. "Leave your wheelchairs and crutches in the corridor," it read. Nice, eh, for a club stricken by injury to get such a greeting? With Mick Leng pressed into service at right back, an 18-year-old debutant in yours truly at left back and Willie Womble called up to play out wide, it really was a patched-up side and perhaps no surprise it wasn't a winning start for me, going down 1-0 to a late goal.

I do recall that a young David Bairstow, the red-haired former Yorkshire and England wicketkeeper and father of Jonny, played centre forward for Bradford that day. He was 20 and it was one of his first games. The next day I got a favourable mention in the match report in the *Sunday People*. The reporter? None other than Freddie Trueman, the former Yorkshire and England cricket legend. He managed to get my name wrong by spelling it *Brekin*. It wouldn't be the last time it didn't appear correctly in print!

Both sides of the coin appeared on my second appearance a couple of weeks later – happiness because we won 2-0 at Swansea, but an insight into how ruthless league football could be because I got "done" by an opponent. A wicked challenge it was, too. As I played the ball down the line, the Swansea player came late and went over the ball with that most cowardly and shocking of challenges. It ripped my sock, took my shinpad and at first I really thought I'd broken my leg.

He'd gashed my shin right down to the ankle. It was like two tramlines. I was stretchered off and had to go to hospital to get it stitched up. With no mobile phones then, it was the legendary former *Star and Green 'Un* reporter John Piper who rang my mum and dad to tell them I was okay with no more than a badly gashed shin. I don't hold grudges, but that player did go into my little black book even if I never did come across him again.

This first team action was at my basic wage of £14, but with bonuses it could quickly increase. You got £10 appearance money and £10 a point. So that win at Swansea meant I'd get £44 on my "top line" for that week. Have a midweek game as well and win that, then win bonus and appearance money meant an extra £30 and suddenly there would be a top-line gross figure of £74 – more than five times my basic wage.

Of course, a first game at Millmoor was always what I'd hoped for, but it was more than two months after the injury at Swansea that I got the opportunity, running out on my home ground for the first time on April 3rd, 1972, and the sheer delight of helping us to beat Mansfield Town 3-1. My first season as a Rotherham United first team player ended with eight appearances in all. I had tasted the "big time" – well, it was to me. I couldn't wait for the following season. But little did I realise what was around the corner during the next season. And it wasn't nice!

***

It often helps to go through bad times. Not only to make you more appreciative of the good times, but also to help you cope whenever things don't go right further down the line. And boy, did I suffer some bad times during what was a wretched year for the club in the season of 1972/73. At the time you don't think: "Put this down to experience." You just know you are having a difficult time and you have to get on with things, work as hard as you can to get through it and come out the other side. Even if the "other side" looked a long way off at times.

The season in Division Three had actually started very well with six wins from the first eight matches. We were second in the table behind leaders Port Vale, who'd been hammered 7-0 at Millmoor! But then things started to slide. Or rather, plummet. First choice left back Dennis Leigh had gone to Lincoln and Mick Leng went in there, not his natural position at all. Finally at the start of November I got the call which coincided with a 1-0 home win against Watford. For a time it went okay. But then things really went bad. Six successive defeats with several heavy ones in there, too. All that early promise had long since evaporated. The talk of promotion was now a distant memory. And the Millers fans weren't happy. Not at all.

I was struggling and, before I knew it, I had the crowd on my back. It didn't matter that I was a young, local lad, trying to make his way; they gave me some stick and I got abuse. I wasn't the only one. But let me tell you, when you're getting it, you notice all right. It was no surprise when, six games from the end of the season and after playing a run of 23 games, manager Jim McAnearney finally left me out. It wasn't nice, but there was some relief. When it was happening, did it affect me mentally? Yes, it did! Was I sleeping soundly at night? No, I wasn't. Was I worrying? For sure I was. Was I looking forward to going out in front of my own critical supporters at the next home game? Have a guess!

Fear was stalking a young man. Back then, if a player was down or feeling a bit depressed because things weren't going right or he was getting criticised, the remedy was instant, simple and stark. "Shake yourself; grow up; pull yourself together." That would be the advice. No one really looked upon it then as it would be regarded today, as a mental health issue, and there are now clubs who employ the services of a psychologist for affected players. In those days? A senior pro acted as an impromptu psychologist – if you were lucky. I was.

Johnny Quinn was there and he most certainly was a good pro. A genuinely nice man, a top bloke and I could talk to him. In fact, I could have gone to him with my life although not to some of the others! Had he not been there, what would have happened? I'd have stayed silent. Bottled it up. Not said anything to anybody. Back then in the early 1970s no one realised that's the worst thing you can do. Nowadays, thankfully, there is far more awareness of mental health issues in football and players are rightly assured of the right sort of support.

However, I did have with me for comfort a special memory – my first Football League goal. As happens in football, you need a bit of luck – and good fortune can often arrive through an unexpected opportunity. We were playing at Brentford in January '73. Losing 1-0 in the second half. Normally I wouldn't go up for corner-kicks because regular centre half Ray Mielczarek always did. However, this was the day he missed his only game that season.

So the manager said I should go up for corners. It was the only reason I was up there. It was at the double-decker stand end at Griffin Park, a corner from the right and, in not dissimilar fashion to my goal at Old Trafford in the FA Youth Cup a couple of years earlier, I made a run towards the near post run and in went the header. Thankfully it earned us a point. And I had to savour it because I wasn't to score again for another two seasons!

It was the season when we ended up going down in the most freakish of circumstances. After flirting with the bottom four, three straight wins meant any talk of relegation looked ridiculous. We were 14th with three games left. A point from any of the last three matches would guarantee safety, but it seemed impossible for us to go down because Halifax had to win all their last four just to draw level. On the last day against York at Millmoor a draw would have sufficed and relegated them. They had to win or were down. They won 2-1 and saved themselves. Suddenly the awful truth dawned on everyone at Millmoor.

Even though we had never been in the bottom four all season – and even weren't there after that final game – we could actually still get relegated. That's because Halifax had one game to play the following midweek. If they won it, we went down. The inevitable happened. Halifax won 1-0 at Walsall and the Millers dropped into the bottom four so would be playing Fourth Division football for the first time.

What rubbed it in even more was a decision by the club that ultimately proved costly. They had loaned Trev Womble to Halifax a couple of months earlier. He played 10 games for them and scored a couple of goals which in the final reckoning proved crucial. He was called back when the warning signs were flashing, but the damage had already been done. Jim McAnearney paid the price with his job.

He also had a team with a lot of experienced players and many of them played for themselves and not the team. I experienced that, expecting more support from such players, but not finding it forthcoming as it should have been. And at only 19 it was also the first time I had seen two players come to blows in the dressing room – one blaming the other over a goal that had been conceded. "*My* man didn't score it," said one. It was an eye opener all round, that season.

Actually my first appearances in the 1972/73 season had been for Darlington back in October. *Definitely* an eye opener. I went on loan, they were struggling in Division Four and my debut was scheduled to be the next day, a Tuesday night game at Gillingham. I did say "scheduled." It was also, as you'd expect, "scheduled" to be as a player. I didn't expect to end up being the trainer! We stopped for breakfast on the A1 after an early start and at the team hotel in Gravesend I was tucking into my pre-match meal anticipating my first game for Darlington when the manager Alan Jones took me aside. "There's been a mistake," he told me. "Your registration hasn't gone through so you can't play tonight. But we haven't got a trainer so sit on the bench with me and run on if you're needed. If it's a bit serious, we'll ask their trainer to go on." What a carry-on. I'd no experience at all, no idea what I was supposed to do if someone got injured and I'd to go on. Fortunately I didn't need to run on with the magic sponge and luckily I didn't play either because Gillingham stuffed them 4-0.

I do recall that sitting in the stand was Leeds manager Don Revie, apparently watching Gillingham's promising left back David Peach, later to join Southampton and win the FA Cup with them in 1976. What I also remember is the shock when someone piped up later: "What's happened to Rotherham tonight?" They'd lost 7-2 at home to Bournemouth and used three different goalkeepers, two of them outfield players in Carl Gilbert and Mick Leng after Jim McDonagh had been carried off.

I played four times on loan at Darlo, including a 2-0 win at Barnsley when I had a really good game. Jim McAnearney had somebody checking on me at Oakwell and, in view of the report he received, decided to bring me back. In I went for a County Cup game at Hillsborough a few days later – against former Rangers and Scotland winger Willie Henderson – and then it was into the Millers side for my first start of the season against Watford. All looked rosy right then, but things would soon change.

6

THE LEPER COLONY

The appointment of Jim McGuigan as Rotherham United's next manager proved a pivotal moment in the revival of the club's fortunes and a turning point in my career as well. The removal of Jim McAnearney after the relegation in April 1973 was inevitable. The appointment of McGuigan, a shrewd, canny Scot, was a masterstroke by the board. It came after the club had started a downward spiral. In fact, a rot had set in. He proved the perfect man to stabilise the club and turn things around. But it wasn't easy.

His managerial record at the lower level was good. He'd led Grimsby and Chesterfield to promotion from the Fourth Division, so knew the division well and how to get success there. My introduction to him was when he went to Holland with us for the under-21 tournament at NAC Breda in May 1973 shortly after the season had ended. As the new manager, we assumed he was familiarising himself with people at the club. But I later found out his main purpose was to check out the young players and especially note those with potential.

This was my fifth and final time going to the Breda tournament when, one year, Wolves were in it with future stars such as Alan Sunderland, Steve Daley and Kenny Hibbitt. I first went in 1969, we won it in 1970, finished runners-up in '71 and won it again in '72, beating Czech side Sparta CKD 1-0 on penalties after a goalless draw. There were only three penalties each then. Alan Crawford scored our first, Jim McDonagh saved two and the Czechs missed their last one. But the 1973 penalty shoot-out success must have set a world record then! It was 47 penalties in all.

The final ended 1-1, Dutch side SC Baronie equalising late on after

Phil Syrat put us ahead. We took them in threes and round after round we'd be level. I took two and missed 'em both. The goalkeeper could have thrown his cap on the first one! The saga seemed to go on forever until eventually Baronie missed and Paul Murphy scored the clinching penalty. I gather 48 is the world record for a shoot-out.

McGuigan intended making some youngsters part of the first team squad. He'd seen how the assembly line was, said we were "a very promising bunch of lads" and planned on us being the club's future. However, there was a snag. Or rather a few snags. There were a number of experienced players still at the club – all of whom had played at a higher level and a couple who even had international caps. We young lads thought they were superstars; they were certainly the top earners. Naively we thought they would do a great job for the club. McGuigan knew otherwise.

Their skill wasn't in question. They had been good players in their day. Some had been better players than I or most of us would ever be. But in this twilight of their careers their commitment – or lack of it – was the problem. McGuigan knew instantly the good professionals from the not-so-good and the bad ones. He'd already got rid of three or four experienced ones who'd been involved in the relegation. And as the new 1973/74 season began to unfold, the situation arose whereby the remaining "superstar" players were steadily squeezed out. In fact, there was an amazing team meeting when McGuigan left no one in any doubt what he was going to do. It was one of the most incredible meetings I was ever involved in. "There's a cancer at this football club," he said. "And when you have a cancer, the surgeon wants to operate. He gets his knife and he cuts it out. Well, I'm going to be that surgeon and I'm going to take my knife and I'm going to cut it out here."

There was silence. Everyone was sitting there stunned, flashing little sideways glances. But he had made his point. The message got across in the direction of those it was intended to reach. And it wasn't aimed at those eager, young lads striving to make their way in the game and hoping to make their mark with the Millers. At one point we had the incredible situation of a group of experienced players, who were not part of even the immediate future, training apart from those who would be figuring the following Saturday. We referred to them as "lepers" or "the leper colony".

They weren't the first players, and by no means the last, to be happy picking up pay cheques or turning up somewhere just for the money. Just another pay day. Those people are no good for your football club. In a way Paul Warne had a similar task when he took over in 2016. There were certain players at Rotherham he knew he had to get rid of and who were no good for the future of the club. So much of the way he handled a difficult situation reminded me of McGuigan – although I never heard of a meeting such as the one we had!

McGuigan had to stabilise the club while integrating the young players, but at the same time sideline an experienced group who might well have ensured things turned nasty when they knew they hadn't got a future. It was a difficult balancing act, but one that McGuigan skilfully and knowledgeably dealt with. The young, inexperienced players among us knew he was the boss. We weren't fearful, but we were respectful, for sure.

As the clearing out took place, some players didn't help themselves. One Saturday we were on the team coach outside Millmoor waiting to set off to an away game. But I needed the toilet and went up into the club offices to use theirs. While in there I could hear McGuigan and club secretary Jim Bennison talking about a player, Eddie Ferguson. He had been missing training and wasn't on the team coach. "He's not turned up," said McGuigan to Bennison. "And I'll tell you something else – I don't think he's going to be coming back." He was right. I have no idea what had happened, but I never saw Eddie Ferguson again. He got sacked for a breach of contract as did, at more or less the same time, Mike O'Grady, a former Leeds United and Huddersfield Town player who had a couple of England caps to his name. Gradually almost all the ones involved in the previous season's relegation were weeded out. By the turn of the year, as we moved into 1974, the ones not wanted were gone.

As experience departed, McGuigan replaced it with ... experience. But players of good character, good people who knew the lower divisions and who he knew he could rely on. Players such as defenders Tommy Spencer, Bob Delgado and Steve Derrett and midfielder Jimmy Goodfellow, who he could guarantee would be an excellent influence on the young players and would operate in a role McGuigan knew would suit him perfectly. Gradually things did turn – we had a great 1-0 Friday night win at Colchester in March when they were top of the table and still unbeaten at home. But with four games left we were still in some danger of finishing in the bottom four, which meant you had to apply for re-election to the Football League and might be voted out, when we headed off to play Workington.

We arrived late Friday afternoon in Cumbria, had a stroll out and came across a village fair. There was a "catch-the-egg" competition, which was hilarious – blokes were having a go at catching eggs thrown from distance, but were getting splattered with yolk. Step forward our 'keeper, Seamus McDonagh. Who else?

"I can do that," he said. Bob Delgado volunteered to throw the egg, hurled it from half-a-field away and Seamus took it perfectly. Unbroken. It won us a crate of beer, which we drank – but only after the match, which we won 2-0. Things were coming together and were emphasised a couple of weeks later in our final game against the new champions Peterborough United at Millmoor. We played really, really well that day, beating them 3-1. It was an indication of what lay around the corner.

***

There was a whole new "feel" to the club when we reported back for pre-season training in the summer of 1974. The atmosphere was different and you could sense good times were on the horizon. It's important for a manager to have good staff around him and we were lucky at that time to have an excellent physio, Alan Smith. His footballing career cut short by injury, Alan was only in his mid-20s, but his enthusiastic, positive approach and his hard work and dedication to the job took injury treatment, rehabilitation and more to another level.

And his bright, cheery personality was just the perfect pick-me-up on a daily basis for lads out with injury for any length of time and perhaps feeling a bit sorry for themselves. You could always see he loved his job. One day I had given Steve Derrett a lift up to Lodge Moor Hospital and on the way back a bloke drove into my car. I broke a bone in my wrist and that night it was really giving me pain. No way would I be able to get a decent night's sleep. I phoned Alan and he came straight across late that evening to give me painkillers. I'm not surprised he went on to have the long career that he did in football, including 11 years at Sheffield

Wednesday and eight as England's physio, receiving a lifetime achievement award from his own medical profession for his work in the game. He did leave football, but you can't say he's ever retired – he continues his physiotherapy business up at Wickersley and still attends Millers Nostalgia Society meetings and the odd game.

The feeling that the good times were coming was a relief for me because I knew what it was like to have the bad times. Having the crowd on my back during that relegation season wasn't nice and definitely hard for a 19-year-old to handle, particularly at my own club and the one I had always dreamed of playing for. You don't expect it and there is no doubt a player's confidence takes a big hit when he can hear the crowd giving him stick. Mine did get hit, for sure. Perhaps it's not surprising when you clearly hear someone single you out. I can still vividly recall on this particular afternoon, over near the left touchline, a bloke piped up: "I don't know why tha'r playing Breckin; tha' were bloody rubbish last time." Others around him laughed. And we haven't even kicked off!

But looking back now, I know it helped to toughen me up. There are lots of bad times, difficult ones in football and you simply have to tough it out. At 19 it was a whole new, unnerving experience for me. But you have to get on with things and I strove to do so, to come back, do better and show the fans what I really was about. Winning the crowd over would make me a better player and a stronger person. I believe both happened. The difference now, as we approached the new season, was that I was with a group of players I could trust. No one was just looking after himself as had happened that previous season. We were a team and Jim McGuigan now had a group of players he could rely on and mould into the way of playing he wanted.

I had a lot of time for Jim and learned a lot. More than I realised at the time. Indeed he was ahead of his time. I realised there was something special happening. The ball work, the passing drills, the way he wanted the game to be played. It felt good to be involved. Much better than ever before. I was still a baby in the world of professional football, but I had grown up enough to sense that better days beckoned. They did.

***

There is always a moment in a season, I believe, when one performance, one result, has a definitive significance to it. Often it can come early. One such moment sticks out for me early in that 1974/75 season and it was indicative of the will-to-win that Jim McGuigan had instilled into us. We'd had a good start to the season with three wins and a draw, but then lost at Reading in the League Cup and suffered our first league defeat at Hartlepool. Two days later, a Monday night, we were at Brentford. A tough place to go – they hadn't conceded a goal in their first four home games – and we found ourselves two down. We came back to level and at 3-3 late in the second half you would have thought: "Let's settle for a point." But no. The will-to-win that McGuigan was about was to prove pivotal. We kept going and got a last minute winner for a dramatic 4-3 victory.

Just as the manager wanted, we had all worked for each other that night. We had shown character to come from behind, been resolute when required and then finished in some style with the late goal. I think it planted the seed in our minds that we could be serious promotion candidates. Indeed we were – helped by one particularly key signing midway through the season. McGuigan sold one striker Ron Wigg and brought in another, Dick Habbin from Reading, to replace him.

Habbin's style of play, the way he led the line, his sure control with his back to goal and how he held the ball up were perfect for how the manager had us operating. The signing proved pivotal to maintaining our promotion push during the second half of the season and Dick also provided important goalscoring impetus, netting 10 goals in his 21 appearances, including some really vital ones.

Talking of scoring, I enjoyed what you can call – ahem – my "best-ever" season. The mighty total of three goals. All were at Millmoor, my first ones in front of the home fans, but one stands out for two particular reasons. It was the late goal against Exeter in November that got us a 1-1 draw with a couple of minutes to go. It was the best I ever scored – although there aren't a lot to choose from! – and understandably I well recall it. Exeter had done their homework and shut us out well and the normally successful left-side triumvirate of Breckin, Goodfellow and Crawford hadn't found much joy this particular afternoon.

I moved up the left and Jimmy's pass found me in more space than I'd enjoyed all game. Jimmy told me later he was shouting at me to give him the ball back, but that I ignored him. I always remember his words about it in print: "It was the first time he'd disobeyed me as captain because I was still shouting at him for the ball when he struck it for one of the best goals I've ever seen."

Although about 35 yards out – that's what the Press reports say and I accept they are correct in this instance! – I made the instinctive decision to shoot. The reaction was good. A great contact, the sort you don't feel, and it departed with some power behind it. Now on many occasions such a hopeful strike ends up sailing way over the bar – I well knew that feeling! – or goes nearer the corner flag. But on this occasion it was a peach and flew into the far top corner. If I may say so, the goalkeeper stood no chance. I almost did a lap of honour.

A vital point then and I felt particularly good as I headed off home to see what my mum and dad thought. As I walked – or rather floated – through the front door, I was still figuratively punching the air in delight. I looked forward to their reaction. Beaming, I asked them what they thought. They both looked a bit bemused. "What about?" they asked. I replied: "My goal; the equaliser." There was an embarrassed silence until my dad confessed: "We missed it; we left 10 minutes from the end because we wanted to get ready early. There's a good turn on at Greasbrough Club tonight."

My other memory from that afternoon is a quite astonishing one and something that certainly could not possibly be handled today as it was back in 1974. Just before kick-off there was an announcement over the loudspeaker, warning the crowd the police had received a call saying that a bomb was due to go off at 3.25pm. It added that the club had left the gates open in all parts of the ground and spectators were free to leave and could return later if they wished. I know it seems too ridiculous to be true, but how times change. Apparently hardly anybody did leave and one report said: "3.25 came and went without anything explosive happening on or off the field, at least until Breckin's thunderbolt near the end."

Promotion – only the second in the club's history – actually came when we were all at home on the Monday night of the last week of the season. We'd beaten Rochdale at home 3-1 on the Saturday and had two games left. So had Chester, but, if they lost at Hartlepool on that Monday night two days later, we were promoted. It was an agonising wait – we had no mobiles back then of course and had to wait until the final score came through. When it did, Chester had lost 1-0. We were up. And I think the old Adam and Eve nightclub had its busiest Monday night ever!

To cap it all for me, I was named at left back in the PFA's Division Four Team of the Year – a great honour. It would have been even better had someone from the club informed me! I'd been at a do at the Brecon Hotel on Moorgate one Sunday night and, when I got back home, Dick Habbin – who was staying at my mum and dad's – said: "Did you know you were in the PFA team?" I didn't. The club had received a letter from the PFA inviting me to go to the awards night and get my medal, but had never passed it on!

After promotion was confirmed, we drew 1-1 at Reading on the Wednesday ahead of our final game at Southport a few days later. We'd got the flip-flops and sunglasses out by then. The fans made it a carnival atmosphere, but we couldn't reciprocate and lost 2-0. But it didn't matter. A special season had seen us put some pride back in the club and given long-suffering supporters some overdue joy.

7

DEREK DALTON – FAN EXTRAORDINAIRE

Of course, the 1974/75 promotion from Division Four was a new experience for all those of us who had come through the ranks. Only 16 players were used all season and eight of them had actually been nurtured at Millmoor, namely Jim McDonagh, Mick Leng, Richard Finney, Trev Phillips, Alan Crawford, Trevor Womble, Trevor Swift, who was a just a few years older than we were, and me. So a bond had formed among the group, which remains to this day and we definitely enjoyed our celebration in the Southport dressing room afterwards, the mood anything but downbeat despite the defeat. A couple of bottles of champagne, some group photographs and plenty of singing saw to that. We were a happy bunch. Then came a knock on the dressing room door. It was a Millers fan.

Might he have a photo with the team? Normally you wouldn't allow it. Let one fan do it and every other supporter quite rightly would want the same access. But this fan was very special. He was special to the club, to all the other fans and special to me, too. He was Derek Dalton, the paralysed, permanently wheelchair-bound polio victim who was also a personal friend. Derek lived and breathed Rotherham United. It was his life – a life we cannot really understand or comprehend, but a life in which he gave so much. He was an example to everyone he came into contact with thanks to an outlook that was always optimistic and positive despite his situation. A shining example even now to all those touched by negativity.

Many people think my friendship with Derek was purely through our Millers connections – me as a player and Derek as a high profile fan. But not so. I knew Derek long before I was connected with the football club. In fact, when I decided to write my story, the first person I thought about having his own chapter was Derek Dalton. That day at Southport, his pals wheeled him into the dressing room to have his picture taken with his beloved team and mark the first promotion he could celebrate, too. The players, who all knew him anyway, got round him holding their bottles and cans and Bob Delgado mischievously knelt down right alongside him and held a whisky bottle to his lips as if Derek was drinking some. Then, as the camera clicked, Bob gently lifted the base of the bottle and Derek had no choice but to take a big gulp of the hard stuff. I gather his journey home was better than he remembered!

When I moved to Clough Road, which was the street that Derek lived on, I was two; the same age he was when he contracted polio, the devastating illness which caused his complete paralysis apart from having limited ability in the fingers of one hand. Derek lived in a specially-adapted bungalow a bit further up Clough Road – the posh end – and, although he was four years older than I was, I'd seen him and knew him from being at Thornhill Junior School. As I walked to school, I would wave to Derek's mum and dad who were always looking out from their kitchen window. Little did I know that I would be required to go in. On an errand. The headmaster, Mr Hammond, had letters and things that needed taking to Derek and, because I lived near him, he would ask me to drop them off. So I was the little messenger boy.

Eventually I started calling in, along with big school pal Pete Wainwright, and played board games, draughts and tiddlywinks with Derek. We became friends. The bungalow was amazing. The inside of some rooms resembled the interior of a spaceship. Everything was automated and Derek could open doors, switch lights on and control the TV from a little control panel attached to his hand. This was the 1960s, don't forget, and such gadgets were not as commonplace as they are today. It was never dull when you were around Derek and, as he grew older, he developed a good personality and became very witty. Back then disability was considered something to be hidden away or shunned, but I think being around someone with such a disability from such a young age helped me to handle such issues among others with the normality that people now expect.

Following the Millers became his life's passion. In fact, it really was his life and he jolly well made the most of it. Certainly more than most fans manage anyway. Home games weren't a problem. Just a few minutes from Millmoor and he got wheeled down there. Many supporters will remember Derek in his Millers-emblazoned wheelchair inside the boundary wall at one end of the ground. Travelling to away games could be a problem, though; not of access but of location. Every evening Derek had to be connected to – i.e. inside – his body-length iron lung which was in a special room at home. Away travel had to be completed in the day. That affected going to some away games down south, but London was a different story. He had a little advantage there. He was regularly checked out by specialists at a hospital in the capital to monitor his condition so he would be booked in. He referred to it as "going down for my MOT."

You can be sure any conversation with him was always lively and time spent was never dull. He was genuinely funny – I remember loads of hilarious moments with him – and he wasn't averse to laughing at his own disability or situation. There was the time Rotherham sent a team to Wentworth CC in a fundraising event for the club and played them on their cricket pitch behind the Rockingham Arms. It was a hot day, good publicity ensured a big crowd and for an extra boost Earl Fitzwilliam, who owned the magnificent Wentworth Woodhouse stately home and probably the entire village as well, agreed to turn up and meet both teams beforehand. I'd invited Derek because he was a celebrity in his own right and had been voted the Football League's No.1 fan.

I asked Derek if he wanted to be introduced to the Earl and he said he'd love to. Derek, whose natural position was virtually to lay in his wheelchair because he could not sit up and support himself, was wheeled on to the outfield alongside the Millers players. Eventually the Earl's limousine pulled up at the entrance and out he stepped. People began applauding and Derek, because it was really sunny, was sporting a big pair of sunglasses, like the ones Roy Orbison used to wear. Sounding a bit agitated, he got my attention: "Breck, I say, Breck, let me know when he's about 25 yards away," Derek said.

"Well, actually," I replied, "he's about that far away now."

"Well, in that case Breck, would you take these sunglasses off? I don't want him thinking I'm f****** blind an' all."

But that was Derek. He did become very well known on a wider national level, notably because of the Fan of the Year accolade, and his wit memorably surfaced on another special occasion. After his MOT at the hospital he went to watch the Millers get stuffed 3-0 at Brentford. That night Derek had been invited as an audience guest on the Michael Parkinson Show when the main guest was one the world's great figures, the nun and peace activist Mother Theresa. Derek and his mother, Hilda, had even been invited into the hospitality green room with Parky and assorted guests – yes, Derek could get anywhere. He rang me after the show that night, still upset about the 3-0 defeat, and said he had been in the green room. I asked him if he'd met Mother Theresa.

"Yeah, Parky brought her across and introduced me to her," Derek told me. "I wasn't very happy 'cos of the defeat, but she moved forward, put her hand forward and drew a cross on my head with her finger and said: 'God will always be with you.' I asked Derek what he thought of that and he shot back: "When she said that, Breck, I thought: 'Well, where was he at three o'clock this afternoon then?'"

His brother Tony noticed that Mother Theresa had gone up quietly, knelt by Derek's wheelchair and had a little word with him. He asked Derek what she'd said. "That when we all go up to the next level, we'll all be the same. There'll be no disability." "In that case then," said Derek, "I'm not sure what I'll do first ... have a game of football or a shag."

His life's devotion was to the Millers and he raised a heck of a lot of money for the club over the years, becoming really well known across football in the process. Derek's personality, and the fact he was disabled, gave him a special profile. He met a lot of famous footballing people and personalities, among them Pelé and Sir Bobby Charlton. You can be sure Derek wasn't averse to asking searching questions, even down to: "Why did you..."

Another example of his quick wit came when the Millers played at Oxford in the early 1980s. Oxford manager Jim Smith, a Sheffielder from Shiregreen, knew Derek and invited him into the boardroom after the game. Jim beckoned over the Oxford owner and chairman, one Robert Maxwell. "Come and meet a good friend from my neck of the woods," he said to the powerful publishing figure, pointing out Derek's fundraising and great support for the club

"Very pleased to meet you," said Maxwell as he bent over Derek in his wheelchair. "I wish we had 20,000 fans like you."

"Oh, I don't think you do, Mr Maxwell," replied Derek. Now Maxwell was the boss of all he surveyed. A big, bullish man whose word was law, he was most certainly not used to having anyone disagree with him and definitely not contradict him. Looking briefly taken aback, Maxwell asked: "Why do you say that then?"

"Because I get in for nowt," said Derek. Cue huge guffaws of laughter, not least from Maxwell.

Derek may even have made an impression on Her Majesty The Queen when she came to Rotherham, handing her a little gift of a Millers pennant. In fact, he cheekily sent one to Neil Armstrong, asking if he'd take it with him to the moon on that inaugural mission. He got a personal letter in reply from the famous astronaut. Derek's fame across football certainly helped with his fundraising and he used it to keep the pounds rolling in. But, to put the record straight, he could also be a bit of a nuisance on the odd occasion. A friend of mine, a club sponsor, was entertaining some big, potential customers and wanted them to have his full, undivided attention. But Derek wanted a word and, despite a refusal, insisted the sponsor pop and see him. Reluctantly he left his guests and all Derek wanted was to ask is if he'd sponsor some horses at a future fundraising race night! My pal told Derek he wasn't pleased and that it could have waited until the next day. "But however hard you try," he told me later, "you just can't fall out with Derek."

***

All the players knew Derek and would chat. Ours was a genuine friendship going back a long way. I enjoyed his company and well recall one particular night when we met up. In fact, I couldn't possibly forget it and it resonates still. It was 1993 and, although I was assistant manager under Phil Henson at the time, I still had an active interest in the youth set-up. On Thursday nights I'd pop to the Millmoor gym to check on the club's School of Excellence, have a word with the coaches and then go for a drink afterwards in the snug at the Millmoor Hotel next to the ground. On this particular night I joined our Brian, my former teammate John Seasman and dear old Cliff Powell, who had been hosting the young fans' Millers United social night at the club down Millmoor Lane. At the last minute I thought I'd invite Derek. By then his mum and dad were quite elderly and he had a nurse helping him. It was short notice and I didn't expect him to come. A bit later the pub door swung open and Derek was wheeled in by his nurse. He'd made the effort.

We had a great night laughing and reminiscing – much of the laughter inspired by Derek, even at the expense of himself. Many times when I felt down or thought I'd got my own share of troubles, I'd call to see Derek. I'd look at him laid there, speaking modestly about his life and, above all, not complaining. It put my life and my concerns into perspective. He had a bit to drink that night, as usual through a straw, and was a merry Miller indeed as he set off home. The next morning at 7am, I was woken up by a phone call. It was Cliff Powell. I knew straightaway.

"It's Derek, isn't it?" I said. He'd died the previous night. In fact, almost certainly as the nurse was wheeling him back on the few minutes' walk to his home on Clough Road. She could hear him struggling and unfortunately he couldn't be saved. I went straight up that morning, gave Mrs Dalton a big hug and commiserated with his dad, Cliff. In a way I'm glad we had that last night together.

As good friends do, we could wind each other up. When I was a player, he would throw out a witty line – but often a cutting one that was bang on the mark – about some aspect of my performance. In retaliation I would impersonate him with his broad Rotherham accent and his high-pitched tone. It was easy for me to mimic him. I developed such a good impersonation that he often told me I sounded more like him than he did. That was Derek, able to laugh at himself if he thought something was funny and I never had a problem taking him off in front of him. I like to think it strengthened the depth of our friendship.

All those years provided me with a lot of memories and anecdotes and, when I did talks or after-dinner speeches, I could relate Derek Dalton stories, complete with impersonation. These would go down well, particularly with Millers fans who knew him or remembered him. If they didn't know him, they certainly knew of him. At one fans' event with Ronnie Moore a few years after his death, I moved into Derek impersonation mode. During the interval I saw Derek's mum was there and I was immediately concerned. She was elderly and suffering with her sight and I thought she might be upset. Not at all. She'd heard and understood why I did the impersonation and she later sent me a lovely message saying she thought it was fantastic. "While ever you are alive," she added, "Derek is alive." God bless her, she's passed away now, but she was an absolute angel with her son. And never can I forget her telling me the story of taking Derek, as a two-year-old toddler, on a day trip to the seaside with his older brother Tony.

"He ate exactly the same as Tony that day except Derek had a tomato, which he ate like an apple," she said. "That night he started to be ill and it turned out to be polio. I always wondered if it could have possibly been something to do with that tomato." It almost certainly wasn't, but that was a terribly nagging thought for a wonderful woman to have carried with her for the rest of her life. Derek's delicate health meant he was always susceptible to any infections or virus knocking about, any of which might have been fatal at any point of his life.

But when he did pass away that night in 1993, just before his 46th birthday, it was still a massive shock. There was a huge turnout at his funeral and I was honoured to be one of the pallbearers. As a youngster Derek was in the Boy Scouts and received their highest honour, the Scout VC. His fame in his home town and the respect he attained for what he'd achieved despite such overwhelming odds meant that he was named Rotherham's Citizen of the Year for 1993. It was the first time it had ever been awarded posthumously.

Today at the New York Stadium he would have loved, the disabled enclosure in the east stand is named after Derek – a courtesy afforded by Graham Moore, chairman of its sponsors Westfield Health and a good friend of his. There is also a blue plaque dedicated to him outside the stadium on the wall at the corner of the west and north stands. The Derek Dalton clock, which was fixed to the front of the Railway End facing the pitch at his beloved Millmoor, has never been allowed to be removed by the ground's owners despite efforts by supporters to re-site it at the new stadium.

It still remains in place, clearly seen by anyone walking across Coronation Bridge overlooking the old ground which looks exactly the same as it did when the club last played there in 2008. Despite the understandable intention of the fans, I'm actually happy it's still there because I think it is appropriate it never was removed – it's the Derek Dalton clock, looking down on where his ashes are buried and where he watched his beloved team. I still tell Derek stories now with that impersonation and I like to think his mum would have approved. I appear on shows with Ronnie and we both acknowledge that Derek, with his vibrant personality, was such an influence on our lives, even if only to make us realise how lucky we were to play football and then to work in football management and be fit and able enough to do both. There is only one way to end this chapter and it is the way Derek would always finish off any phone conversation.

Up the Millers.

8

JUST A STEP AWAY FROM GLORY

There is always excitement – mixed with a touch of trepidation, it has to be said – when you prepare to start off in a higher division following promotion. But the way things had unfolded under Jim McGuigan and then developed and improved during the promotion campaign, we felt there was nothing to fear stepping into the Third Division for season 1975/76. Things had turned around both for me personally and the club in general. After the tough time I'd had a couple of seasons previously, getting stick from the crowd, I had won them over. It had been a great honour being recognised by my peers who voted me into the PFA Division Four team and the supporters felt proud of their club again and more connected.

The connection often went further than previously because some of the players, particularly the local lads, would often get together socially with supporters in pubs and clubs. The night we clinched promotion I went to the Adam and Eve nightclub in town with Seamus, Crawf and a few others. There was backslapping from supporters, we bought each other drinks, no trouble at all. Not sure you could do that today; in minutes you'd have fans uploading pictures on Twitter and all forms of social media. After a few drinks you can imagine what subsequent photos might look like and the misinterpretation if you got caught as your eyes were half-closing. Then the comments that would be posted as well. Not all – if any! – of them complimentary. Ah, the naive, innocent days of the 1970s, eh!

There was a significant introduction to the first team for the opening game in the new division – a young giant at centre half in Paul Stancliffe, who was only 17 and still an apprentice. What a great asset for the football club he turned out to be and he formed a super partnership in centre defence with Tommy Spencer, another shrewd McGuigan signing. Like the influential Jimmy Goodfellow in the promotion season and beyond, he provided invaluable experience and know-how for what was a young team. A 3-0 defeat at Brighton on that first day was a rude awakening, but there were typically uplifting words from Goodfellow, our new skipper, after drawing our opening home game 1-1 with Hereford United – when I got my only goal that season.

"Look," he said, "we're on our way. Yes, we wanted to win, but it's a point and it means we are off the mark. And, trust me, just getting that first point on the board is important." It put things in perspective when we were feeling just a little bit deflated and he was right. It was also a much better result than it seemed at the time; Hereford ended up champions. Interestingly the opening gate for that first home game after promotion was ... just 3,825. It was a season of consolidation. We got huge praise for our football when drawing 0-0 on the club's first league visit to Hillsborough for 18 years. It was even better a few months later, March 1976, when Dick Habbin's goal sank Sheffield Wednesday 1-0 at Millmoor.

Despite numerous home games against them since then, the Millers fans had to wait until a League Cup tie in 2013 to beat them on home soil. It's a great pity no fans were in the ground for the 3-0 win over them in October 2020, the first at home in the league since the 1976 victory. Yet during the same period the Millers have a great record at Hillsborough with wins and draws all over the place. It's strange that we couldn't beat them at home for so long – yet have so often won and done very well at their place.

***

The best of the McGuigan years in terms of football played – even allowing for the promotion season – came in the following campaign, 1976/77. We played some wonderful stuff that season and got so agonisingly close to promotion into what's now the Championship. We could hardly have come much closer. There are a couple of remarkable statistics from that season and it probably indicates why we were so consistent.

No fewer than NINE players played more than 40 games and SIX appeared in all 46 league games – Tom McAlister, Paul Stancliffe, Tommy

Spencer, Trevor Phillips, Dave Gwyther and Alan Crawford. Three others – me, David Pugh and Jimmy Goodfellow – played 43, 44 and 42 respectively, while Richard Finney appeared in 34 and only a two month injury absence stopped him being an ever-present. There was a spell of 18 consecutive league and FA Cup games in which the team remained unchanged – and we even had the same substitute in all of them, Barry Wagstaff. Not once did he get on the pitch in that time, which has to be some sort of record, surely?

In fact, we lost only once in a run of 24 league games between mid-October and early April – away to eventual champions Mansfield. Such continuity in personnel meant there was a familiarity among the players; we knew our jobs individually and in the team framework and it nurtured a trust and understanding throughout the team, not least with partnerships forming. When you play week in, week out as a particular partnership – as, for example, Paul Stancliffe and Tommy Spencer did in centre defence, or Dave Gwyther and Trev Phillips did up front – you understand each other more and work together better. There was a real desire in that team to work hard and pull for each other.

By then I was well established and Jimmy Goodfellow used to tell people about my impressions – he reckoned I could take off the manager perfectly. I would stand on the dressing room table and sing *Just one cornetto* from the TV advertisement. Anything for team spirit, eh? An early highlight that season was the 3-1 win at Sheffield Wednesday one Tuesday night in November. We outplayed them and one thing I can remember is that, when we got our third goal late on, I suddenly became aware of thousands of Wednesday fans giving up on their team and heading for the exit. I do remember, just before the final whistle, looking around the stands at Hillsborough and all I could see were thousands of empty seats.

At the end of March we were joint top with Mansfield. There were 12 games to go and, although we didn't know it at the time, an incident in our next game was to have an ultimately crucial effect on the promotion outcome. Our opponents at Millmoor were Crystal Palace, five points further back and they'd played a game more as well. We were leading 1-0 when the referee, Peter Willis, awarded a free kick in the second half against our goalkeeper Tom McAlister for exceeding the four-step rule. This was a rule brought in to curb time wasting and referees were generally slack on it, but goalkeepers knew they had only four steps available to them before getting rid of the ball.

You can check out the footage on YouTube – it was the main highlights game on Yorkshire Television's *Goals on Sunday* the next day – but it was a decision that is harsh in the extreme. In fact, I believed at the time and do so now, having seen it again, that Willis was looking to even things up, having penalised the Palace goalkeeper in the first half for the same offence. While we didn't score from our free kick, Palace did so. The game finished 1-1. It was petty, but Willis was the sort of officious referee who had his head in the air, projecting a supercilious attitude. Eight years later he was the first referee to send off a player in an FA Cup final, Manchester United's Kevin Moran.

I cannot recall a referee making two such "four-step" decisions in the same match all the rest of the time I played! As I said, I did not realise at the time the huge effect this would subsequently have. Not to bleat, but another dubious decision a few games later proved very costly indeed. It was a goal ruled out at Wrexham which would not have been disallowed in this modern era. Back then, such long range goals were wiped off, usually on the whim of a linesman – as with this one.

Wrexham were third; we were fourth. It was the game in hand both clubs had on the two above them, Brighton and Mansfield, with three teams promoted. At 1-1 Mark Rhodes struck a stunning 25 yarder into the top corner. What a goal it was. We celebrated. But the linesman had his flag up. In an offside position, but out on the wing and nowhere near play, line of flight or anything else, was Richard Finney. In those days, if a referee saw a linesman with his flag up, he simply acknowledged it and ruled out the goal. It was a criminal decision because no one could possibly have interfered with Rhodesy's screamer – and certainly not Fin. It was a perfectly good goal. In the changed modern climate the linesman doesn't flag in such a situation unless the offside player is deemed "active." Finney, in splendid isolation out wide, would no way have been deemed active. But that's today and this was then. We should have been 2-1 up. Instead we lost 2-1.

My belief about those two games and those two cruellest of decisions is that we would have had a total of two extra points and most certainly an additional one. But as we came to the final Saturday of the season, we had to win by six clear goals at Port Vale to overhaul Palace, who had completed their fixtures, in the third and final promotion place. We also needed Wrexham not to win and they drew. Of course you simply don't win 6-0 away to order.

We led 2-0 at half-time and late on made it 4-0. Immediately afterwards, with 10 minutes to go, we were so close to 5-0, and really had a chance of the miracle, when hitting the bar. But all the time tempers were rising with the tension because Vale had become more physical and set out to stop us in any manner possible. At times we responded. When Dave Gwyther – our big, strong Welshmen who didn't take any prisoners – was sent off, we knew that was it and Vale rubbed it in with a late consolation goal.

The final table showed we had finished on the same points as promoted Palace, but they had a better goal difference by three. Reflecting on that near miss after the game, my thoughts flashed back to six weeks earlier at Millmoor and the decision of referee Willis which so benefited Palace, enabling them to get a point which, as we all now knew, had enabled them to finish third and not us. And you can throw in that Wrexham one as well. One or the other and we would have got promotion. Top scorer that season was our slightly-built left winger Alan Crawford, a local lad from Wickersley. He scored 31 goals in all, 23 of them in the league, and it is a club record for a winger. A number of them were penalties, but they still have to be scored.

It was to be the peak for that set of players. As can often happen to a team who just miss out so narrowly on promotion, there can be an adverse reaction the following season. The team began to lose some of their major influences over the next couple of seasons and McGuigan, always asked to run a tight ship by the board, had to rebuild and needed to recruit well again. The rebuild proved difficult on the back of some inadequate recruitment, although you certainly wouldn't describe an unknown right back signed from non-league football in the North East as inadequate. Gerry Forrest proved to be one of McGuigan's best signings.

But the cracks started to show. On and off the pitch.

9

RED MIST, EXPLOSIONS, BUT THE BEST OF PALS

Players make many friendships across their years in football. Some are lasting and endure; some are fleeting and almost a case of ships passing in the night. One of my most enduring ones is a friendship I loved and continue to treasure – and what a character he was. Goalkeeper Jim McDonagh. Known to all and sundry as Seamus because of his part-Irish ancestry, he was brought up in Canklow which, in 1960s Rotherham, was no place for faint hearts or dilettantes. Seamus was neither.

We started out at Rotherham United at the same time, him just a few weeks ahead of me because he left St. Bernard's RC School at Easter as I left school in the summer. We were renewing acquaintance, having played together for Rotherham Boys at under-15 level. The traditional apprentice's boot polish "initiation" ceremony, mentioned previously, was led by good old Seamus. Thanks for that, pal! So we grew up together, played together and might even have been that bit closer because we were goalkeeper and defender. He certainly provided me with some memorable moments although not all of them were on the football pitch. He was quite a character.

Apart from the fact he would turn out to be a very good goalkeeper – he was an England youth international – what I soon learned was that he wasn't someone to take liberties with. He was hard, had a fierce determination to win and didn't take prisoners. When he felt he had been wronged or not treated fairly, then it might put him in a bad mood; if that happened, be careful. If the red mist came down, then the siren sounded for those in the firing line. He wasn't afraid of a fight. In fact, I would tell people that I used to hold his jacket!

A fairly early example of his willingness to take forward steps and not a backward one, came during a youth trip to Holland. Wolves were on the same tour and we were out with them one night when four Dutch locals were riled by a couple of the Wolves boys. They set off running back to us, followed by the Dutch four chasing them. We turned round and Seamus set off towards them, taking off his jacket as he did so, ready for a confrontation. They stopped in their tracks and ran off. Another occasion was on the team coach. Seamus wasn't in a good mood. He was vying at the time with Roy Tunks for the first team spot; and Tunks had got it.

Seamus had brought Goal magazine with him. It was passed down the bus, but, when it got back to Seamus, it had a rip in it. "Who's ripped my magazine?" he roared down the bus. It wasn't normally something that might cause the red mist to descend, but his mum always bought him that every week and I know that's what upset him. Tunksy owned up: "It was me, sorry." Seamus wasn't in the mood for apologies. He set off down the bus, Tunks stood up, too, and reserve centre half Tony Henderson bravely attempted to intervene to stop a scene. He got brushed aside, thrust back into his seat. When intervention to the altercation was made seconds later, Seamus had Tunksy by the throat!

Roy was a very good goalkeeper, but it was obvious the club couldn't keep both, not with McDonagh now pushing through. Roy was the one for the club to cash in on at that time. He was sold to Preston for their then-record fee for a goalkeeper and went on to have a splendid career at several clubs, topping 800 games in all. So the name of McDonagh became the regular No.1 on the teamsheet although things didn't run exactly smoothly because of a fan on the Tivoli End who took to giving him some stick and shouting things to wind him up. Once he even remonstrated with the fan, pointing up into the crowd. A bit later the fan got "rescued" in an extraordinary incident.

Four or five of us were having a coffee after training in the old Ring O'Bells cafe on the corner of Church Street. All of a sudden Seamus sprang up out of his chair and dashed outside. Naturally we followed to see what was up and Seamus has this young bloke cornered, up against a shop front a bit further down the street. The bloke looked petrified as Seamus kept hold of him, explaining: "This is the fan who's been abusing me from behind the goal for weeks." Fortunately we were able to stop anything further and the fella was saved from a possible good hiding. Seamus just happened to see this bloke walk past the cafe and recognised him as the abuser. The fan got the message because I never heard of any further stick for our goalkeeper!

Seamus didn't mind whom he confronted if he felt it was justified. Including the manager! He was the regular No.1 until suffering a broken leg midway through the season after promotion in a home game against Chesterfield. Our only sub, striker "Willie" Womble, went in goal and we won 2-0. A month or so later Seamus, his leg in plaster, and I went to have our regular haircut at Pete Morris's salon on Wellgate. Pete was a big Millers fan and most of the lads went there; we'd even take new signings. At least one club chairman got his hair cut there – except that, while we paid Pete in cash, the chairman never did. Instead he gave him a couple of tickets for the next home match which Pete would have been going to anyway! And this chairman was supposedly a millionaire!

Anyway, on this particular day we were in adjacent chairs, the shop was full and the radio was tuned to *BBC Radio Sheffield*. When the sports news came on, the presenter announced that Rotherham had signed on-loan goalkeeper Tom McAlister on a permanent basis from Sheffield United. I thought it made sense as our No.1 would be out for ages and we needed someone. But when I looked at Seamus, he was clearly not sharing the same view.

His face was like thunder. He was livid and when Seamus was not pleased, get ready! He raised his hand. "Hold it, can I borrow the telephone, please?" he asked. Pete Morris brought it over. Seamus stood up, hair half-cut. "Will you switch the radio off, please, while I talk?" he asked. A deathly hush descended on the salon. Nobody spoke; the hairdressers even paused cutting hair. As he waited for his call to be put through, his face was getting redder and redder. Finally, he was through to manager Jim McGuigan. Seamus asked if what he'd just heard on the radio was true, that he'd signed Tom McAlister. Yes it was, came the reply. There was a long pause before Seamus didn't just ask for a transfer – he demanded one. He didn't wait for a response either. He slammed down the phone and handed it back to Pete. Suddenly, aware of the stunned silence in the salon, he raised his hand again and, still wearing his protective cape, bowed to the row of waiting customers. "Okay, carry on," he said, before sitting back down in the chair for the resumption of his haircut. That was Seamus. But it wasn't the end of that particular episode.

He actually limped up to the manager's office the next day to hand in his written transfer request – even though his leg was still in pot, would be for ages and he couldn't play anywhere for months. It wasn't to be the last altercation between player and manager concerning this particular matter. In Seamus' absence for the rest of the season, McAlister established himself as the No.1. The following pre-season McGuigan intimated he might alternate his goalkeepers. When it didn't happen, Seamus took issue.

At the team meeting the day before our friendly with Bolton, McGuigan began naming the team. "McAlister, Forest, Breckin..." The manager had barely got my name out when Seamus piped up from the back of the room. "Hold it, hold it," he said. "You told me that we goalkeepers would be playing alternate games. It should be my turn tomorrow, but I suppose I'll be playing at bloody Goole on Tuesday night." McGuigan reacted: "I'll see you later on," and ordered Seamus from the room. Before he left, the angry goalkeeper repeated his claim – with the odd swear word chucked in – that the manager had told him the 'keepers would be alternated and added, pointing around the room at all us players: "They are all witnesses in here; I want a transfer." McGuigan replied that he could have one, to which Seamus further addressed his teammates: "You've all heard that!"

The team room was close by the players' tunnel and, as McGuigan was outlining what he expected from us against Bolton, singing and the sound of a familiar tune suddenly started to drift into the room from the tunnel. I thought it was Frank Sinatra and Fly Me to the Moon, but no, it was a tuneful Seamus... "Sell me to the Spurs and let me play among the stars. For I just want to get away, I'd even play on Mars." Inside the room every player was absolutely bursting to laugh and we were all biting our knuckles, trying not to. It was a hilarious moment. But there was still another clash to come.

We'd had a training session soon afterwards and in the subsequent meeting McGuigan told us: "I've had a player come to see me and he's told me he's not happy; he's told me he's a grenade and what do I do if I've got a grenade in my hand? You don't pull the pin out. Well, he says that I've pulled the pin out and he's going to explode." Again Seamus butted in. "Hey, that's personal," he said. "That's not on. You don't care, you didn't come to see me when I was in hospital with my broken leg, you never bothered about me then, so you can f*** off." Nothing could survive that.

His departure to Bolton quickly followed and he went on to enjoy a splendid career, playing for them and Everton in the top flight. It didn't surprise me. Although born in Rotherham, he was capped 25 times for the Republic of Ireland, qualifying through his father who came from County Mayo. After becoming a goalkeeping coach, he enjoyed a fruitful relationship with Martin O'Neill at Sunderland, Aston Villa and Leicester City and also with him at international level as the Republic of Ireland goalkeeping coach. Another man who thought highly of him was O'Neill's assistant, Roy Keane. He is not a man to suffer fools gladly, but was complimentary about Seamus in his autobiography.

On the occasions when he is able to get to a game, Seamus loves coming back to Rotherham and catching up with old friends. It's always great to see him, he's always wonderful company with a few tales to tell and, y'know what, I even think he's mellowed a bit! He is a great lad to have grown up at the football club with and, of all the youngsters who came through together in our era, he was the one who achieved the most on the football stage. But it's never gone to his head. He's still the same old Seamus whenever he does come back. He was the best goalkeeper I ever played with and I would always want him in my side and on my side.

***

Seamus and I, with another local lad, left winger Alan Crawford, were as one before the start of the 1976/77 season. We all asked for a transfer! The McDonagh one has been noted, but my reason and that of Alan was different. We were unhappy with the terms of the new contract we had been offered. As you can imagine, it made headlines in the local papers. Of course, I didn't really want to leave. It was all about trying to get the sort of money I felt I deserved after three and a bit seasons as the first choice left back.

It was always felt that local lads, those who had come through the ranks, were short-changed when it came to wages compared with those who were signed from elsewhere. You shouldn't be penalised for being local, getting less money, so we felt we had to make a stand – not only for ourselves, but also for others who would follow. We always seemed to be the poorer relations as we noted new signings on more money. It didn't stop one of them, however, pleading poverty and asking to borrow some cash.

This particular player asked me if I could lend him £100 – twice my basic wage at the time – for a deposit on a washing machine because his signing-on fee hadn't gone through as yet. I lent him the money. I'm still waiting to be paid back! Some time later I mentioned this to a teammate. "That's funny," he said. "He asked me to lend him hundred quid for a washing machine and I've not got it back either." We believe it all ended up in the bookies!

During the previous season I had been on £50 a week, plus whatever accrued through the incentive scheme the club introduced and which was so complicated I couldn't even start to try to explain it. None of the players had a clue apart from Richard Finney, who was the brainiest of us all. So, towards the end of the month, Rich had worked it all out for each player and would tell us what we were due in bonuses. The club was run very well, but we weren't up there with the best paid in the division. In fact, we were in the bottom half. Of course, fans don't like players asking for a transfer, but I did say publicly at the time that it wouldn't alter my attitude on the pitch. I would still give 100 per cent out there.

Jim McGuigan pulled me one day and said: "You've not re-signed." My reply was: "No and I'm not going to either on those terms." Not long afterwards vice chairman Lewis Purshouse took me aside at a club function and asked what it would take. What happened back then – and no agents were representing players in those days – is you went to see the manager about a new contract. I'd ask for a £10 rise, but the club would say they couldn't do that and you'd get offered £5. On this occasion I decided to stick out for what I felt I was worth. In the end I got what I asked for, a tenner, which took my basic wage to £60.

McGuigan never held it against me in any way and, in fact, two years later made me club captain after Jimmy Goodfellow's free transfer at the end of the 1977/78 season. It was a great honour and meant backing up captaincy at youth and reserve team levels. My game had started to improve, particularly as a defender, because there had been queries against the defensive side of my game in the early years and it was said I was just an attacking full back. But by the age of 24-25 I had grown up as a defender. The manager was generous in his reasoning to the Press: "John's game has matured well, both on and off the field," he said. "He has maximum regard for the club and his responsibilities towards it." It was really nice to read that and be acknowledged in such a way. But little did either of us realise that a year later the captaincy would be removed because I again put in a transfer request – this time for different reasons.

10

END OF AN ERA ... AND THE START OF ANOTHER

It was an unprecedented scene that stunned everyone on the team coach. And it probably signalled the beginning of the end for Jim McGuigan as Rotherham United manager despite the fact it was still to be two more years away. One thing we had, young and old in that team, was respect for McGuigan. His name deserves to have a worthily high place in the modern history of the club because he stabilised and righted a sinking ship and had the vision, the courage and the trust to put his faith in a core group of homegrown players. Both manager and players were extremely good for each other during that rebuilding period of the mid-1970s when, had the board made a poor choice of manager, the club could have been marooned in Division Four for who knows how long.

But McGuigan was the right man at the right time. His particular way of playing produced some outstanding football and his introduction of new ideas stimulated a group of players either young and eager to learn and do well or experienced ones with enough nous and football intelligence to grasp it and carry out his wishes. I learned a lot from him, not least in his wisdom and the way he used those wise words. One team meeting occurred with us on a good run and immediately after a very good result. Naturally we were feeling pleased with ourselves. Enter the manager.

He touched on the good performance from Saturday and then made his point. "You'll all have looked in the paper and seen the eights and nines out of 10 and patted yourself on the back and got the reports in your scrapbook," he said. "Well, make sure to read it when you've got fours and fives out of 10 and put those in your scrapbook as well. And make sure you always turn back to that page before you shut the book."

Jim had made his point and very succinctly. Keep your feet on the ground. He had lots of little sayings, very smart ways of getting his message home, and I would find myself repeating classic McGuigan phrases and sayings to players in my future coaching years. But the night of his outburst, a couple of months into the 1977/78 season, was a shock. After the narrow promotion miss, we actually started this next season quite well. After seven games we were joint top, had beaten both the top two, Colchester and Oxford, and had a game in hand as well. On a Tuesday night we were at Shrewsbury, promoted with us a couple of years before and with whom we had established a little rivalry. The meetings were always close, but on this occasion we were well beaten 4-1. We all knew what time we'd leave after a night game and all the very disappointed and deflated players were on the team coach at the appointed time. But not everyone was.

And we waited ... and waited ... and waited. The manager had still not turned up. The wait continued until patience – probably shortened by the defeat, too – snapped and it was decided that someone should go and investigate what had happened to the manager. It turned out not to be the best idea. The designated search party returned with news that he was still enjoying a drink with Shrews' boss Alan Durban and staff. The search party actually threw stones up at the office window to get attention and indicate they were still patiently waiting. It was an action which didn't go down well at all with the visiting manager inside.

We waited and waited a bit more until finally the coach door opened and on walked a rather ruddy-faced and clearly unhappy manager. He stood at the front of the bus and started to address everyone on it, including a couple of our local Rotherham Press guys who were allowed to travel with the team back then. When they realised what was coming, they tried to do the diplomatic thing and got up to leave – only for McGuigan to order them to sit down and listen as well.

It was an angry rant, berating the players in a lengthy tirade; the sort of drink-fuelled outburst I imagine many people may have come across on a night out. Except this was a respected manager acting in a manner none of us had ever witnessed before. We were stunned, but in the minutes that it went on it became an embarrassment and you simply wanted it to stop for his own sake. When it did, he shocked us even more.

"I've done. I'm f***ing finished," he said. He instantly dismissed the notion of travelling back with us and got off the coach, to be followed by his faithful assistant Charlie Bell. Vice chairman Lewis Purshouse got off to try to talk him into getting back on board, but McGuigan wouldn't be persuaded. We did indeed set off back without the manager and his assistant. What fuelled the outburst that night, I don't really know. There is a theory that Jim felt his way of playing had been sussed out. Durban was Shrewsbury's player-manager and that night he dropped into a role that perfectly nullified what was a major attacking strength for us – down our left side. Whatever we seemed to do, Durban seemed to be one step ahead and often snuffed out the threat.

The next afternoon we were all called to a meeting at Millmoor. We were convinced the manager was going to confirm his threat of the previous night and tell us he'd resigned. But he apologised to the squad and the club for his behaviour and said that having too much to drink, as he drowned his sorrows afterwards, was at the heart of it. "I'm never going to touch another drop of whisky and you should take my advice – you stay off it, too," he said.

He had been man enough to stand up in front of the same group of players and apologise for his actions. A bad result had got to him and sometimes you do lose it a bit – that's what can happen in sport. It was soon forgotten – we won the next game four days later – but I think he did lose a bit of respect because of that incident and some people viewed him slightly differently as a result of it. It wasn't the only team coach "incident" either!

We drew 1-1 at Bury and, as time approached for the team coach to leave, a couple of players were still inside the ground. McGuigan got on the coach and at the appropriate time told the driver to set off. He was prepared to leave those players behind. As the coach started to move, vice chairman Purshouse told the driver to stop. McGuigan responded in his Scottish burr: "Drive on, driver" and, as the bus started again, once more Purshouse intervened: "Stop the bus."

McGuigan told the driver to drive on once more and Purshouse overruled the order again. The poor old driver was in a right pickle, following one order and then receiving a contradictory one. But in the end, of course, there was only one outcome. The vice chairman is deemed in overall charge of club affairs in such a situation and McGuigan had no choice but to back down. The missing players came running back and got on the bus, saved only by the vice chairman's intervention.

Talking of missing players, there was a humorous incident on the once-a-season "working holiday" McGuigan organised every year. It was at the former FA coaching centre at Lilleshall, where we would have four or five days doing two or three sessions a day. It was a good bonding exercise, but damned hard work. The place was great and had everything but a bar, leading three players – Dave Gwyther, Trev Phillips and Mark Rhodes – to decide one night to go out to the nearest village. It wasn't that near because the Lilleshall complex is in the middle of nowhere and it is a heck of a long walk back up the drive from the main road. It was about 11.30pm when the three lads heard a car on their way back. They realised it belonged to McGuigan, who had been out to a Tuesday night game, and dived into the bushes to avoid detection.

When they eventually made it up the drive, they decided not to get back in through reception, but instead through Gwyth's first-floor bedroom window that he had craftily left ajar. Trev Phillips, being the smallest, was lifted up to lever it open. "I'll go in and put the light on, Gwyth," he said. He climbed in, clicked on the light and jumped back in amazement. Sitting on the bed was Jim McGuigan. "Er, hello, boss," said Trev – and, hearing that, Gwyther and Rhodes ran off.

"Why are you coming through the window?" asked the manager. "We've been for a drink, boss," came the reply. McGuigan let it be known to the squad the next day he wasn't happy. "You have everything here you need, yet three players decide to go out of the complex to the village pub," he said. "So I will be punishing them." We had an extra tough session that day and I was one of a delegation who went to see the gaffer later, asking him not to punish the trio. As it turned out, he didn't fine them, but we, and particularly those three, knew that we had better not let him down in the game a few days later. Fortunately we didn't, drawing 3-3 at Lincoln with Gwyther, one of the missing three, scoring twice.

It wasn't the only time McGuigan had pulled us up about having a drink. When the wife of physio Alan Smith had their first baby, a lot of us went out with Alan to the Adam and Eve nightclub to wet the baby's head. Tagging along was the new addition to the coaching staff, Barrie Claxton. Next morning Barrie innocently mentioned to the gaffer that he'd had an enjoyable night out, having a celebration drink with the lads. McGuigan was not best pleased to hear it and called everyone together.

"So, someone's wife is having a baby and you think that's a good excuse to all go and have a drink, do you?" he asked. "Well, what will it be next time? I know; one of you will have a pimple on your arse and, when it bursts, you'll all cheer and decide to go out and have a drink to celebrate. Well, drinking isn't on. Charlie – run 'em," he ordered his assistant. And we had to run and run and run that morning. If there was any of the previous night's beer left, it came up in the most unpleasant way for some of the lads. It was a lesson learned a really hard way.

***

Although a core of the team remained good, there was a definite weakening around the edges and after two below-average seasons the denouement came in the opening months of the 1979/80 season. The controlling Purshouse family, chairman Eric and his son Lewis, decided to put the club up for sale. In stepped self-styled millionaire Anton Johnson, an Essex businessman complete with big fur coat and loads of promises. He was actually a butcher from Thurrock in Essex – a fifth generation of the family in that particular business – so there must have been plenty of money in that game if he was a millionaire. Ironically Eric Purshouse had originally been a butcher in Rotherham!

To the fans – and indeed everyone else who was hooked – it seemed an enticing prospect. A fresh start and a new era, ambitious talk of spending money contrasting greatly with the steady, frugal and financially stable regime operated by the Purshouses, who treated the club's money as if it was their own and ran the club sensibly, ensuring that it stayed in the black. Not all the new breed of owners coming into football then would necessarily have the same mindset.

This flamboyant newcomer was offering an exciting future and plenty of money to throw at it, as you'd expect from a so-called millionaire. So it was strange that it seemed to take so long for him to come up with the £62,500 needed to buy the club. In fact, it went into the Purshouse bank account only five minutes before a final deadline in December 1979.

At first all was well in the early part of that 1979/80 season. The team had a great start and were top of the table when at the beginning of October it all started to come crashing down – as did the boundary wall at the Tivoli End when a crowd surge during the 20,000 full house, top-of-the-table clash with Sheffield United led to injuries to some of the spectators. Results began to slide and, as negotiations with Johnson dragged on through the autumn, fans turned their ire on the Purshouses, particularly so in a home game against Oxford United at the start of November. Eric was at home with his ill wife, but the abuse aimed at Lewis was so vile and personal that he left the directors' box within minutes of the kick-off. He vowed never to return and was turned off football forever.

The way was clear for Johnson, who made several high profile appearances at home matches, to settle the deal and take over. But McGuigan realised that what was coming was not for him. He had his doubts and suspicions about the future management style and methods and decided it was time to go. He had probably come to the conclusion some time earlier that under the Purshouse family – whose philosophy actually probably suited Jim's character and way of operating – he had gone as far as he could or would be able to go. On November 10th, 1979, we played at Wimbledon and McGuigan didn't even go to the game. The rumours that swirled around proved to be true. He left Millmoor a couple of days later after six and a half years in charge.

I have often wondered how my playing career would have turned out had Jim McGuigan not arrived when he did and I hadn't been guided by his shrewd, disciplined, but compassionate management. My best achievements still lay ahead of me, but I have never underestimated the grounding he gave me, firstly from a playing viewpoint, but also learning so much from what he said and did, including repeating those classic McGuigan phrases he had used to us in squad meetings.

"Sometimes," he said, "you help a lame dog over a fence. You get over the fence and it bites you." It was his way of saying that you can help people, but they can let you down – that must have happened to all of us and I know it has to me. He reckoned that everyone is basically lazy and used an example of a housing estate with a grassed area where a really nice pavement had been laid to walk around it. But there is a worn track right across the lovely patch of grass because people take shortcuts. "Everyone takes shortcuts if they can," he said. "But I don't want anyone taking them in my team."

But his team ethic one is timeless and has always remained with me: "It's not liking what one wants to do – it's liking what one has to do for the team." I didn't slavishly follow him and didn't agree with everything he said, but playing under him, particularly in key developing years of my career, was a good learning curve and most definitely helped me in the future. Yes, the right man at the right time. He left at the right time, too. The "new way" and how things were going to operate would not have been to his liking.

11

GREAT TIMES - AND I NEARLY MISSED OUT

Perhaps pause a moment as I give a little shudder. It's when I think how close I came to leaving Rotherham United and missing some great times, including the best season of my playing career. It certainly looked on the cards in the summer of 1979. Fortunately I didn't dive in and be lured by temptation. And as luck would have it, it was fortunate the board of directors didn't succumb to temptation as well.

I had actually asked for a move during that summer of '79. Unlike the transfer request three years earlier, which was for better terms, this one was because of growing disillusionment with what was happening at the football club and the atmosphere which had developed around it. There were several indications that the club might have passed a peak and I felt I'd got a flavour of what the future might look like.

One of the factors was a result of what happened in one particular home game earlier that year and suggested a burgeoning discontent among the fans who were witnessing a failure to build on the very good season of the promotion near-miss. This was now the second below-average season after that and they were reacting to seeing their hopes fade away. However, it does not excuse anyone cheering an injured player – particularly one of your own!

We played Swindon Town at home, a game I well remember because of a horrendous colour clash. We wore red shirts, white shorts and red socks while Swindon had white shirts, red shorts and white socks. All you could see was a mass of red and white. It was confusing at times and almost certainly led to the collision in which Richard Finney suffered a badly gashed head. As he was being stretchered off, our fans were cheering at his misfortune and you could hear abusive remarks being shouted from the terraces aimed at the players in general.

I was angered, and so were the rest of the players, supporters could do that to one of their own. Suddenly I found myself thinking about my future. Having experienced abuse previously, would it be coming my way again?

Two or three clubs were interested in signing me. One of them did all they could to entice me. Another made a clandestine approach. The other club I found out about only by accident. Last one first. This nugget of information was revealed to me only decades later during the period of chaos engulfing the Millers at a time of takeovers and acute financial problems. One day I was in the club offices and the huge safe, where all sorts of documents were kept, was open. My file was in there and curiosity got the better of me. I took it out and had a look. One entry stunned me.

It noted a letter to the Rotherham United board from Swindon Town in 1979. The wording is still clear to recall even now. "We wish to make an offer of £70,000 for your player John Breckin." It was a pretty sizeable sum back then and particularly for a left back. Millers legend Danny Williams was Swindon's general manager at the time with Bobby Smith the manager. Obviously the directors had turned down the offer, but no one had ever informed me of any approach. More than 20 years later this was the first I knew of it. But I certainly knew of the second club's interest. It had a Rotherham connection.

Blackpool – managed by Bob Stokoe, who won the FA Cup with Sunderland in 1973 – were throwing money at a promotion attempt in our division and fancied this attacking left back at Rotherham. So in 1979 I went over there with my fiancée Elaine. I was met by Bob Waite, formerly head of the commercial department at Millmoor who had moved to Blackpool in a similar role. Bob knew me well. Stokoe was introduced to me and we shook hands. I was taken to the training ground and my first thought was: "Crikey, it's windy here." Bob even took me and Elaine just down the coast to Lytham St Annes to look at houses and check out the area for when I moved over.

We even talked about a job for her and reckoned she would easily get one in a hospital, considering she was working in the NHS at Rotherham Hospital. That's how close it got. But I stayed here. Thankfully. It wasn't a decision I ever came to regret. Ironically Blackpool had their final game of the season at Millmoor in desperate need of a point – not for promotion as the previous summer's big spending plans had been geared for, but to avoid relegation! As it happened, they beat us and stayed up.

The other club to get in touch were Chesterfield. I got a message to drive to a particular car park in Chesterfield and meet their manager, Arthur Cox. It was dark and I got out of my car, only for Arthur to come marching across and order me back into my little VW Beetle. He got in the passenger seat. With his close-cropped hair and his no-nonsense, disciplinarian manner, Arthur was the sort to strike fear into any young player and he opened up with a warning. "This meeting hasn't taken place and I have a witness over there," he said, pointing to a little fella sitting in his car, "that it didn't happen because I was somewhere else at this time tonight. So this interest from my football club had better not get out into the papers."

I knew Chesterfield wanted me because the phone call setting up the meeting came from a confidant of Arthur's at the club. He had opened up on similar lines: "Breck, this call has never taken place ..." I do believe Chesterfield offered £80,000, an increase on the Swindon offer, but still the Rotherham directors would not let me go. About that time there was speculation I was unhappy at the club which probably fuelled the interest from elsewhere. The truth is I was looking to my future and, with an eye on my personal life and aiming to get married, I wanted some security as well as better terms. A new three-year contract and the prospect of a job on the backroom staff when my playing days were over was the offer from Rotherham. It was gratefully accepted.

When Jim McGuigan left, I must admit it did unsettle me a bit. I felt my position was safe while he was there and I'd learned a lot from him. I need not have worried although the next managerial choice – and, therefore, the high profile, cigar-smoking, allegedly helicopter-flying new chairman's first appointment – was hardly dynamic. A player from Sheffield Wednesday reserves with no previous first team coaching to his name, Ian Porterfield. He was an excellent player – scorer of the winner for Stokoe's Sunderland in their 1973 FA Cup final shock against mighty Leeds – but we had no idea of his coaching abilities. We had swapped an experienced manager for a novice. It seemed a strange move on the face of it. Any fears were misplaced. This also proved to be the right man at the right time.

Ian, appointed on New Year's Eve 1979, steered us away from the relegation zone – although I missed the last two months with a knee injury which required a small operation – and it was all systems go for the following season. But one of his first moves was a non-footballing one. In the summer Ian organised a re-painting job at the ground. The crush barriers, boot room, lockers ... you name it, he had them redone in red, regardless of the colour they were before. Apparently it was an idea he had picked up from Brian Clough who did something similar in his first managerial post at Hartlepool United.

He was very much a tracksuit manager. Hard working, diligent and hugely enthusiastic, he threw himself wholeheartedly into the job. His training sessions were longer than we'd had previously. We hadn't quite expected the intensity of the schedule and he was certainly determined to get us fit. As fit as, if not fitter than, any team in the division. And the "new" training venue had the most picturesque backdrop of any in the country – Wentworth Woodhouse, the magnificent stately home in Wentworth's picturesque village on the outskirts of town. It has the longest frontage of any house in Europe and nowadays very much a desired location for major films and TV series.

To ensure our fitness was up the scale, he brought in a pal of his from the North East, a successful long-distance runner called Jim Dixon. I had a sense of déjà vu when he was introduced. When I started at the club in 1968, Tommy Docherty had brought in someone regarded to this day, and rightly so, as one of this country's finest-ever middle-distance runners – Alan Simpson, very much a man of Rotherham. I'd heard of him because he was Britain's top middle-distance runner during the 1960s and lost out on a 1500m bronze medal at the 1964 Tokyo Olympics by 1/10th of a second. He held British records and set an indoor 5000m world record in 1965, all while holding down a full time job in the steelworks. He took us for pre-season training and what an athlete he was. None of us could match him. Fit? You bet.

He had us doing laps of Herringthorpe Stadium, including over the steeplechase barrier, but it was when Alan took us to a favourite haunt of his that we really got put through it. Big time! It was more or less at the back of St. Bernard's RC School on Herringthorpe Valley Road. He had us in Herringthorpe woods and in there was this really steep hill. It was hard enough running up it once. He had us going up and down it in sets of three! When Docherty left, Jim McAnearney carried on with Alan and I recall our flying winger Neil Warnock – yes, him – saying after one such session: "Somebody's going to have a heart attack one day running up there." That remark earned it the nickname "cardiac hill" and whether on the track, in the gym or up the hill, Alan worked us really hard and it got us fit.

When he finished his fine athletics career, Alan had more than 20 years in charge at the former Herringthorpe Leisure Centre – adjacent to where Herringthorpe Stadium athletics track is now. He remains a very good friend and, although turned 80, he still kept himself fit – which I certainly could vouch for – and for some years I've had a standing invitation to use the gym at his house just up the road from me. It is an honour and a privilege to have one of our country's all-time great middle-distance athletes, originally a working class lad from Thrybergh, as one of my match day guests from time to time at the New York Stadium.

So here I was 10 years later with a runner leading the way. Morning and afternoon sessions in front of the palatial house. The morning one would often be a seven mile run, out by the dams to Greasbrough and Wingfield, which was my patch having been brought up there. The training at Wentworth Woodhouse was during pre-season. It was at Lady Mabel College, a women's teacher training college, but this was during the summer break when the students were on holiday. At lunchtime we would go to the George and Dragon pub in the village where the son of the landlady was a massive Millers fan, known as Duke.

When the students returned, we had to go elsewhere and ended up at Grange Park at Droppingwell, using a football pitch on land belonging to Rotherham Borough Council. Because we actually shouldn't have been there, we would have to go on a run whenever council workers came to cut the grass or whatever. It was public space so anyone could use it, rather like the bloke out walking his dog who walked straight across the pitch while we were having a practice match one day. When we pointed it out, he was unperturbed. "I walk my dog across here every day," he said, "and I'm not stopping for you lot." I guess he wasn't a football fan and certainly not a Miller. In fact, we called it "dog-shit alley." But the upshot of it all was that we were all supremely fit when the 1980/81 season started.

***

There was excitement for the fans just a week before our first league game. Rotherham United splashed the cash like never before – and it was to be a long time before they matched such an outlay as well. We spent £100,000 on centre forward Ronnie Moore from Cardiff City, where he'd had a difficult time, and a total of £180,000 went on the Millwall pair of Tony Towner and John Seasman. Seasman was the bargain makeweight in the deal at just £30,000, meaning Towner was the club's record signing at £150,000 – and it was to be the next century before that figure was topped.

To be honest, he proved to be worth every penny. A small, impish right winger with blistering pace, he instantly became a crowd favourite. The fans adored him. Every Millers follower of that era recognises his nickname "Tiger." He was tagged by Millwall fans after a Shell petrol advert at the time, depicting a cartoon tiger with the slogan: "Put a tiger in your tank." With Tiger in our tank, we were certainly supercharged.

Bringing those three in, along with central defender Jimmy Mullen, a snip at £35,000, was a great boost for everyone. It seemed that Anton Johnson, the flamboyant, publicity-conscious new chairman and owner had, in contrast to the more staid, frugal Purshouses, shown his stated ambition and kept his promise to the fans to splash out. Of course, had the fans known at the time how close the takeover nine months earlier had almost fallen through for wont of the small sum of £62,500, they might have queried how he'd managed to come up with near enough £300,000 so soon after – a pretty huge sum, equating to seven figures today. Perhaps a check on the club finances at the time might have provided an answer – the Purshouses had built up shares in an oil company that were worth about £285,000. If my maths is right, that was roughly the amount of the big pre-season signings. Then again, perhaps those shares didn't do it! You decide!

We had a great season and a very good side. Well, bad sides don't win titles. We actually didn't have the greatest of starts and, although half-a-dozen games is hardly any guide, we were 17th in the Division Three table. What followed – a 2-0 win at Walsall when Tony Towner absolutely murdered their left back Kenny Mower – set me thinking. This was one of five successive wins, including a great day for our fans when we won 2-1 at Bramall Lane. That spell got us right up in the thick of things at the top and proved crucial in establishing ourselves as promotion challengers.

We didn't have a settled side in the opening few months. Cruelly we lost Richard Finney in October to the knee injury that was to finish his career. And when Millers fans of the time go back to that season, one thing they always fondly recall is Rod Fern scoring so many vital goals. "We'd win 1-0 away and Rod Fern would have scored it," they tell me even to this day. Well, the incredible thing is that, while that's true to a certain extent, Rod never played in any of the first 17 matches and his first goal didn't come until mid-November. Indeed it was only then that he formed the partnership with Ronnie Moore which was to be so devastating and so prolific. In the 28 games they played together that season, they actually scored 27 goals between them. That is some partnership.

Ronnie finished the season with 25 in all and Ferny had 11 which included the goals in four 1-0 away wins and in two 1-1 away draws. He was certainly the man for away games and his record wasn't bad for someone who started the season on the transfer list because he wanted to play in midfield. He wasn't even in manager Ian Porterfield's plans because he was never going to play him there. So he didn't play him at all until he put him in up front.

I really got a sense that something special was around the corner on Boxing Day when we played really well and won 2-1 at Hull City. I started to believe then. There was also an unusual mid-winter boost for the lads which proved very smart indeed. After a little blip with two draws and a defeat in four matches, Porterfield said: "Turn up with your passports on Monday morning." We'd no idea why. It turned out we were off to Benidorm for a few days. The manager didn't go – assistant Barrie Claxton took us – nor did chairman Anton Johnson, but two big minders went instead.

You wouldn't call it a football break. What training we did was on the beach or even the hotel car park. The place was empty; after all, it was January. One morning we looked in the car park and there was a camel walking round it. We were supposed to train at Benidorm FC, but the car park was in better condition than their pitch. There was a drinking culture in football at that time and it was as much a booze trip as anything. One morning we started doing sit-ups and one player threw up as the previous night's drinking left its mark!

But Porterfield knew that psychologically it would be good for us. We all relaxed, it was a bit more bonding for a group of players who were close anyway and then he could hit us with his message on the return. We got back Friday afternoon and the next day we had an important home game against Portsmouth, who were in the top six just below us. On the Saturday morning Porterfield had us doing some shadow play in a training session. After it, he got into us.

"Shake yourselves," he said. "You've had a week off, all nice and relaxed, having a drink and enjoying yourselves. Now it's back to business, serious stuff and it's a big game." The message hit home. The club had just looked after us, given us a nice little break. Now it was our turn to look after them. As an individual, you're thinking: "I'd really better perform this afternoon." We beat Pompey 3-0.

We also had another great 3-0 home win a few weeks later in a real promotion crunch match – some said it could be a title decider. We had gone top with a 1-0 win at Millwall the week before – yes, another Rod Fern away winner – and the visitors to Millmoor were the team we'd replaced in top spot, Charlton Athletic. Top versus second. There were six games left and excitement was really mounting. Porterfield, having seen Charlton struggle on a mudheap and lose at Bramall Lane a month earlier, decided to have the pitch heavily watered, getting the fire brigade in to do their annual fire drill practice at Millmoor the day before the game. Their hoses did a job on the pitch.

However, Porterfield hadn't bargained for the overnight rain that followed. Groundsman Albert Wilson arrived first thing the next morning to find the pitch near enough flooded. Panic stations. The match might be off. It was all hands to the pump, literally, and even Porterfield dashed down and helped with the forking. Fortunately it was okay, but, if a heavy pitch didn't suit Charlton, it wasn't going to bother us. We stuffed them 3-0 with a brilliant performance in front of a 13,515 crowd who made it a great atmosphere.

It set us up superbly. In the end promotion came in a rush, but had sort of crept up on us because no one expected it on this particular Easter Saturday. We'd won five on the trot without even conceding a goal to go from third place to clear at the top and within touching distance of promotion with five games still to play. The equation for promotion that April afternoon was simple to fathom, but looked far harder to achieve. Win at Carlisle, who hadn't lost in their previous 18 home games, and at the same time Huddersfield, then fourth, had to lose at bottom side Hull, who had just been relegated anyway and so had nothing to play for. Huddersfield had lost only two of their previous 11 away games and rock-bottom Hull hadn't won any of their previous six at home. So everyone expected Huddersfield to win or at least draw at Hull.

What Millers fans were really gearing up for was a promotion-clinching party two days later on Easter Monday at Millmoor. At home to ... Hull. Rod Fern scored in the opening few minutes at Brunton Park and, although we got a real grilling in the second half from a Carlisle side including a young, but very skilful and talented Peter Beardsley, we dug in with typical tenacity, the sort of defensive resilience we had shown all season, for another of those 1-0 away wins for which we had become famed. We got back in the dressing room, no one any wiser about what it all meant. I was in the bath when someone shouted: "Huddersfield have lost at Hull." We were promoted!

We all began jumping about, but there was no champagne to celebrate with. No one thought to bring any because no one really expected it to happen that afternoon. When some appeared, it was from the Carlisle boardroom. There were still four games left and that is some achievement to have clinched promotion with so much football still to play. All that remained was to make sure we now finished as champions. We did over-celebrate a bit – who could blame us? – and it probably affected us in the next three games when we got only a point. It meant we needed a draw from the final match at home to Plymouth Argyle.

It was a carnival occasion. Not a great game in all honesty on a really difficult, typical end-of-season pitch, but all those there won't ever forget all the celebrations after the 2-1 win. Fittingly Ronnie Moore got his 25th goal of the season early on and, although Plymouth equalised before half-time, we weren't to be denied. Film of the winner, about 10 minutes from the end, shows a pass from the left back which fortunately gets a flick off a defender to carry it into the path of Rod Fern. He seemed to take an age, but knew what he was doing before slotting the winner to spark a pitch invasion and confirm only the second title in the club's history. And there's been only one more since.

There was definitely champagne in the dressing room that day. Plenty of it. TV cameras were in there, too, and a few of us were interviewed by Martin Tyler, who later became a key figure in Sky Sports' Premier League coverage. It was an unbelievable night with the Millmoor gym turned into a disco. Fans had paid to be at the function although many players spent much of the night in the boardroom and drank it dry! It went on well after midnight and I recall one fan standing outside Millmoor waiting for a taxi, accompanied by a small tree he'd pinched from the disco!

We actually still had one more match to play. My testimonial game two nights later on the Monday. Derby County pulled out at the last minute, but fortunately Bolton Wanderers agreed to step in. We were presented with the Third Division championship trophy and everybody enjoyed themselves. We won 2-0 and I got the chance to take a penalty. The referee was John Key, a Football League official from Rotherham and he said with about 10 minutes to go: "If you get in the area, go down and I'll give a penalty." He was as good as his word.

Of course, there was only one person who everyone wanted to take it. The goalkeeper was Dennis Peacock, a lovely fella and former teammate at Doncaster Rovers. He sauntered off his line towards me, smiling, and whispered: "I'm diving to my left." I trotted up and slotted the pen to his right. I remember a fan saying to me afterwards: "That was a great penalty, Breck, you sent him the wrong way ... you ought to have taken them for us." If only he knew. It was my one and only penalty success – and I even needed a bit of help with that!

About 6,000 fans turned up, support for which I was grateful, with the trophy presentation the highlight. So we all got the chance of an additional celebration and an amazing 12 months came to an end. The best of my football life. What a great future lay ahead. Or so I thought!

12

A BIG NAME – BUT A BIG DISAPPOINTMENT

There was a confidence from everyone at Rotherham United that we would be all right moving up to Division Two. We could certainly hold our own, we all felt, if not more so. The promotion side had lots of things going for it; we had players with differing abilities and qualities and complemented each other in so many respects. It was a great dressing room, a really good spirit among the lads.

We had just gone through the season unbeaten at home so wouldn't be fearing anybody there. Ray Mountford had developed into a fine goalkeeper; Paul Stancliffe and Jimmy Mullen were a great partnership at the heart of the defence and me and Gerry Forrest at full back had both enjoyed great seasons. We both loved to attack – Gerry was a real thoroughbred who glided down the flank – and brought something extra and special. He deserved his eventual move into the top flight at Southampton, but was 28 by then and could have gone and played up there earlier. People would say we couldn't defend. Well, we were part of a defence who conceded only eight goals in all our home games and our goals-against tally of 32 was by far the best in the division.

In midfield Mark Rhodes was an unsung hero, having adapted superbly to his particular role in the side; Micky Gooding had really come on and John Seasman had obvious class; these two vied with each other later in the season. Out wide were two contrasting figures – Tony Towner, a mercurial right winger, feted by the fans for his speed and trickery and a real penetrating force, and on the other side Phil Henson was the ultimate team man. He was unselfish, worked for 90 minutes, took responsibility and was the man who always minded the back door when I bombed forward.

Then we had our front two, Ronnie Moore and Rod Fern, who had evolved into such a devastating partnership in the second half of the promotion season. Yes, we were confident. Then came the bombshell. Ian Porterfield was the man who had moulded that team into the way he wanted it. He'd got the cake mixture spot on and the end product tasted lovely. A young, eager manager had driven us on to that promotion. Then he shocked everyone by moving to Sheffield United, who had gone in the opposite direction, having just been relegated to the Fourth Division for the first time. It was a surprise, but in a strange way it wasn't. No one expected him to leave, but whispers were already growing about what was happening behind the scenes at Millmoor and Ian felt it was time to go and grasp the opportunity to perform a rescue act on an ailing giant. It was a blow because I honestly believe he could have taken us on to even better things.

The place was buzzing and promotion was just what the new chairman Anton Johnson had promised the fans when he'd taken over 18 months earlier. He was an Essex businessman and a nightclub owner. After one game in London all the players were taken back to visit his club, Croc's, in the Essex suburbs. It was so-called because there was a crocodile – only a small one, note – in something not much bigger than a fish tank. There were strippers, but the turn who opened everyone's eyes – and made them water at the same time – was Johnny Bollocks. Now I thought I recognised his face because he'd been the guy serving behind the bar. He went on the dancefloor and arranged two chairs, before stripping off below the waist and standing with a leg on each chair. He then got another, tied it to his testicles and swung it to and fro between his legs. To say I've never seen anything like it is an understatement. I could now understand his stage name. Minutes later I went to the bar and there he was, back serving again.

Johnson had promised a big name as Porterfield's replacement and at that time none came much bigger than the former captain of Liverpool and England, one Emlyn Hughes. He entered to a fanfare of huge media coverage and again, rather like when Tommy Docherty arrived, the club were in the national spotlight. Emlyn was then at Wolves and in the latter stages of his playing career, but still insisting on playing and he was appointed as player-manager. It was his first managerial job.

It seemed to everyone a great appointment on the face of it. I thought the same but straightaway me and Emlyn didn't hit it off. There was no one incident to spark it and I had no problem with him as manager; I was open minded. But I couldn't understand his cold attitude towards me and noticed pretty quickly that he was the same with the skipper, Jimmy Mullen. I came to the conclusion that, because me and Jimmy occupied the left-side central defence spot and the left back role respectively, then we may have been perceived as a threat to his own aspirations to both play and manage.

Emlyn, of course, made his career in the exact position Jimmy played, but could easily slot in at left back as well. Then John Seasman also appeared to get the cold shoulder, yet it didn't seem that would clash with Emlyn because he was a midfield player. I can think only that there was something else. I was by now a senior professional with longevity at the club. The other two were among the more senior professionals, too.

It was hard to work out why me and Jimmy Mullen were treated as we were at training. I'll bet Millers fans who watched training down at Silverwood were puzzled, too. We'd be down there with the rest of the squad and Emlyn would send across his assistant, Barrie Claxton, to tell us we wouldn't be involved in this session. So we had to jog round the pitch while the rest trained. Naturally after even a short time fitness levels dropped. I used to do my own work to try to keep my level up. Maybe he saw us as a threat to his leadership. I accept managers are human beings and have their own vulnerabilities, even top stars, but it was hard to work this one out.

***

It didn't take too long for tensions to surface in a dressing room bust up. It was only the ninth game of the season, we were at Crystal Palace and winning 1-0 at half-time. We'd played well, were bubbling and feeling pretty good. Well, Emlyn tore into us and had a right go. It was as if we were 4-0 down and not giving it our all. I couldn't understand it one bit. It flattened us, we went out quite demoralised for the second half and ended up losing 3-1.

Back in the dressing room after the game he started reading the riot act again. So I challenged him about the fact he'd had a right go at the lads at half-time when we were winning – at which point an angry Emlyn lost it and lunged towards me, grabbing me by the neck. I stood my ground, but, when it looked like getting really ugly, some of the other lads jumped in and pulled us apart. I made my way to the bath. I was shocked and almost in tears with anger. "What a mess," I thought. "What is this all about?"

It was a sad day for me because I'd never experienced that with a manager before – and didn't afterwards. While I was in the bath, he came in and apologised. "Come and have a word," he said. Fine. I eventually got out and, with still wet hair and just a towel wrapped around me, I went to see him. And guess what? He started having a go at me again and made another lunge, grabbing me again by the throat. This time Ronnie Moore and John Green pulled him away. "You're bang out of order," Ronnie raged at the manager in no uncertain manner.

For the manager to do something such as that, not once but twice, is naturally unsettling and I was definitely badly upset – so much so that I thought I would make my own way back to Rotherham. I wasn't going on that team coach with him. Then I remembered we were at Crystal Palace, a really difficult place to get home from. It wasn't as though we were somewhere not far away. So that thought didn't last long! I did get on the coach and within minutes Emlyn was shouting for me to come and join in the card school. I politely declined – although, I must admit, there wasn't much politeness in the refusal.

So things hadn't got off to a great start with the new manager. These things hurt, but none more so than one incredible occasion midway through the season. A harsh start to winter 1981 meant no league games from December 5th through into January. So to get some much-needed match practice, there was a quickly-arranged friendly with Nottingham Forest, but it was to be played in Jersey. We trained as usual in the morning, but nothing was said about any forthcoming practice match. That evening I had invited Mum and Dad round for tea and, while I was in the kitchen, they had the local evening news on TV. The presenter said that, in an attempt to beat the big freeze, the Millers would be playing a practice match in Jersey the next day.

When I came back into the lounge, my mum said: "You kept that quiet; you didn't tell us you were going to Jersey. It's just been on the local news." I glanced at the telly and back at my mum and dad. "I'm not," I said. "I don't know anything about it." I don't know who was the more stunned, me or them! We sat in silence as it emerged the squad had flown out that afternoon. No one had told me. And very quickly I found out I wasn't the only one who didn't know.

The phone rang a couple of minutes later. It was Jimmy Mullen. "I've just seen the news; I didn't know anything about this game," he said. "That's two of us then, Jim," I replied – only to discover another one a few minutes later. John Seasman called this time. And reserve goalkeeper Graham Brown didn't know anything about it either. We'd all been left behind and not told a thing! I could only think then – and believe the same now – that it was rank bad management, not even to have the decency to tell me or the others that we wouldn't be going. Jimmy had actually been sidelined after the first half-a-dozen games of the season; Seas had sort of been on the fringe, playing the odd game as a substitute here and there; Browny never figured at all under him.

Despite not having been given any instructions or messages, the four of us decided it would be sensible to report for training as usual the following day. We did so and waited and waited, but no one else turned up and there was no communication from anyone at the club. So, having hung around for a while, Jimmy suggested we go and have half a lager up the road at the Green Dragon at Kimberworth and that's what we did. But the entire incident left me with a really confused impression of our new manager. Yes, he was a fantastic player for Liverpool and England and someone you would expect to be an ambassador for football at all levels. With his laughing face and cheerful public persona, Emlyn was someone hugely popular with the wider general public. Yet he didn't have the grace and good manners to tell me – and the others – I would not be going on this trip.

From then on, unsurprisingly, communication between us became difficult and, if I'm being honest, I never did see eye to eye with him or got on with him. It gives me no pleasure writing this in view of Emlyn's life being taken so tragically early by a brain tumour at only 57. But I recall reading the autobiography of his Liverpool teammate and defensive colleague Tommy Smith who said there was a lot of animosity towards Emlyn in the Anfield dressing room and after one incident he never spoke with him outside a football pitch again.

In fact, Tommy titled a chapter about him: "A man of many faces." One day Emlyn walked into our dressing room and someone had placed Tommy's book on the table in the middle of the room, leaving it open at that particular chapter so that he couldn't miss it. It was cruel, but indicated the general feeling. The worst treatment of all was to Graham Brown. He was coming towards the end of a good career in the game; a solid, well liked and reliable professional who didn't deserve what happened.

He was told to report in an afternoon and be fully kitted out, including his gloves, at two o'clock every day. He would do that and then a few minutes later Emlyn's assistant Barrie Claxton – acting on orders – would turn up and say: "You can get dressed now, Browny, and go." I don't know if Emlyn wanted him to get fed up and pack it in one day or whether he knew Browny had his own shop in Mansfield where he would go in an afternoon, but such treatment was shocking.

How do you actually go on and play for a manager when you've been treated that way or how he treated me? Well, what got me through was playing for the shirt and being determined to do the best for myself and for my football club. If I went on to play well, then it would be more despite the manager than because of him. But it was probably my worst time at Rotherham, even allowing for the barracking early in my career.

People do fall out; I've had fall-outs and they're part of the game, but there is a right and a wrong way to treat your fellow professionals. He could have got rid of us. Perhaps he wanted us around just in case. After all, me and Jimmy were defenders. He may not have wanted us in the team, but to have shipped out two defenders would have left him short of cover at the back and he may have feared it could have left him personally exposed if things didn't go right. And you can't blame players who aren't there!

A two month absence at that time resulted from an injury during a home game with Barnsley. In the first half I suffered a subluxation – a partial dislocation – of the shoulder after a challenge from Trevor Aylott. It was really, really painful and I should have been taken off. But Emlyn didn't make the change and I had to struggle on, not having complete use of that arm and clearly restricted. What happened after the game was a joke and indicates the lack of care and professionalism at that time – nothing at all like the proper attention afforded injured players nowadays.

The physio was soon changed and off; he'd be on his way to the boardroom for a drink and a chat. I was left in real agony and so restricted I couldn't dress myself because I couldn't lift my arm up. I was still struggling and the only one left when a long-time pal, Carl Luckock, stuck his head in the dressing room to see where I'd got to. He had to help me to put my shirt on. Luckily, and thank goodness, my wife Elaine took me straight to Rotherham Hospital and, because she was a radiographer there, got me X-rayed straightaway to find the damage. Just as the nation had reason to thank the NHS during the 2020 coronavirus pandemic, so did I back in 1981. If she hadn't had such access because of her job, I'd have been left to fend for myself and go home that night in absolute agony.

Her boss at the hospital was brilliant – and a football fan – and he arranged for me to see a physio there for my rehabilitation. Note, the club did not do this, nor did they oversee my rehab. To get fit again, I went running round the woods. Ironically, after a seven-match spell out of the team, I got back in it in time to enjoy the most remarkable month's football Rotherham have probably ever been a part of. Not least because it was a record-breaker of sorts.

It was February 1982. I'd got back in for the final game in January, a 2-1 home defeat by Graham Taylor's Watford who were heading for the top flight – a game in which the wind-aided winner was scored from *inside* his own half by Watford defender Ian Bolton. When February arrived, we were third bottom and had a relegation fight on our hands. Or so we thought. Nothing could have been further from the truth by the time the month was out! The first game was the most amazing of the lot. Derby County at home on a cold Tuesday night. New midfielder Gerry Gow had been brought in to add experience and bite to the midfield. Too much of the second attribute, however. In only his second game he made himself a spot of football history, albeit of the wrong sort.

Inside the opening minute he had got himself booked. Before the two-minute mark was reached, he was looking at a red card as well for a challenge which ended with Derby right back Steve Emery suffering a broken leg. There have been faster red cards and faster yellow ones, but it is believed to be the fastest a player has ever received separate yellow and red cards in different incidents – and this certainly wasn't a second yellow either. If you take into account the stoppage in the game while the referee dealt with the yellow card, then it was about 90 seconds of playing time. Down to 10 men in the opening couple of minutes, we were losing 1-0 at half-time and not long afterwards Ronnie Moore missed a penalty. How much more could go wrong? Nothing, as it turned out, as the 10 men came back to win 2-1.

It sparked a winning spree. A 2-0 home win over Crystal Palace meant eight straight wins in February – the most number of successive victories ever in a calendar month, its shortest one too. Those eight games were in just 26 days and we ended the month third top after starting it third bottom. An incredible turnaround. Fab Feb indeed.

A 3-0 win at Oldham followed to make it nine, Ronnie scoring after using his elbow to nudge the ball out of the 'keeper's arms, and it would have been 10 on the trot, but for Tony Towner having a stoppage-time penalty saved at home to Newcastle. We were right in the thick of the promotion fight to get into the top division. Another missed penalty in stoppage time – this time by Gow – stopped us from beating runaway leaders Luton Town, the eventual champions, in a 2-2 draw at Millmoor that was on Match of the Day. Actually those two missed penalties – both in added-on time – were more significant than it seemed at the time. Because they were so late, they would certainly have won us those two matches, providing an extra four points in total in what was the first season of three points for a win. It would have meant us going into the final game of the season in third place, an automatic spot then, and knowing a win would have taken us to the old First Division. Even a draw would have done it as it transpired.

Instead we headed for already-relegated Wrexham knowing we couldn't catch Norwich, but still had a chance of securing fourth and so finishing as Yorkshire's top club in Division Two. The night before the game Emlyn said in the high-pitched voice many will remember: "Come on, lads, you've had a good season, we're going out." And we went out to the pub and had a few pints. We lost that last game 3-2 and ended up seventh, Wednesday and Barnsley jumping over us on that final afternoon!

It rather summed up what the club had become behind the scenes despite the success on the back of what became known as "Fab Feb." Incidentally eight successive wins in a calendar month has been achieved only twice since – by Bristol City and Brighton. Clubs may have won more on the trot, but not in the same month. In fact, it's not often teams play eight league games in a month and, if you do, it takes some doing to win them all. It was a remarkable feat.

13

FAREWELL TO MILLMOOR

Perhaps there was a clue in the traditional pre-season team photograph. The body language probably hinted at something. The one before the 1982/83 season has me sitting right in the middle of the front row. Not a hint of a smile. Pretty sombre if I'm honest. It was the start of the second season under Emlyn Hughes and, considering his treatment of me in the previous nine months or so, it's hardly surprising I don't look a bundle of joy.

Okay, I hadn't missed a game since getting back in the team after injury at the start of 1982 and I was destined to be the regular No.3 when the new season opened. But something told me that things were about to take a turn for the worse despite the seventh-place finish on the back of the astonishing revival of fortunes the previous winter. That Jersey affair still rankled – although I did eventually make it over there. At the end of the season there was a jolly to Guernsey and Jersey. We played a friendly on the islands, but this wasn't a football trip. It was a piss-up, if you'll pardon the expression. In keeping with Emlyn's way.

Ian Porterfield had twice taken us down the pit, at Silverwood and Thurcroft, to open the eyes to what life as a miner entailed – many miners were Millers fans and, in fact, had been players in the past – but Emlyn took us to a brewery in Sheffield where we got sloshed on free booze. On the day we played Guernsey we were round the pool, all enjoying a drink – some more than others!

We lost 2-0 and Emlyn told the Press back in Rotherham we'd won 2-0. Then we hopped to Jersey. We got on the bus to go to the game, looked out of the window and could see Gerry Gow still drinking in the bar. "I don't think Gerry's going to make this one," somebody said. He didn't and we were 2-0 down in this one, too, before we sobered up a bit and won 5-2. That gives you an idea. It was like a Christmas club.

We had gone from the training regime of Porterfield – where it had a structure, we were ultra-fit and knew what we were about as a team – to the exact opposite. Everything had deteriorated. Training was geared to Emlyn really. We'd go on a run, he'd be at the front and he'd say: "Nobody comes past me." We'd all be jogging behind at a nice, easy pace and it was doing nobody any good. The ball came out and it would be five-a-side. He reckoned that, if it was good enough for Liverpool, then it was good enough for us. But the big difference was they were internationals, top players, and we weren't near their level. We needed more than that.

From early on I could tell he was not going to be a manager. Not that I hadn't admired him as a player and had nothing but respect for his achievements. All those international caps, European Cups, league championships, FA Cup – those honours speak for themselves when describing what a great player he was and I wasn't within lots of country miles of him as a footballer. In fact, it was often an education playing alongside him; I certainly learned things from him. We went to Chelsea, having beaten them 6-0 on that famous occasion at Millmoor and expected some sort of backlash at Stamford Bridge. Well, after going a goal down early on, we turned it round to win 4-1 and Emlyn "refereed" the game that day.

He would say to us: "Lads, the referee's name today is Paul. So, if you speak to him, then make sure you address him by his first name." Well, he rarely left him alone. "Well done, Paul," he said. "Great decision, Paul" ... "Paul, what was that for? Right, okay Paul, your decision ..." and so on and so on with both praise, query and criticism. We got some decisions that day you would not believe. Whether the referee was flattered to have a household name praising him loudly in front of all the players or intimidated by him, I don't know, but Emlyn Hughes clearly got into his head and was a major influence on the game that day. It was an education all right.

One of my last games for the club happened to be Emlyn's return to Liverpool for a League Cup tie in November 1982. It was an eye opener, too. If we didn't know already, we soon found out from some people around Anfield that he wasn't as popular as a lot of the general public thought he was. We lost 1-0 late on against a full-strength Liverpool side who were to romp the league that 1982/83 season and also win the League Cup. Emlyn had by then gone back into centre defence, ending his midfield partnership with Gerry Gow, who showed how invaluable top flight experience can be.

An early ruse of Gerry's left us smiling. Before a game a linesman would come into the dressing room to do an inspection of everybody's studs. Gerry would lift his leg up for the boot check. As soon as the linesman had gone, he took those boots off, put them back in his bag and got another pair out with the longest set of studs you've ever seen. Gerry was a hard man – we called him The Guv'nor – and he had this reputation, but he could play as well. You don't make as many appearances as he did in the old First Division if you can't play.

Left out of the side shortly after the Anfield game, I played just once more. I felt down and went to see Emlyn after a spell on the sidelines. At my age – I was then 29 – it was no good me being out of the side. I wanted to be playing. So he agreed to let me go out on loan. Jim Iley, manager at Bury, came in for me and I went on loan there with a great arrangement for me. I trained at Millmoor in the week with the lads and then travelled over to Bury on the Friday with Ray McHale who was on loan from Sheffield United. At least I can thank Emlyn for allowing that. After a couple of months Emlyn came over during a training session and said that Bury, who were top of Division Three, wanted to make the move permanent.

It was a day I had dreaded whenever the thought cropped up. What a tremendous wrench it would be leaving the club I loved. But while it was a tough decision and I didn't really want to go, I could see only reserve team football at Millmoor. So after some thought I decided to sign for Bury, but only to the end of the season. What I didn't know is that had I waited a bit longer, I wouldn't have left!

I went to Millmoor on the Monday as usual for training and Emlyn called all the players into the dressing room. It had been a bad weekend – the Millers had been hammered 4-0 at QPR and rumours were floating round about certain things that went off down there. I reckoned this would be the "inquest," so had to stand outside because technically I wasn't a Rotherham player any longer. But rather than hang around, I decided to go and wait in the gym. I walked in and to my utter amazement one person was standing there on his own. George Kerr, the former Grimsby Town manager! He was there for one reason only!

A couple of minutes later Emlyn had said his "farewells" and was being escorted from the ground. No longer Rotherham United manager. He'd been sacked. Into the dressing room walked George, to be introduced as the next boss. It was as quick as that. After he had spoken to the players, George came to me and asked how long I was on loan at Bury. I told him that, unfortunately, just three days earlier I'd signed permanently to the end of the season. He just looked at me and shook his head. So that was the end of Emlyn and the end of my Emlyn Hughes saga. And sadly, the end of my playing days at Rotherham United. I'd have happily been a one-club man for my entire career. But it was not to be.

Indeed it was to be all change at Rotherham at a time of great upheaval when it became close to financial ruin. In fact, many feel the club were never really able to recover from the acute financial problems inflicted during Anton Johnson's time at the helm. It has been well documented – and is apparent from the club's financial statements of the time – that the Purshouses left the club in a healthy state, very much in the black to the tune of more than £250,000 in cash assets – a creditable sum by 1979 standards – with no overdraft. But by 1983 it was heavily in the red with the club's financial documents showing that they were now £285,000 in the red. There was a bank overdraft of £129,000 and other liabilities amounting to £131,000, figures which have been previously well publicised.

There had been lots of rumours flying around for some time. Remember, Jim McGuigan quickly reckoned he wasn't going to hang around when change was in the offing and Ian Porterfield decided he would leave and go elsewhere, even at the height of his success and popularity. The relative success had covered up the deteriorating situation behind the scenes. The relegation at the end of that season, in May 1983, meant the way in which things operated was simply not sustainable back in the third tier.

Johnson had been a flamboyant character, but for all the success he brought in a short space of time – and it did include my best year in football in 1980/81 – the club was now back where it was when he took over and considerably – dangerously so – worse off on his official departure a few months later in September 1983. By then he had become majority shareholder at Southend United, having also been investigated by the Football League about his alleged involvement there and at other clubs, including Bournemouth, as well as a highly-publicised incident – not least at the club's AGM – that Rotherham had actually loaned Derby County money at one point to pay wages. Johnson was subsequently banned by the EFL from football for life.

In going to Bury, I had swapped a relegation scrap for a promotion battle and, incredible as it sounds, was getting better wages at a Fourth Division club, £220 a week, than the £190 a week I was on two divisions higher with Rotherham United! On the last day a home win over the Division Four champions Wimbledon would give Bury promotion. But we lost 3-1. That Saturday night I'd arranged to meet up with Ronnie Moore for a drink and he was drowning his sorrows, too. The Millers had been relegated that afternoon after drawing 2-2 at Elland Road when a win would have kept them up.

Later on we decided to head to the Adam and Eve nightclub in the town centre and bumped into Ian Snodin. He too had sorrows to drown. Doncaster Rovers had also gone down, dropping back into Division Four. Little did I realise then that Ian and his brother Glynn would be my teammates the following season at Belle Vue.

***

It was my old Millers colleague Dave Bentley who sounded me out. Billy Bremner wanted to sign me for Doncaster. Dave was coaching under the former Leeds United and Scotland star at Donny and I agreed to meet them. Billy made it clear he had a number of other experienced signings in mind and was determined to put together a team, blending youth and experience to get Rovers out of the Fourth Division at the first attempt. He was passionate and ambitious about the challenge ahead. I liked what I heard, was immediately up for a go at promotion and didn't hesitate in signing a 12-month contract. What an amazing 12 months it turned out to be. I loved that year at Donny and with Billy, who was brilliant with me. When you look at the team he put together, there was no wonder they were promoted.

The Snodin brothers were both talented, young players with obvious potential and were on the verge of bigger opportunities. Both went on to play top flight football and it was clear then they would. Ian was only 20, but what a prospect. He was Nijinsky – a real thoroughbred. I used to look at him late in a game and think: "He's not even out of breath." It was no surprise he went on to play in the Premier League, starring with Everton and Leeds and getting England under-21 caps. Glynn, with that lovely left foot, had spells at Leeds and Sheffield Wednesday on his CV. How Rotherham United missed out on two talented lads on their doorstep will always remain a mystery to me.

Billy Russell, who I was to work with so much at Millmoor, was at Donny and they signed three experienced stalwarts – centre half Bill Green, midfielder Andy Kowalski and that evergreen centre forward Ernie Moss. All had enjoyed success in their careers, not least at Chesterfield. I remember looking round the dressing room in pre-season and thinking: "Nothing is going to stop this lot from going up." I had moved on from one football legend, Emlyn Hughes, to another, Billy Bremner; the captain in that great Leeds team of the Don Revie era. I found them as different again. Billy was an absolute pleasure to work with, great in the dressing room and on the training ground. The only problem for us with Billy was his contribution in training. He was undoubtedly the best player on the pitch even at 41. It was almost impossible to get the ball off him. He just loved head tennis and was so good at it. He also had a persuasive tongue as I found out in one extraordinary incident.

I was lying in an operating theatre waiting room ready for my knee operation; the only downside of my time at Doncaster. During a Tuesday night game I'd landed awkwardly after jumping for a header and hurt my right knee. It was swollen and uncomfortable overnight and a visit to a consultant noted some cartilage damage, so surgery was recommended. It was going to be an arthroscopy – keyhole surgery – which wasn't as common then as now. In fact, it was only the second one this surgeon had done. I was lying there on the Friday afternoon when the nurse came in ready with my operation pre-med. But before she could administer anything, there was a knock on the door. "Mr Breckin, there's a Mr Bremner on the phone and he wants to speak to you. Says it's urgent." I'm thinking: "This is a player having a joke." But surely not. So I got out of bed, wearing the theatre gown, and went down to reception to take this call. It indeed was Billy Bremner.

"John, are you okay? Can you play tomorrow, we've got a crisis and I've no left back." So I say that, not having done any training all week, the knee has gone down and feels fine. "If you're desperate, then I'll play," I said. "Good," Billy said. "Well, it's Chesterfield and all I want you to do is to mark Alan Birch, stick right to him, nothing else. Job done."

Can you imagine that? Anyway the operation was off. Elaine had to come and pick me up from the private hospital where the club had booked me in and the next day I turned up at Belle Vue to find myself the butt of the dressing room jokes from all the players. My right leg had been shaved and there was a question mark and a big X written in black-marker pen on it. Did they take the mickey big time or what? Anyway I did the job I had to do – no overlapping runs that day – and managed to nullify Birchy as we won 2-1.

The following Monday I was back in the hospital for real and the job was eventually done with half-a-dozen little bits of cartilage in a jar as a souvenir. It cost me quite a number of games that season, but, even during the period of inaction, Billy Bremner involved me and insisted I was in the dressing room. It was shrewd because he knew I would contribute to the atmosphere, helping to motivate others. He kept his promotion promise as Rovers finished runners-up in Division Four, but I was released at the end of the season. Billy went out of his way to explain why he was doing it and that it was a genuinely hard decision. He thanked me profusely for supporting him so well, too, particularly when he'd asked me to be in the dressing room when unable to play.

In the dressing room I'd found myself quoting my old boss Jim McGuigan and using some of his pertinent one-liners. And it's very important to have a sense of humour in there, especially for the young players because it helps them to relax. The waiting before a game can make it a tense and nervous place. Fortunately I've been blessed with a good sense of humour and hope I made the atmosphere lighter than it would have been. I loved that year at Donny and Billy was great with me. It was probably the all-round experience that gave me the idea I might enjoy the management and coaching side of the game when my playing days were over – which was fast approaching, even though I was only 31.

***

It was a time to contemplate finishing as a full time footballer. When I look back now, it can be easy to see much of my time with rose-tinted spectacles to think everything was better in my day. Well, what I see of the Rotherham United way now – and clubs in general – it is frankly another world these days and so much better in so many respects. Yes, many players I played with had the skill sets to have performed with the Rotherham of today. For sure. Ronnie Moore scored 24 goals to finish top scorer overall in what's now the Championship. Are you telling me he wouldn't be an asset to Paul Warne? Anyone who saw Gerry Forrest play knows the right back position would be sorted. And perhaps I could start a debate for those able to compare the two – Tony Towner or Chieo Ogbene on the right flank. Sort that one out then!

No, it is all that surrounds footballers and a football club nowadays which has moved it to another level for the players. For a start the pitches are far better. No more mudheaps or bare, bumpy, rock-hard surfaces in the final months. And the training grounds are better, too. I have noted how some of my managers worked us and got us really fit, but not with the measured strategy employed today. I recall one day a week when we were run into the ground and the trainer was happy only if you were physically sick. It was all measured with a stopwatch. And you were expected to go faster than last time! Nowadays it is all structured. They have heart monitors plus implements to record how far they've run, and everything is measured. They even give urine samples. Work harder? Not if the fitness coach's analysis suggests that it wants easing back.

Diet is such a factor, too. The emphasis is on nutrition and players get a breakfast at the training ground – not a full English either, but a healthy, nutritional one. When they come off the training ground, they are then eating on site and have to do so within 20 minutes at the prepared buffet; again protein-rich because it's important to be eating the right food to replenish them after a hard session. When we finished training, it would be off to Josie's Cafe just up from the ground to get tucked in, probably pie and chips. They were nice pies, though! By the way, old wrestling fans will remember top wrestler Mike Marino. Well, he would often be serving behind the counter at Josie's and one day he chased Bobby Ham out of the cafe after he had made a light-hearted remark suggesting it had been Mike's turn to lose the previous weekend. There is food on the team coach after away games now. We might have had a bag of crisps. Sometimes we stopped at a fish and chip shop on the way back. But players nowadays generally look after themselves better and there certainly isn't the drinking culture I recall from years ago.

The club have two physios, a couple of masseurs. Hydration is important – you'll see a break in play and players take on water on the touchline. Well, we weren't allowed to have water. They said it gave you stomach cramps. So at half-time we had a cup of tea, well sugared. On a hot day you'd be gasping, but there were no bottles of water to have a swig from. In fact, you might get lucky when the trainer came on – although how "lucky" often varied. On he'd run with his magic sponge in water in an old football bladder. Wipe away blood from a cut, a quick sponge over and back in the bladder. Next injury and on he trots again. Same sponge. On a red hot day you might very well take advantage of a lovely wet sponge – he'd pass it to you and you'd bite on it and suck the water out. It was so refreshing – and it never even crossed your mind that it had wiped away somebody's blood about 10 minutes ago or been rubbed on a teammate's sweaty face.

I was fortunate we had an excellent physio. Alan Smith eventually went to the top, but they were a one-man band back in the 1970s. At least he was qualified. Now the physio will go on the pitch with a doctor and the overall medical supervision is so much better. There are many stories of players carrying on after being knocked out, even still pretty dazed – the old "not knowing where they were." That wouldn't happen now. Neither would the pre-substitute situation whereby, if a player got an injury that restricted him, the manager would tell him to go and stand on the wing and be nuisance value because "someone has to mark you." The fact that you couldn't actually run or might well be making the injury worse was overlooked. Better than playing with 10 men, they reckoned.

Yes, players are looked after far better and it has moved on for their greater good. One thing is for certain; there was more tackling back then and certainly more fouls, particularly from behind. Attackers would take some fearful punishment, not least in the early minutes. There were challenges which went unpunished then – and refs never dished out a booking for the first one – which would have been a straight red card today. So players can be grateful that aspect of it has been improved. Dirty games with hard men on either side exacting revenge and vendettas raging as tackles flew in are thankfully things of the past. Back then you could not be seen to pull out of a 50-50. Do that and you were in big trouble from the gaffer. Nowadays I've seen players reluctant to go into such challenges, perhaps because the leniency level is so much lower among referees. If you just "catch" an opponent and he ends up writhing on the ground, whether hurt or feigning, then you could be looking at a red card, certainly a yellow. The game is cleaner and, you would say, all the better for it.

And talking of 50-50s, an old friend of mine was at a First Division club as a youngster in the late 1960s and a well known international midfield player taught lads how to go over the top in a sly, crafty manner that would enable them to get away with it. In the process it might cause serious injury to the opponent. Yet some people believe the game was better back in the day. Believe me, the improvement in so many areas makes it better for today's players and, with that, a better game. But we still had players who would have flourished in a Rotherham shirt today – and how much better would they have been in modern conditions?

***

Without finishing with football, I decided it was time to look ahead and to ensure some regular income. There were offers to stay in the Football League. Exeter, where Jim Iley had gone after Bury, and Port Vale both wanted me, but I got the chance of a "proper" job and also to continue playing at a good level. Thanks to my brother Brian, a manager at Northern Dairies at Bramley, I heard of a milkman who was selling part of his round, so I moved in. It was in Maltby and, as luck – or ill-luck – would have it, the national miners' strike of 1984-85 was just getting under way. It was hardly the ideal time to be starting a new business, but I must say the miners and the people of Maltby were absolutely brilliant with me. If I didn't know them beforehand, I certainly got to know plenty of them and I won't hear a bad word said against all those people from Maltby who I had to deal with.

As we know, these people are the salt of the earth and the support I got was wonderful. It was as if they realised that I was someone just starting a new business and they did their best to support me, even during their troubled times. I hope I reciprocated. If they were struggling to find the money, I'd tell them pay me when they could and what they could. I can't recall anyone ducking out of paying and everybody settled up eventually. I had to work hard at it, but reckon I provided a reliable service – and even left a few eggs or dropped off a bag of potatoes for someone who might be feeling the pinch during the strike.

I was up at 4am six days a week with the first pint on the doorstep by five – and one of my first customers was Millers player John Dungworth, who had just got a house in Maltby with his wife. There was another football connection, a promising schoolboy player called Andy Crosby. I delivered for his mum and dad and sometimes me and Andy would have a kickabout outside. He was about 13 or 14 at the time and I hoped my persuasive chat might work, but he ended up going to Leeds. I still see Andy now and again and he's become a trusted No.2, working now with Grant McCann at Hull after their time at Doncaster Rovers.

The football call this time came from Neil Warnock, who was in charge at Burton Albion. They were in the Northern Premier League – which was then the sixth tier, equivalent to the National League North today – and he said to come and play part-time and help out with a bit of coaching. It was ideal and worked well until things began to creak. Literally. The knee began to play up at times and I needed to rest it if I got a knock. But I still had to be up early and in and out of the van delivering milk.

We had a splendid FA Cup run, winning six ties including one at then-league side Aldershot, which earned a third round tie with Leicester City. They were in the top flight, five divisions above us. The game was switched from Burton to Derby County's former Baseball Ground and in front of 30,000 fans Burton lost 6-1 with Gary Lineker among the scorers. But a replay was ordered because our goalkeeper Paul Evans was struck on the head by a wooden object and a coin thrown from the crowd. It affected him in the second half when five of the goals were scored.

The replay was at Coventry's old Highfield Road ground and I have some idea what the Millers players went through in 2020 because it was played behind closed doors. I was on the substitutes' bench, went on in the second half and it ended 1-0 to Leicester this time. I can't honestly say I have much recollection of what it was like other than obviously it was very strange with no one there. The comments at the time of Leicester manager Gordon Milne are interesting, however, particularly in view of what has been happening in football since the pandemic stopped crowds attending back in March 2020. "It is unfair to ask teams to play in that environment," he said. "And I would not like to think any professional side would have to do it again. The crowd is part of the game and you cannot perform without them." With the experience of clubs and supporters from the past year, I think we'll all nod to those words of 35 years ago.

I loved that spell with Neil. It was just the one season, but it was obvious to me that he would be moving on and up. Indeed he was soon climbing higher on the management ladder, going on to have an incredible career. I'm pleased to say that I played a part in him coming to Rotherham in 2016 when he helped the club to pull off that miracle escape from relegation in the Championship a few months later. He was my guest in hospitality at a game against his former club QPR and, when he went down on the pitch to do the half-time draw, he got a great reception. It was the response from the Millers fans throughout the day which helped to persuade him to come to Rotherham when Tony Stewart spoke to him.

In fact, we had a great arrangement at Burton which ultimately suited us both that season – although a couple of incidents did help to persuade me that fitting in the milk round and playing at that level might clash. One night we played over the Pennines – Mossley, I think – and about 20 minutes from the end the fog started to come in. It was getting thicker and thicker and I was thinking: "I've got to get back home in this and be up at 4am ... By the looks of it I might not even get home and people might not get their milk."

One morning I wasn't there to deliver. I was in hospital. I played an FA Trophy tie at Stevenage and was knocked out in an aerial collision. The game was held up for a long time, the ambulance came on the pitch to take me to hospital and they kept me in overnight, putting six stitches in my head in the process. Fortunately our Brian and my wife Elaine came to the rescue by delivering the milk the next day. But it made me realise the perils of juggling both.

If I wasn't in the team, Neil Warnock wanted me to ensure I kept fit for when I might be needed. So it was ideal when my old Millers pal Dick Habbin knocked on my door and suggested I turn out for Maltby Main in the Northern Counties East League on a Saturday. Neil was happy with the arrangement and it meant I could still play and keep match-fit for when the Burton call came. But at the end of the season my body was telling me that my high level playing days were about at an end, so I left Burton after the one season with Neil. My football then expanded to Sundays.

One day there was a knock on my door. It was a massive Millers fan from up the road, Tim Albiston, with his mate Gary Willis. He wondered if I fancied playing for their Sunday team. So I agreed along with a pal, Steve McVann, a good local player and kitman for the Millers until a couple of years ago. The team was Brecks Rangers so appropriately, it was Breck playing for Brecks. It was a success, too, because we romped Division Three in the Rotherham Sunday League that season. I actually played on occasions in the Midweek League on a Thursday for Rotherham Fire Brigade and also moved up the Sunday League ladder. In the side at Maltby were some lads who played for the Joker, the crack Rotherham Sunday League club who, remarkably, are still a top side 35 years or so on. The Joker manager, Paul Dewick, who had persuaded me to turn out for the fire brigade, got Dick Habbin to see if I fancied playing for them. As I obviously knew some of the lads, I was interested and it turned out to be a good move, too.

It was the 1986/87 season, we won the Rotherham Sunday League Premier Division title and I was to make what would be my final playing appearance at Millmoor – in the Rotherham Sunday Cup Final when we beat Thurcroft Hotel 1-0. Our big league rivals at the time were Sportsman and we had ding-dong battles with them. They were runners-up. I do recall a key game that season at Ferham Park against an up-and-coming side, Bradgate WMC, who had enjoyed a couple of promotions and had done well in the top flight. We'd heard they wanted to knock us off our perch.

Using my influence, the Joker lads were able to use Millmoor to get changed in some comfort and we walked over Coronation Bridge the couple of hundred yards to Ferham Park. I was playing in the centre of defence and Bradgate had this really tall guy up front and against me. I gave him a few verbals during the game, a bit of winding up on occasions, and we ended up beating them. Afterwards he came walking towards me and I thought: "Aye, aye, I hope he's not upset ... he's a big lad." He put out his hand and shook mine. "Well done," he said. "It's been a pleasure to play against you, but you were too good for us today." Which I thought was gracious and dignified in defeat. It was Paul Douglas ... and I never thought I would be coming across him many years later in his present-day role as chief operating officer at Rotherham United! You never know who you might come across in football!

14

"COME DOWN TO T'SCRAPYARD"

The phone rang at home one Sunday morning and I didn't recognise the rather gravelly voice on the other end. "Errr, is that John? It's Ken Booth here. Can you come down to t'scrapyard and see me?" I agreed. "Come in about an hour, drive up to t'gates, pap t'horn and I'll come and let thee in." Everybody who lived in Rotherham knew of Ken Booth or at least knew of his scrap metal company, CF Booth Ltd. And every Millers fan knew those big cranes which towered over the back of the Railway End at Millmoor were Boothy's.

The wealthy owner of a multi-million pound business, he wasn't interested in any copper or spare metal I might have hanging about and I didn't reckon it was to give me belated thanks for having actually worked down at his scrapyard a few years before. Yeah, me and skipper Bob Delgado were offered jobs during the close season in the mid-1970s, doing some labouring work in the scrapyard. At snap time we'd even have a kick around in the yard with the blokes who at least could say they'd played with a couple of Millers!

We were burning rubber off copper cable and we were black at the end of the day, so me and Bob would pop into Millmoor and get showered. It was the first time I'd got to meet Ken. At the end of the week he would come and see us to pay us. In cash! And it was a bit more than I earned working by driving limousines at funerals with my Millers colleague Trev Womble. I enjoyed it, even at only £1 a funeral. Where there's muck, there's brass. Hence the scrapyard.

No, it was a football reason behind the call. Ken had just rescued Rotherham United. It was the spring of 1987. The club, financially crippled and still suffering the aftermath of the early 1980s' ownership, had fallen into administration and needed someone to come in and save it or else it was finished. Ken, a long-time supporter of the club, had been on the fringe of the previous well-meaning ownership, Rotherham businessmen Syd Wood and Graham Humphries, who were big supporters, too. They had stepped in to try to turn things around, but found it a financially draining and thankless task and ultimately a hopeless one. Ken had helped them out at times, but knew when not to get involved – and when it would be timely to do so.

I arrived at CF Booth's gates, which are nowadays overlooked by the New York Stadium, and Ken walked out and undid the padlock. He was the only one there. He locked up behind us and took me into his office, the place where so many scrap deals had been hatched and agreed, almost always with a spit on the palm and a shake of the hand. That was the contract signed! He took off his flat cap and put it on his desk, which looked like an antique. Indeed it was like stepping back in time.

"Errr, I've heard you're doing a bit o' scouting for Billy McEwan at Sheffield United and helping out with Rotherham Boys," was his opening gambit. He was right. My old teammate Billy was manager at Bramall Lane and he'd roped me in to do a spot of scouting for him and, yes, I was doing some coaching with Rotherham Boys' under-11s.

"Well, errrr, as you know, I've just bought t'football club and I want to get a youth policy going," he said. "We haven't got one. I want you to come in and sort it out and run it." Inside my head I was instantly elated. It was the chance to come back to Rotherham United, my club. Not only that, it would be in running the youth set-up, something that was close to my heart. But I initially demurred. "But you've got a youth-team manager, Mr Booth," I said. "Have you agreed it with Norman Hunter [the manager] that it's okay if I can come in? Shouldn't I speak to him first?"

Ken was typically blunt in his reply. "I'm the owner. There's no need to ask Hunter or Barrie Claxton [Hunter's assistant] or anybody else. I'm asking you to do it. Do you fancy it?" I didn't need asking again. We agreed – and I don't think we even had to shake hands, let alone spit on the palm! I was back at my football club. I was overjoyed. I couldn't wait to get started. I sold my milk round sharpish and was back in football full time. It felt great.

I was in charge of the youth development department. But there was virtually nothing to be in charge of at that moment. It had been run down so badly; the lack of finances meant nothing had been spent. Even the gym roof was leaking. It was basically starting from scratch. The club's School of Excellence had collapsed. Everything connected with having a youth policy had gone tits up. All the schoolboys had gone. Any lads who were there were free to go if they wished. There was no system at all for recruiting and nurturing young players in the hope that some would develop into full time professionals and hopefully first team players one day. It was a challenge all right, but one that I really did relish getting stuck into.

Rather than grumble about it and get all negative, I looked on it as a blank canvas. The first thing I did was to get some sort of background structure in place, something that could form a framework and then enable us to get a youth policy underway – from the bottom up. So the first person I phoned was Micky Hukin. He was a great guy with a great reputation and I knew what I'd get from Micky. He'd had involvement with the School of Excellence before it closed, leaking gym roof and all! In fact, I will go as far as to say I couldn't have done it without him. He was different class.

The first person he rang was a young lad still short of his 13th birthday – Paul Hurst. There was a danger we might lose him to another club because of the mess we were in. Thankfully Hursty agreed to stay. Little did anyone realise then what a great piece of work that would turn out to be. He was a great servant to the club and is the second-highest appearance-holder in the club's history with 494, behind only Danny Williams. An incredible achievement. I wish we could pick another up like him now and he was also a great lad to boot.

I made the next signing straightaway – my nephew, Ian Breckin, son of my brother Brian. That didn't turn out to be a bad one either! Ian was among the lads I was coaching at Rotherham Boys' under-11s. A familiar name to many Millers fans, Ian was to come through the ranks, enjoy a successful time at the club – including the 1996 Wembley triumph – and go on to have a good and successful career with promotions at Wigan Athletic, including into the Premier League, Nottingham Forest and finally in his second spell at Chesterfield. Two players signed. It was a start.

Micky Hukin knew everyone, including all the junior clubs in Sheffield, and we actually took over a top club called Hillsborough Celtic. We changed the name to Millmoor Juniors – not the present-day club of the same name – and the intention was for them to become a feeder club for Rotherham with players at various age ranges. Of course I had to get a network of scouts as well. So I got some excellent people in to work for me to look for good, young lads – people such as Graham Flint, Brian Tonks, Alan Stables from local club Redscorpions, Bob Unwin, Tony Morton, Brian Stuart, Roger Longden, Paul Toy, Trevor Ford – whose son Stuart eventually played for the Millers as a goalkeeper – and later on, a massive Millers fan Mick Bagnall through his club Bethesda.

Mick actually linked Bethesda with the club a few years later, as a sort of Millers A team playing in the County Senior League. It was a great grounding for those teenagers to play in a men's league – I would sometimes turn out and actually played alongside a young Ian Breckin – and on occasions we could give game time to a first team squad player on his way back from injury. Unfortunately we had to pull out of the league because of the FA disciplinary punishment rulings of the time.

Once the network had been set up, all the scouts were called to a meeting. They were shown a map with a 20 mile radius ring around Rotherham. "Right," I said. "I want to know about every talented kid there is inside that ring. Let me know the best players. Get out and watch all the age groups. If there's one that we ought to bring in, then let me know and I'll go and knock on the door and speak to their parents."

Obviously other clubs were doing the same and we were up against both Sheffield clubs, the other local ones around Rotherham and such as Leeds and Nottingham Forest. Even Manchester United had involvement in the area, but it didn't faze me. I always reckoned that I could pull a lad our way if I could get in and speak to him and his mum and dad. We did that, but one signing I remember more than any didn't involve a visit. He was brought to me.

It was a lovely, sunny, summer evening and we had our School of Excellence running that night down at the Hooton Roberts training ground, which Ken Booth had funded. Graham Flint, who did a great job in the scouting team for me, was walking across the field with this blond-haired lad, 13 years old, and his dad. He was a prospect all right because both Sheffield United and Sheffield Wednesday wanted him. "Hello," he said. "I'm Chris Sedgwick. Nice to meet you."

I took Chris and his dad into the office, told them how it was and how it would be and said he would definitely get a chance at this football club. The rest, as they say, is history because he signed and proved a wonderful asset to Rotherham United, making more than 270 appearances, including two promotions. He also "earned" the club about £400,000 when joining Preston North End. In all his time in the game Chris – as nice a fella as you could wish to meet – made more than 650 appearances, which is some career.

With four local feeder clubs linked to us and providing a stream of potential talent, close tabs on Rotherham Boys, the School of Excellence back up and running – oh, and the Millmoor gym roof repaired – we were on the way and rebuilding things. The idea of providing a conveyor belt of potential first team players was under way. It was hard work and time consuming, but I loved it.

It was extremely rewarding. There are fewer things more satisfying for those involved in the youth development at a football club than to see lads progress and break through, particularly if they make it to the first team. Quite a number of the lads we brought in – and by we, I am including all the scouts – from the middle of 1987 developed really well and enjoyed success, even if they didn't ultimately make the first team. A lot of them did, though.

By success I include winning things at your own level. For example, in 1990 we won the Northern Intermediate League Cup against all the odds. We drew 1-1 at home to Newcastle and then won the second leg 3-1 at St. James' Park – capped by a goal I still remember, an astonishing 30 yard dipping volley from Enrico Ojeda. Think Alex Revell, Wembley 2014, and you get the idea!

A Spanish lad, we called him Sanchez because at Real Madrid at the time was the Mexican star Hugo Sanchez. He scored plenty of goals with spectacular overhead kicks and guess how Enrico scored our first goal that night? Yeah, with an overhead kick Hugo would have been proud of. So Sanchez proved an appropriate nickname. Neil Booker got our other goal and the Sanchez wonder strike was a few minutes from time after Newcastle had pulled one back.

Newcastle's side included Lee Clark, Steve Howey, Matty Appleby and Lee Makel, to name just four who eventually had really good careers. Howey even played for England. By that time I was youth coach, in charge of that team, and it was a game from which I got immense satisfaction. In the first leg we were second best, basically because they were a very good side indeed.

So having learned from that game, in the week before the second leg I worked with the lads at Ferham Park because our training ground was being re-seeded. I tweaked things and changed our system to 4-3-3 because we had the players to adapt to it and played a certain way which I reckoned would cause Newcastle problems.

It worked a treat. We fully deserved the win and it certainly shocked the Geordies. After the game Billy McEwan, the Millers manager at the time, and his assistant Phil Henson came into the dressing room to congratulate us. Phil leaned over and said: "Well done, you were far better than they were tactically." The remark meant a lot and acknowledged the work and preparation put in. The important thing was that it had paid off.

The side included five players – goalkeeper Stuart Ford, central defenders Julian Watts and Mark Hodges, left back Andy "Nuffy" Taylor and striker Jonathan Howard – who all went on to make first team appearances. A couple of others went close. One of them, Fraser Foster, moved into coaching in our School of Excellence, later became head of the club's Football in the Community Scheme and has done really well for himself in America, where he runs his own international soccer camps and has close connections with the universities out there.

And I am sure our Spanish lad, Sanchez – who had never played on grass until he played for us – would have made it had he been given a chance and persevered with. We sold Julian Watts to Sheffield Wednesday inside a couple of years, such was his initial impact when he got in the first team. The really unfortunate tale surrounded Mark Hodges.

A left-sided centre back, he would have gone right to the top in my belief. I will go as far as to say he was the best prospect I ever dealt with. He didn't run, he floated across the ground and he really was a thoroughbred mover. He played a handful of games before a persistent back injury meant he wasn't able to pursue a Football League career. He would have moved on one day for very good money, I'm sure of that.

That same season several of them featured in the successful reserve side who clinched promotion to the First Division of the Central League, doing so on a memorable night when we beat Sheffield Wednesday 3-1 at Hillsborough. It meant moving up to play the second strings of all the country's top clubs in the north and midlands, including Manchester United, Liverpool and Manchester City. Doing so was an invaluable experience – not only for the younger players, but also for the more experienced ones.

Back then even the top clubs would include stars in their reserve sides in addition to talented prospects, many of whom would ultimately go on to become stars in their own right in the Premier League. Many fans remember – I know because they have reminded me across the years – the midfield masterclass from Jan Molby for Liverpool reserves at Millmoor. It's not just the young lads who can learn during the 90 minutes. More experienced players would, too. Manchester United had a number of promising young players, among them both Neville brothers, Nicky Butt and a talent called Ryan Giggs coming off the bench.

It was all early reward for the effort and hard work put in by a lot of people when the youth policy was restarted from scratch in 1987 after Ken Booth's takeover. Little did I realise that I would "step up" from my role as youth liaison officer after only a few months and be asked to take charge of the first team, albeit only for a couple of games. In such a short space of time it was certainly a big jump from the milk round and Sunday League football.

15

SURVIVING THE SACKINGS

When a faltering Norman Hunter was sacked after a disastrous 4-0 FA Cup defeat at Macclesfield, Ken Booth needed someone to hold the fort before the next appointment. He turned to me as caretaker manager. So I was plunged pretty quickly into the deep end although I didn't have to swim for long. I had two games proudly in charge, if only temporarily, and my first was at home. Unfortunately it ended it in a disappointing 2-1 defeat to Gillingham on a Friday night. The second and last one would have tested Sir Alex Ferguson ... away to Sunderland, who were to romp the division by a distance. The 3-0 defeat was no surprise.

On Christmas Eve, Dave Cusack was appointed manager. A Rotherham lad from Thurcroft, he came in as player-manager and had a great start, too – three straight 1-0 wins. One was at home to his old club, Doncaster Rovers, where he'd also had the dual role but was fired this same season. The three wins were as good as it got at Millmoor for Dave. Results went on the slide, relegation loomed and chairman Booth made it two sackings in a matter of months. There were only three games left of that 1987/88 season and the club looked doomed to go down to Division Four. I reckoned I knew who was needed by the club. So, too, as it turned out, did Ken Booth. He stopped me very soon after Cusack's sacking: "Billy McEwan? What's tha' think?"

So I went to see Billy, my old teammate, at his home in Rotherham. He'd been manager at Sheffield United until he was sacked earlier in the year and we had kept in touch because of the spot of scouting he'd had me doing. Billy gave me his typically warm welcome when I knocked on his door. "Do you want the job at Rotherham?" I said bluntly, not beating about the bush. Billy didn't either. "Yeah, I'd love to do it," he said. "Right, come on then. Go and have a meeting with Ken Booth; I'll arrange it." The appointment was a formality.

However, not everything went quite so smoothly, humorously so when Billy was officially presented to the players. They all gathered together at Millmoor and, with Billy hidden from view, it was up to the chairman to address everyone. But Ken Booth wasn't one for speeches and he kept the introduction as brief as possible: "I'd like to introduce our new manager ... Billy Bremner" before quickly realising his error and correcting himself: "Err, I mean Billy McEwan," by which time Billy was appearing from behind the curtain. He got the chairman off the hook perfectly. "I'm glad you didn't introduce me as Billy Graham, chairman," laughed Billy – a reference to the American evangelist who was making a much-publicised appearance in Sheffield about that time.

Neither of the other two Billys could have started as well as the McEwan version who inspired two immediate wins, giving an indication of what sort of philosophy he'd have. In the first game he gave a debut to a very promising 18-year-old midfielder, Shaun Goodwin, and called up Martin Scott, only 20, after six months out. Unfortunately Scotty was injured in that 1-0 home win over Aldershot and couldn't return until nine months later.

The two wins – the other at Gillingham – meant the Millers went into the last game of the season as one of six clubs looking to avoid finishing in fourth-bottom place which back then meant a relegation play-off. Unfortunately the last-day opponents at Millmoor were Sunderland, runaway champions and far better than any other side. Anybody but them and we might have managed it, but, as it turned out, a win would have been needed anyway. We lost 4-1. The play-offs also involved three teams from the Fourth Division and Rotherham lost by the odd goal over two legs to Swansea in the semi-final so went down.

Although relegation feels awful and in certain circumstances can feel like the end of the world football-wise, this wasn't. With hindsight relegation wasn't the worst thing to happen at that time. It was a good thing. It meant Billy was able to regroup and rebuild. He was an excellent coach and did a great job. I learned a lot from Billy and he was the one who made me go to the FA coaching centre at Lilleshall that summer and gain my FA "full" badge. I was grateful for that and for him appointing me youth coach. In that role I knew Billy would be encouraging the development of youngsters and would give worthy ones a chance. He'd already done that in his first three games.

This also meant working with the reserves on their match days with Phil Henson who had been appointed Billy's assistant. It was a three-way partnership which dovetailed perfectly. Billy led the club to the Fourth Division title the following season, 1989. Pride was restored in the club and among the fans. There were some great performances and fans still mention the 3-1 win on Easter Monday at promotion rivals Crewe to this day. It was a tactical masterclass by Billy and topped by a hat-trick from top scorer Bobby Williamson – a great signing by Billy and one of the best free transfers in the club's history.

The appointment proved a turning point for the club and we had two great years. But the truth is that the financial backing he expected to facilitate another promotion push didn't materialise. It was during this time there was the strangest substitution I have ever known in my career. We came in at half-time and Billy wasn't happy. He got into full flow and told midfielder Mark Dempsey that he was coming off.

Demps wasn't happy at all. Off came the boots, socks, the lot; all flung about angrily before he marched off to the bath. At this point another midfielder, Shaun "Raggy" Goodwin, indicated he wanted me. He was rubbing his calf. "I'm really struggling, Breck," he said. "I can't go back out." I had to wait until the gaffer was finished to inform him quietly that Raggy couldn't carry on. "Tell Demps he's back on," said Billy.

I went to get Mark Dempsey and he was actually submerged under the water, blowing bubbles. "Come on, Demps, you're going back on," I told him. Like a submarine surfacing, Mark emerged and said: "What? No, fuck him, I'm not going back on."

"Demps, hurry up, get ready, we're out in a few minutes," I implored of him. "Not likely," came the reply before he slid back down in the water. By this time some of the lads had come in to see where he was and had to persuade him to get out of the bath. "You're doing it for yourself and you're doing it for us, so come on Demps," they told him. Suitably persuaded and still with hair dripping wet, Demps paddled back into the dressing room to locate his kit, which he had scattered in his annoyance. I remember him grovelling around on the floor, chuntering away, and looking underneath the benches trying to find his shinpads. He couldn't find them. He never actually got dried and went back out with his hair still wet through. It did teach me one thing... never make a substitution at half-time until you've checked that everyone is okay.

This was near the start of Billy's third season when results began to turn and players weren't responding to his methods as they had done previously. A 5-0 defeat at Swansea on New Year's Day, 1991, proved the end for him. Ken Booth showed him the door. It was a sad day because he had put his heart and soul into it and done a great job. No one could accuse Billy of not giving his all. He did that every day. But he had become frustrated by the lack of backing and his natural drive and intensity was no longer bringing the appropriate response.

Phil Henson was promoted to take temporary charge and asked me to assist him. We'd little time before the next game, the long trip back to Swansea four days later for an FA Cup tie in the third round. Ken Booth offered an incentive, obviously with the prize money in mind. "There's £2,000 in it for the players if we can stay in the cup," he said. We did so thanks to a 0-0 draw. The chairman repeated the £2,000 incentive to win the replay. We did, 4-0. Ken provided the necessary thousands in cash in a brown envelope and the captain distributed it to the players. I'm not sure whether it was within the FA rules or not, but Ken was happy and so were the players.

But we couldn't halt the slide in results or get out of the bottom four in the second half of the season, which brought me into managerial opposition, for the first and only time, with Ronnie Moore. He was assistant to John King at Tranmere when we went there one Friday night and pulled off a shock 2-1 win. But Ronnie still had the last laugh when Tranmere went up via the play-offs that season.

I also remember the game because it was one of the handful which featured Mark Hodges, the young defender who I eulogised about previously. It was his fourth and last appearance before the injury which was to curtail his career – one that I remain convinced to this day would have been an extremely good one. His performance that night, a tough gig at a Tranmere side up near the top and in front of a partisan crowd, confirmed my belief.

It is extremely upsetting when a talented young player such as Mark, who you have watched progress, receives the awful news that he has to quit the game because of injury. That's bad enough, but at least you as an individual are not responsible for his departure. That's down to bad luck. But in charge of the youth set-up, you are responsible for crushing the hopes and dreams of starry-eyed young footballers.

Make no mistake, telling them they will no longer be staying at the club is the worst job in the game. Whatever you say and however you say it, you are basically telling him: "Sorry, son, but I don't think you're good enough." It's a cruel moment of devastating realisation for a lad who had arrived with such hopes, who had dreamed of a future as a professional footballer and who had probably worked so hard for years to try to achieve his ambition. In the aftermath you are probably the most unpopular person on earth, not least with the parents, and I've known those who blamed me, the club, anybody and everything except taking off the blinkers and acknowledging the obvious. A few parents did get angry with me and gave me criticism. Fortunately plenty of parents didn't react that way.

We'd say that, while the door had closed here, others may well be open elsewhere. We'd suggest they had to work on certain things, what they were and that I hoped they would go and take the constructive criticism on board and prove me wrong. As far as I can recall, none did so. I would have happily patted them on the back further down the road had they done so. Yes, there are plenty of examples of lads being released and then finding a way back. We'd advise them to play at the highest non-league level that they could. Who knows, they could get spotted – Jamie Vardy anyone? But a lot would go and play with their mates, go socialising, enjoy a drink with them. There's nothing wrong with all that, but with no more full time training they soon put on a bit of weight – and it then becomes really difficult to find a way back.

So that was one aspect of the job I wasn't disappointed to leave behind when, after Phil Henson was handed the manager's job permanently, he asked me in that summer of 1991 to be his assistant. It was the right step up the ladder at the right time. I had worked for four years with the junior players and the reserves. I was ready for the bigger challenge of regular first team involvement; let's see if I could handle things at this higher level.

***

Things went well from the start and it proved to be another back-in-one promotion from Division Four in 1992, this time as runners-up. But it didn't cost Ken Booth a penny when it came to paying out promotion bonuses to the players after the success. This was due to a remarkable "insurance system" which isn't allowed now and hasn't been for some time. Basically you put a bet on your own team to go up. And the winnings covered the cost of the bonus payments!

A betting company invited the club down to a race meeting at Sandown. You didn't pay tax if you laid the bet at a racecourse. I went down with Phil Henson, director Carl Luckock and commercial manager Dave Nicholls, who is sadly no longer with us. Down there we met Harry Redknapp, who was in his first managerial job at Bournemouth, with Frank Lampard senior and a very young Frank Lampard, who was only 13. Other clubs were there, all invited down by the betting company, too.

I do know that through Ken Booth we laid a bet of £10,000 on ourselves to get promotion from Division Four, a couple of months after our relegation. I recall a woman writing the bet down in a big ledger. I'm not sure of the odds, but you can work it out when noting that, including the stake, the club got back £55,000 at the end of the 1991/92 season – so Ken had virtually nothing to pay out for our promotion. We nearly ended up with something else from that trip to Sandown. I made an "approach" to the young Frank Lampard! We'd heard from his dad and his Uncle Harry what a good prospect he was and I did say: "Well, Frank, if you want to come to Millmoor, we'll make sure you get looked after." But I think that was one path already mapped out.

Ahead of that promotion season Phil made some particularly astute signings, notably Chris Hutchings, the front two Tony Cunningham and Don Page – Cunningham is the best header of a ball I've worked with – and also Dean Barrick who had been signed the previous season. We also made Billy Mercer the regular goalkeeper, but what brought me an immense amount of pleasure that season was several appearances each from Julian Watts, Andy "Nuffy" Taylor, Stuart Ford and, in the last couple of months of the campaign, Jonathan Howard. I had brought them all through and although not all of them went on to make it, I was proud that the youth development process had borne fruit. It made all the hard work seem worthwhile.

Another who had come through the ranks, Shaun Goodwin, was a regular that season, too, although he was already in the system when I returned. Even so, I was always able to use Raggy's elevation to the first team as a selling point when speaking to young players and their parents, saying truthfully that we were a club who gave young players a chance. There was also involvement in a spot of football history that season – the first FA Cup penalty shoot-out. We beat Scunthorpe 7-6 on penalties in the replay at Millmoor, Ally Pickering getting the winning penalty. I've still got the commemorative T-shirt somewhere with all the shoot-out scorers on it!

So it was back up to the third tier and one of the two signings that summer was Chris Wilder from Sheffield United. If we'd taken note of something Gerry Forrest said, we might have got him about six years earlier! Gerry belatedly got his chance to move up to the top flight when he joined Southampton right at the end of 1985. A few months later I was speaking to my old full back partner and he said: "I don't know why they've signed me; they've got a young lad here who's better than I am. You want to have a look at him."

That young lad was an 18-year-old Wilder. Chris was released by Southampton in the summer of 1986 and went to his boyhood club Sheffield United. Phil Henson, who had been at Bramall Lane under Billy McEwan, had worked with Chris and knew his attributes. He was a great addition to the squad. His is one of the great modern-day stories of football management, the way he has fronted so much success at his previous clubs and what he did after taking over at his beloved Sheffield United in 2016 when they were at a low ebb. Getting them into the Premier League and having such a great first season up there in 2019/20 was rightly lauded across football.

I'm not surprised how well he has done, to be honest. He was one of the leaders in that dressing room. Not afraid to speak up, if and when necessary. Straightforward and with good sense. A good competitor and a great lad, he captained the side for spells, which was indicative of his leadership qualities even then. Chris was also brilliant out in the community, too. He'd back whatever we were doing. When a top darts player at the Millmoor pub next to the ground was struck down with a terminal illness, me and the landlord got together to arrange a special darts night to raise funds. I rang Dennis Priestley, the 1991 world darts champion, at his home in Mexborough, explained what the event was for and asked if he would help. To his credit, Dennis said: "Yes" straightaway.

So me and the landlord both chucked £50 in and said the £100 goes to anybody who can beat Dennis over just a single leg. It dragged in the best darts players in Rotherham and Dennis said he was happy to take on all-comers. No wonder. I recall the first three darts he threw that night all went into the treble 20. It took place on a Saturday night after a home game and Chris turned up to support it, taking Dennis on as well. Like the rest, he couldn't beat the world champion either!

At Christmas that season we were second and went to Stoke, who were top. We lost 2-0. It was the peak. In similar fashion to what happened to Billy McEwan, it did to Phil Henson. He had wanted to strengthen just before Christmas, doing so from a position of strength. But Ken Booth kept a hold of those purse strings. Loans were allowed rather than the sort of permanent signings me and Phil felt would improve us and keep us as viable promotion contenders.

Mid-table finishes in two seasons indicated progress had stalled, and it had. The club was stagnating again. Fans started to get restless and when the 1994/95 season opened with an awful 4-0 home defeat to Shrewsbury, the crowd reacted badly. Some fans staged a sit-in protest afterwards on the pitch and chairman Booth came under fire. Gates had slumped to less than 3,000, even in the opening month of a new season when optimism is supposed to be highest. When we lost 3-0 to Bristol Rovers in the third home game, the writing was on the wall. It certainly was halfway through a training session at Hooton Roberts the following Monday morning.

Phil sidled over to me and sang a line from a song: "There may be trouble ahead ..." before nodding his head in the direction of the other side of the training ground. Standing there was Ken Booth with Archie Gemmill. Me and Phil knew what that would mean, and were soon proved correct. Frankly it is totally unacceptable behaviour to do that. But, as Ken Booth said when he took me on and I queried over whether I should speak to the manager, Norman Hunter: "I'm the owner; it's nowt to do wi' 'im." He probably thought it was "nowt to do wi' Phil" who he took to the training ground. He had already met Archie at his office at the scrapyard so the blokes who worked there would have had an idea what was happening.

Anyway Archie was appointed with his old Forest teammate John McGovern and, because neither wanted to be assistant, they had the unusual title of joint managers. Phil was relieved of his duties, but it wasn't the end. Just the start of a new role. Club secretary Norman Darnill was made redundant and Booth decided that the club didn't need a secretary – "The girls in the office can do that job," he reckoned – so he made Phil the chief executive. Which I imagine is the only time a sacked manager has then been asked to run the club!

It was left to me to step into the breach, helped by Billy Russell and Chris Hutchings, for the home game on the Tuesday night against future champions Birmingham City. Archie and John decided they would have a watching brief from the directors' box. But it didn't stop them coming into the dressing room at half-time. We had put on a great performance in the first half and were winning 1-0. The door opened and in walked the former Forest duo. I imagine they would have done the same had we been losing! Anyway we were pushed to one side and they took over. It finished 1-1, still a pretty decent result. I expected that would be me finished at the football club. Perhaps this contributed to a little outburst that, you may think, was totally out of character.

It was after the match. We'd been in the dressing room, the players were getting changed and I headed off back to the coaches' room. But something was burning inside me. How could they have played so poorly previously and then, with their new bosses watching, responded by playing really, really well that night? They couldn't do it for the manager who'd signed them and handed out new improved contracts, but could turn it on for those two sitting in the stand. I turned and headed back to the dressing room.

I pushed open the door. "By the way, lads, thanks a lot for that performance ... you shower of shit." I just wanted to get it off my chest and not just grumble to myself and my coaches. The players knew what I meant. But if they didn't, no one came and challenged me. Had they done so, I was ready with an explanation and to stand up for myself. I guessed I might be out of the door with the new duo wanting their own people in, but it didn't prove the case. I went back to dealing with the youth development aspect and helping Billy Russell, who was youth coach, with both the youngsters and taking the reserves. I even got a fancy title – youth liaison officer. To be fair, Ken Booth didn't want to lose me and I soon settled back into that environment.

***

The joint-manager arrangement was a bizarre one in my opinion. I understand it came about because Archie wanted John McGovern to join him. But John wanted equal billing if he came. One man, one boss is the sensible way. It provides clarity. They were certainly different characters. Archie was abrasive and he said in just about the first meeting I had with him: "I don't get on with people very well." I had no issues at all with him, but John was a different type of person; I found him a nice bloke, a gentleman and got on well with him.

Archie's remark did come back to me later on in their first season. It was a reserve game and an angry Archie was forcibly making his point to quite a number of the players at half-time. Pointing at them individually, he went round the room: "You'll not be here next season and you'll not be here next season ..." After "informing" some of the players, he got to Imre Varadi, a striker who had played at the top level and done well for the club, but hadn't figured much under the pair other than as a substitute.

Archie paused and then, again jabbing his finger, said: "And you'll not be here next season, either." Imre didn't remain silent. "I could have told you that," he said. Archie visibly steamed and started to go round the small table that was between them – only for a flying boot that had just been removed from Varadi's foot to strike the little Scot on the head and draw blood. Archie was removed to the treatment room for stitches and spent the second half sitting at the back of the Main Stand. I know because I was alongside him.

The pair couldn't improve the league position during their two seasons, but they did provide a moment of club history and the enduring memory of Rotherham United's first Wembley appearance in 1996. I also learned a heck of a lot from those two that Wembley weekend about the importance of preparation and how to approach and prepare for such a game and such an occasion. Lessons absorbed then proved invaluable years later.

Me and Billy Russell were invited to go with the team and we stayed on Friday at Waltham Abbey, where England would stay ahead of home internationals. We had a light training session on the Saturday morning where I stood alongside Sky commentator Martin Tyler, identifying players for him. In the afternoon it was off to Stamford Bridge to watch Chelsea play Leeds United.

Afterwards we walked through Chelsea to the cinema to watch *Trainspotting*. I'm not sure if that was Archie's choice, but the film includes the famous footage of his brilliant solo goal for Scotland against Holland in the 1978 World Cup in Argentina. Then the bus picked us up, we went back for our evening meal and Archie and John went off to their room, leaving me and Billy in charge with the message: "Look after them."

The entire weekend was relaxed. The whole approach took their minds off the game ahead on the Sunday and I am sure it contributed towards what was a very good performance to beat Shrewsbury 2-1 in what was then called the Auto Windscreens Shield, the cup competition for the bottom two divisions. I paid attention to how Archie and John did it and how it all seemed to help the players. I thought that, if I ever got into this position, then I'd do something similar because if it was good enough for two European Cup winners, then it would be good enough for me. One thing I would like to have seen relaxed, however, was the restriction on goal celebrations. Under Archie and John you could not jump up off the bench when a goal was scored. I guess that was pretty much the Brian Clough influence.

However, that trophy success did not protect the pair when they made a disastrous start to the following season with seven defeats in the first eight matches. Rotherham also lost both legs of a League Cup tie to Darlington, who were struggling in the bottom division, and a swift end was inevitable after that set of results. Ken Booth was heard to comment that results were bad, adding: "And I'm paying wages to two managers, not one." When that thought crossed his mind, the joint managers were doomed.

16

"WHO THE F*** IS THIS RONNIE?"

A familiar football anthem reverberated around Millmoor. The "Three Lions" song had been *the* sound of Euro '96 in this country a year before, but the Millers fans had tweaked the words just a little bit this particular afternoon to suit their own ends. *"He's coming home, he's coming home, he's coming... Ronnie's coming home."*

It had started in the Tivoli End and, as more fans picked it up and it got a bit louder, everyone knew what it meant. Everyone except one man. Danny Bergara was the manager in charge of Rotherham United as the disastrous 1996/97 season drew towards its close. With the crowd in full cry Danny turned from his position on the touchline, looked at me in the dugout and asked: "Who the fuck's this Ronnie?" I said: "It's Ronnie Moore. Got 50 goals in two seasons in the early 1980s and was a hero to the fans." Danny looked startled. "That doesn't look very good for me then, does it?" he said. He theatrically flung his notepad to the ground. "Well, that's it then, me out of job."

Although I felt sorry for him in that moment of realisation, I desperately wanted to laugh and, as Danny turned back to face the pitch, I had to stuff a towel in my mouth. The other staff on the bench, coach Billy Russell and physio Ian Bailey, were also having to stop themselves from laughing. We weren't laughing at Danny, but simply at his reaction and the funny way it all came across. The little Uruguayan had replaced Archie Gemmill and John McGovern the previous September, but here we were, doomed and simply waiting for the relegation axe to chop us down. It did so with four games left. Danny went just afterwards.

By the time the season ended, just about everybody in Rotherham knew who the next manager was going to be. But when it was announced

– and Ronnie was actually "home" – I heard the news out in Finland. A Rotherham lad out there had approached me about doing some coaching and I went to Tampere, an industrial town about 30 miles from the Russian border.

The John Breckin Soccer School had been set up and I went out for a fortnight every year for about three years, coaching 30 lads in a morning and another 30 in the afternoon. This year was to prove the final year and I took two ex-Millers players with me, Chris Dolby and Mark Todd, to help out. With club director Neil Freeman helping with funding, we also took a couple of teams from our School of Excellence to play in a tournament there. Obviously it wasn't just for the trip – might there just be a little Finnish gem to be unearthed?

Thankfully I was back in time for Ronnie Moore's big coming-home party at the Zone nightclub in Masbrough. What a night that was. The place was packed to the rafters; the fans were overjoyed that their blond-haired, one-time goalscoring hero was back. When he spoke, you could have heard a pin drop; when he'd finished, the place erupted in a cacophony of sound. It was a totally euphoric night for all concerned.

Ronnie, who had been managing Southport, was living on Merseyside and I'd invited him back to stay overnight at my house after the do. We'd had a great night, a few beers, too, and it was after midnight when we got in. I made us a cup of tea and we started chatting about the club and things. Mick Hennigan, a real football guy, had been on the staff as a coach and appeared to be lined up as Ronnie's assistant before he received a very good offer from Nigel Worthington at Blackpool to be his No.2. It meant a vacancy for an assistant manager at Millmoor.

Ronnie took a sip from his cup, remarked: "You make a decent cup o' tea, Breck," and then made his pitch. "You know the club inside out, we get on well, I'm not looking anywhere else. Do you fancy it?" I was happy doing what I was doing, dealing with the youth set-up and helping out Billy Russell with the youngsters and the reserves. I had enjoyed a lot of success at those two levels with cup wins and promotions. It was a great opportunity and I was flattered to be asked, but I decided not to jump in there and then. "Look," I said. "We've had a good night, we've both had a drink, we're both in high spirits. Let me sleep on it and we'll have a look in the morning." When he came down the next morning, he didn't take long to raise the subject. I'd barely got the milk on my cornflakes and

Ronnie was straight at me. "Have you thought about it then?" he said. "You were assistant to Phil Henson, you've got all the experience, you know the club, you love it to bits, you know the town and the people inside out. So will you be my assistant?"

It was a big decision. I was happy and content and job satisfaction is important in any line of work. I'd enjoyed working with young players and on the youth side of things and got a lot of satisfaction at seeing various aspects of success in those roles. But here I was, getting the chance to return to a previous job. The big support act for the manager – something which I had also enjoyed and in which I'd had success, too. Although we had kept in touch, we'd had only minimal contact during the previous 14 or 15 years after going our separate ways. But me and Ronnie went back a long way, experiencing those great days as players together, and we had got on so well. In fact, getting back together that night was as if we'd never been apart. It might be that this chance might never come again. I reckoned there was only one answer. "Yep, I'll come with you," I said and we shook hands.

"I'm glad you're on board – and this train isn't stopping," said Ronnie.

It didn't pass me by that assistant manager is a more vulnerable role than that of youth coach. The turnover is much higher with front-line staff and, as Ronnie has always reminded me: "There's only one certainty as a manager – eventually you get the sack, but you just don't know when." But we weren't thinking along those lines. This was to be the start of an unbelievable journey in management that neither of us could have envisaged. A fantastic eight years at the club we both loved and where we had enjoyed success as players. There was plenty more ahead that we simply could never have imagined.

***

It was great to know the fans were right behind Ronnie. Everyone had just experienced it in the nightclub. After such a poor season with supporters disillusioned again – the average attendance was less than 2,900 – we could be sure we would be given a chance by them. The first job, however, was not so much a shortage of fans, but a shortage of players. Being back in the basement of Division Three did give Ronnie chance to rebuild in a less challenging environment. We still both knew that, as one of the "bigger" clubs, we would be expected to be at least challenging for a play-off place, if not more. But there was a lot to do. There were only about half-a-dozen players under contract in that close season of 1997 and our first priority was keeping one who wasn't, star striker Lee Glover. Archie and John knew him from their Forest days and had signed him from Port Vale for £150,000 the previous summer – but surprisingly on only a one-year contract. What's more, Lee had really struggled in a floundering team and actually went out on loan in March to Huddersfield.

However, I convinced Ronnie he would score goals in the bottom division and we should push the boat out if necessary and get him on a longer contract. You might think that was the first bit of trust and teamwork between us in our new partnership. Ronnie took the views on board, but it was his decision in the end. Lee got a three-year contract and it was a good one, too – £500 a week and £300 a goal plus appearance money. And the chairman threw in a rent-free house. We had to do all that and make it an attractive package or he would have walked away because there were sure to be other clubs ready to pounce. The reckoning was, if he got 20 goals, then that would be only an additional £6,000 during the season and you would almost certainly be up around the top if you have a striker getting to that 20 figure. It was to prove money well spent.

Anyway the club had just dropped on a nice little windfall – about £120,000 for a promising young goalkeeper who had played just twice in Phil Barnes. A Rotherham lad from Treeton, Phil had been given his chance in the first team in the final two games of the season at just turned 18. He showed his potential in the second of them, the last game of the season, a 2-1 win at Bristol Rovers. He was outstanding. The opportunity had been handed to him by Mick Hennigan who, as assistant manager, had taken charge for those last two games after Danny Bergara's departure. Now Mick came back for Phil to take him to Blackpool, having just gone as assistant to Nigel Worthington.

Phil was a good goalkeeper who did exceptionally well for Blackpool and I was pleased for him. He'd come through the specialist goalkeeper coaching sessions we had set up at the School of Excellence some years earlier. When we signed Phil, I noticed he had part of a finger missing, the result of a boyhood accident with his bike. When I asked one of our coaches why he'd never mentioned it in the couple of years he'd been up there, he said: "I didn't notice it; he always had gloves on."

The specialised goalkeeper-coaching set-up helped us to land an even bigger goalkeeping "fish" than Phil turned out to be. Matt Clarke. Micky Hukin alerted me to the fact Matt wasn't getting any specific goalkeeping coaching at Sheffield Wednesday and he wasn't happy at that. So, when he learned of ours at Millmoor, he got his dad to bring him down. It proved attractive to him – even though he was a Sheffield lad and a Wednesdayite to boot – and he eventually joined us. It proved to be Wednesday's loss and they had to pay about £325,000 to get him eventually, a month after he lifted the Auto Windscreens Shield as captain in our 1996 Wembley triumph. Tot up the fees for two talented young goalkeepers and setting up something we hadn't previously specialised in before my return had paid off handsomely.

The blank canvas me and Ronnie had on starting out, now had our first "signing" in Lee Glover. Certainly we had to learn the art of wheeling and dealing quickly. There was no bulging purse and being in the bottom division can make it that bit harder to sell the club to potential recruits. But both of us worked hard on that aspect and there were some handy signings. Alan Knill's move had actually been set up by Mick Hennigan before he left – thanks, Mick! – and others such as Steve Thompson and Vance Warner proved good acquisitions. A less than successful one – but a player fans tend to remember despite only fleeting glimpses – was Gijsbert Bos, and his white boots.

Ronnie remembered a friendly against a non-league side, Lincoln United, when this big striker caused real problems. We watched him and thought he was worth a punt, particularly for just a few thousand pounds. The feeling was that we could hardly go wrong and if he did happen to come off ...! It proved to be a big "if." Gijsbert's first game was in a second XI sent to Gainsborough Trinity for a pre-season friendly. We stood on the terracing and after 10 minutes Ronnie tapped me on the shoulder. "Breck, I think this could be my first bloody boo-boo!" he said. I could only agree.

Actually he wasn't too bad, but no one was wearing white boots back then and those white size 14s had the fans laughing when things didn't go right for him. He could look clumsy although he did score four goals in his first nine appearances. He soon lost his place because of injury, but on his return in the reserves there was almost an astonishing chance to sell him for a big fee.

Big Gijsbert played really well in the first half and caused Bradford City's reserves no end of trouble. At half-time the Bradford chairman was so impressed that he went to the dressing room and insisted that his club signed the big striker. He was ready to give us £100,000 for him. However, former Miller Chris Hutchings, assistant to Chris Kamara, had the good sense to persuade the City chairman that such an outlay would not be advisable. Or any outlay for that matter. Chris was right, of course, but what a sale that would have been! Gijsbert was a reserves regular thereafter, making only a few more first team appearances before departing at the end of the season, taking his white boots with him!

That first season went reasonably well, a particular highlight being an FA Cup replay win over Burnley – who were a division above us – at Turf Moor, which was our first "live" game on television other than the Wembley final of the previous year. Burnley's player-manager was Chris Waddle, but Ronnie tactically outdid him, not least in detailing Paul Hurst to do a man-marking job on the former England star. Hursty did it perfectly, but the memorable moment of the 3-0 win was a brilliant goal from little Trevor Berry, a veritable candidate for Goal of the Season anywhere.

In view of the integration of new players and the necessary chopping and changing during the season, it was a decent achievement to arrive at the final game of the season still in with a chance of making the play-offs. It required Barnet to lose and us to win. Well, Barnet lost, but unfortunately our final game was away to the champions Notts County, who had run away with the division under Sam Allardyce. We actually led 2-1 at half-time, but in front of a full house County were not going to have their party pooped and we eventually lost 5-2. As you can imagine, there were plenty of celebrations going off from the home supporters and players, and Ronnie wasn't happy.

He had his say and then ordered our dressing room door to be opened. The sound of celebrating and singing flooded in. "Just listen, can you hear that?" he said, sweeping his hand towards all that was going off. "That's what we want at this football club. That's success. That's what we want next season and I want all that sound at our ground." Then he shut the door. He had made his point. Not all those players would be at the club the following season. But he had left those who would be in no doubt that he meant business at Rotherham United.

Left: A rare family photo at the seaside with Mum, Dad and Brian. I guess it would be on the East Coast

Below: The second year team at Wingfield Comprehensive School with teacher Alan Archer to whom I have always been indebted

Telephone: 2434

ROTHERHAM UNITED FOOTBALL CLUB LIMITED

Secretary:
J. L. HOLMES
Manager:
T. DOCHERTY

MILLMOOR GROUND,
ROTHERHAM.

Our ref: TD/HB 27th June, 1968.

Mr. & Mrs. Breckin,
78, Robinets Road,
Wingfield Estate,
Rotherham.

Dear Mr. & Mrs. Breckin,

Thank you very much for your quick reply to my letter.

I see your son leaves school on the 19th July, but will not be 15 years of age until the 27th July. If he could report to us for training at 10.30 a.m. on the morning of the 22nd July this would be suitable to us. If you wish to come along with him we can fix up your son then as an Apprentice Professional.

Thank you once again for your letter.

Yours sincerely,

T. Docherty.
Manager.

ıe squad that reached the FA Youth Cup quarter-finals in 1970. Note the neat haircuts - most of them urtesy of Pete Morris! Back row: Phil Bendig, Mark Mitchell, Kevin Ball, Jim 'Seamus' McDonagh, Mick ıng, Dave Abrahams, Les Saxton. Front: Paul Short, Steve Kulic, Alan Crawford, me, Bernard Coop, Trev ıillips. Not pictured are Alan Epton, Doug Hemmingway and John Ryder *(Sheffield Newspapers)*

ght: The ticket stub ɔm my Millers debut, New Year's Day, 1972 Bradford City's Valley rade. We lost 1-0

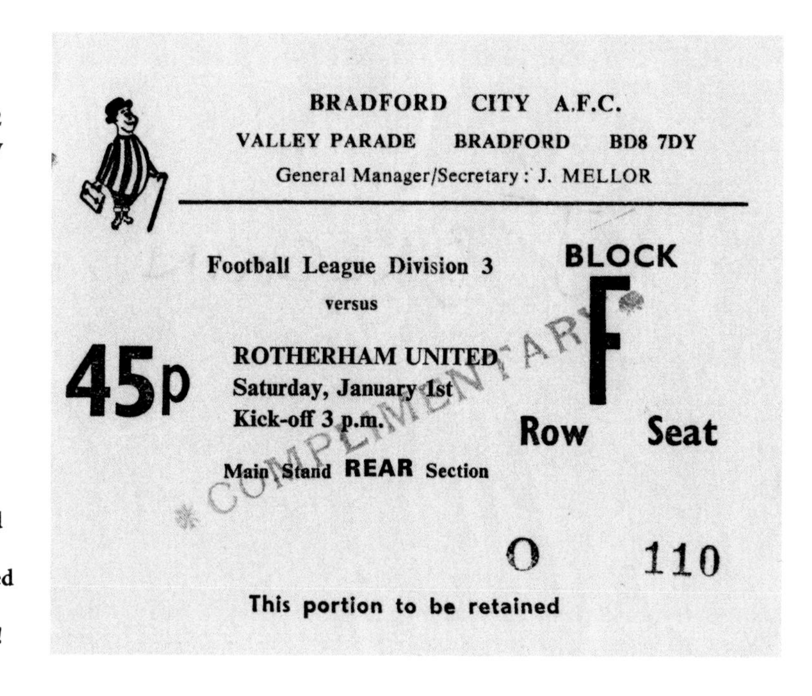

BRADFORD CITY A.F.C.
VALLEY PARADE BRADFORD BD8 7DY
General Manager/Secretary : J. MELLOR

Football League Division 3
versus
ROTHERHAM UNITED
Saturday, January 1st
Kick-off 3 p.m.

45p

Main Stand REAR Section

BLOCK
F

Row O
Seat 110

COMPLEMENTARY

This portion to be retained

ft: A valued letter, ;ned by Tommy ɔcherty, asking me to ɔort for my first day Millmoor. His initial ter, offering me a ree-year contract as apprentice, was dated th June, 1968 - so my ım and dad had wasted time in replying ıstantly to the first one!

The 1974/75 Division Four promotion squad. Standing: Jim McGuigan (manager), Charlie Bell, Trevor Swift, Jim McDonagh, Tony Henderson, Brian Peck, Trevor Womble, Graham Haslam, Barrie Claxton, Alan Smith. Middle: Bob Delgado, Phil Syrat, Tommy Spencer, Mick Leng, Alan Crawford, Freddie Robinson, Jimmy Goodfellow. Front: Trev Phillips, Richard Finney, Ronnie Wigg, myself, Nigel Davey, John Woodall, Steve Derrett. Missing are Dick Habbin and Barry Wagstaff *(Rotherham United)*

You can just make me out in the distance, scoring from long range against Blackpool *(David Blakesley)*

hallenged by Eric Potts. It was March 1976 - the last time we beat Sheffield Wednesday at home in a
ague game, until the 3-0 win in October 2020. Dick Habbin scored in a 1-0 win *(Sheffield Newspapers)*

Above: Striking the opening goal in the amazing 6-0 win over Chelsea soon after getting back into Division Two (nowadays the Championship) in October 1981 ***(Sheffield Newspapers)***

Left: Being put through my paces by physio Alan Smith, after breaking my foot. Alan went on to have a great career at the top, including eight years as England physio until 2002 ***(Rotherham Advertiser)***

A pre-match meal back in the day! Still the best and tastiest pies around. Lifelong fans Eric and Matthew Twigg - of Eric Twigg Foods Ltd. - have been generous sponsors at the club since 1981 *(Barry Payling)*

The 1980/81 squad with the Division Three trophy. Back: Mark Rhodes, Rod Fer Ronnie Moore, Ray Mountford, Graham Brown, Phil Henson, John Seasman, To Towner, Barrie Claxton (assistant manager). Front: Richard Finney, Gerry Forre myself, Jimmy Mullen, Paul Stancliffe, Mick Gooding. Inset: Boss Ian Porterfiel who soon after left to join Sheffield United *(Rotherham United/Sheffield Newspaper*

Above: With my teammates (some not in view) at my testimonial match two days after clinching the Third Division title in 1981. Back row, from left, Rod Fern, Ashley Taylor, Mark Rhodes, Ray Mountford, Paul Stancliffe, Steve Winn, Ken Tiler, Graham Brown Front, from left, Richard Finney, Tony Towner, Ronnie Moore, myself, Jimmy Mullen, Gerry Forrest, John Seasman

Below: With Phil Henson, Ronnie and the championship trophy *(Barry Payling)*

HANDS OFF BRECKIN MESSAGE TO OWLS

WITH good, young and improving players like Richard Finney, John Breckin and Alan Crawford, Rotherham United's future looks bright.

But if manager Jim McGuigan allows Alan Clowes's suggestion in last Saturday's Green 'Un, that Sheffield Wednesday should buy John Breckin, to happen then Rotherham will get nowhere.

RESCUER BRECKIN

Brentford 1, Rotherham 1

A distinction this week for Rotherham United defender John Breckin was his choice at left-back in the Fourth Division's representative team, chosen by the players.

THE SUNDAY PEOPLE, JANUARY 2, 1972 PAGE 23

Unfit Rotherham fall to Hall's last-gasp goal

By FREDDIE TRUEMAN

the end.

The Rotherham defence did not have one experienced full-back and indeed Brekin, an 18-year-old, was making his first team debut and for me here is one to watch. He hardly put a foot wrong and at times he even came up the field in an attacking role.

absence to remind us how steadily

TAKE THAT . . . Manchester City's Gary Owen (left) and Willie Donachie can only watch as skipper John Breckin slams in Rotherham's first goal

Rotherham foiled

expense of Ashley Taylor was soon emphasising his particular values.

Charlton match and today's game at

Various newspaper cuttings from throughout my career - including one, above, by the great Yorkshire cricketer Freddie Trueman after my Millers debut. He may have misspelled my surname, but he was a good judge of a player.

New Millers skipper

JOHN BRECKIN, the Rotherham United left-back, is to captain the team next season.

The former Rotherham schools player and ex-Millers' apprentice succeeds Jim Goodfellow who was not retained.

Breckin, the professional

AMID the infusion of Ronnie Moore, John Seasman, Tony Towner and Jimmy Mullen to Ian Porterfield's Rotherham United team, one name remains constant.

By IAN VICKERS

Left back John Breckin seems to have been with Rotherham for such a time it's a little surprising that he's only just past the mid-twenties mark. Breckin has been with Rotherham for over 12 years, working his way up from schoolboy level to the point where he's now one of their best-known players.

Yet there was a blow last season. He had been an ever-[illegible]nt in the side [illegible] [illegible]arch, when he w[illegible] [illegible] [illegible]ers. John is [illegible] [illegible]tive de[illegible]er, his gr[illegible] st[illegible] going forward."

A testimonial looms for the local-born defender, who will be used to the derby atmosphere of next Saturday's home match against Barnsley.

John Breckin: works hard.

[illegible] Richard Dawson corner, during the Millers' early flourish which included three corners in the opening couple of minutes.

The day Elton met John!

Confirmation has come through this [w]eek of a top level meeting at Watford's [V]icarage Road ground following Rotherham [U]nited's recent match there.

Taking part — and swopping sugges[ti]ons — were Millers skipper John Breckin [an]d none other than the Watford chairman, [su]perstar Elton John.

But there was nothing sinister behind [th]eir get-together . . . no plans to make [Joh]n the first £1 million full back; they were just asking a favour of each other!

It started with John looking for the League's best known chairman to collect a few autographs and our sports writer Les Payne, who had been chatting with Elton, helped the Millers' skipper track him down.

Sitting in an office, quietly opening his mail, Elton — in black fur coat, shiny black trousers tucked into black pointed leather boots and checked cap — recognised John even without an introduction and welcomed him in.

"He said we deserved a point and asked us if we'd now play as well against the other promotion candidates and take points off them," said John (Breckin that is). "I said we would, and asked him to get Watford to do the same for us by beating everyone else to give us a chance to get into a top spot.

"We both had a laugh about it, but he's a great guy and he really loves his football."

'Breck' ready for the 400th

Rotherham United defender John Breckin is set for a double milestone when he turns out against Swindon Town at Millmoor tomorrow.

It will be his 400th appearance for the Millers in League and Cup and he will also be reaching his 350th game in the League alone.

COLOURS:
RED SHIRTS, WHITE SHORTS

Ground:
COUNTY GROUND · SWINDON

SWINDON TOWN
Football Company Limited
League Cup Winners 1968/69

Finance Manager/Company Secretary: R. A. MORSE
Administrative Manager/Club Secretary: R. J. JEFFERIES
Team Manager: R. W. SMITH
Commercial Manager: D. BUSWELL

Registered Offices:
COUNTY GROUND - SWINDON
Registered No. 53100 England

10th September, 1979.

Mr. J. McGuigan,
Team Manager,
Rotherham United Football Club,
Millmoor Ground,
ROTHERHAM.

Dear Mr. McGuigan,

In confirmation of our Team Manager's telephone conversation with you today, I am instructed to offer your Club the sum of £70,000 (seventy thousand pounds), for the transfer of registration of player John Breckin and I look forward to your favourable reply as soon as possible.

Mr. Smith our Team Manager will discuss the terms of payment of this fee with you in due course.

Yours sincerely,

R. Jefferies

R. J. Jefferies.
Administrative Manager/Secretary.

Above: The official offer from Swindon Town for Rotherham United's left back. The Millers reply, right, shows them turning it down. I knew nothing about the offer until many years later, when I discovered the letters in a safe at Millmoor!

Mr. R. J. Jefferies,
Administrative Manager/Secretary,
Swindon Town FC.,
County Ground,
SWINDON.

12th September, 1979.

Dear Sir,

I write with reference to your letter dated 10th September, 1979, addressed to Mr. J. McGuigan, concerning your Club's offer of £70,000 for the transfer of registration of John Breckin. This has been discussed by the Board of Directors and I have been instructed to inform you that your offer is not acceptable at this particular time.

Yours faithfully,

G.A. Somerton
SECRETARY

im Albiston, left, and Gary Willis, who both came
o my door to ask if I'd play for Brecks Rangers

Looking after Derek Dalton along with Richard Finney during the 1981 celebrations - although Derek could look after himself whatever the subject but particularly the Millers *(Barry Payling)*

onnie, chairman Ken Booth and I in natural poses at the annual team photo *(Sheffield Newspapers)*

Above: We could smarten up when required. With one of the managerial awards Ronnie received during his success years. Inset: Bloody but unbowed. Chris Swailes with his 'cuts man' - popular physio Denis Circuit, one of the nicest blokes I ever worked with *(Rotherham United)*

The best squad I worked with? You can be the judge of that! Back: Rob Scott, Guy Branston, Richie Barker, David Artell, Mike Pollitt, Ian Gray, Chris Swailes, Alan Lee, Martin McIntosh, Andy Monkhouse. Middle: Alan Knill, Ian Bailey, Rhodri Jones, Marvin Bryan, Chris Sedgwick, Nick Daws, John Mullin, Shaun Barker, Darren Byfield, Denis Circuit, John Bilton. Front: Jose Miranda, Mark Robins, Darren Garner, Stewart Talbot, Ronnie, Myself, Paul Warne, Chris Beech, Paul Hurst, Danny Hudson (*Sheffield Newspapers*

close partnership - and they still are all these
ears later. Paul Warne (with hair) and Richie
arker in action against Burnley in 2002. I had to
nclude this one didn't I? *(Sheffield Newspapers)*

Two key figures in the Millers success years at the
start of this century, midfielder Kevin Watson
and striker Alan Lee. The real stories behind the
transfers are interesting *(Sheffield Newspapers)*

ottle time with Ken Booth and Ronnie in the dressing room at Hartlepool after securing promotion in
000. Chris Beech is bare-chested, and the forehead belongs to Trevor Berry *(Sheffield Newspapers)*

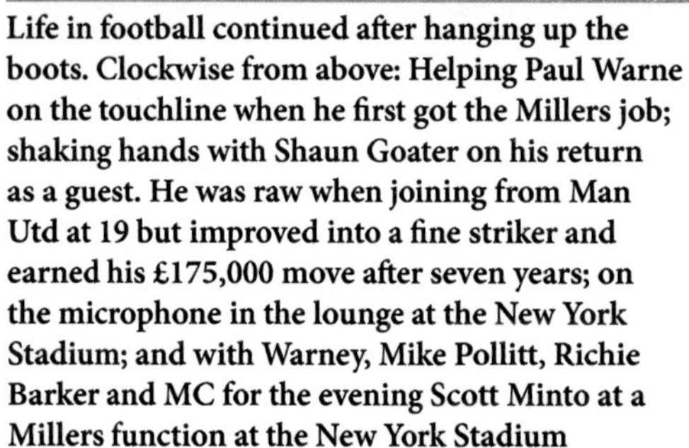

Life in football continued after hanging up the boots. Clockwise from above: Helping Paul Warne on the touchline when he first got the Millers job; shaking hands with Shaun Goater on his return as a guest. He was raw when joining from Man Utd at 19 but improved into a fine striker and earned his £175,000 move after seven years; on the microphone in the lounge at the New York Stadium; and with Warney, Mike Pollitt, Richie Barker and MC for the evening Scott Minto at a Millers function at the New York Stadium

Above: Receiving the honour of Life President from chairman Tony Stewart, a man to whom every Millers fan owes their gratitude *(Rotherham United)*

Left: With Warney after he won his first trophy in management, the 2018 League One play-offs. He has done a fantastic job and the club is fortunate to have him in charge *(Rotherham United)*

Above: Relaxation and happiness on the morning after the tension of the great day before as Warney led his staff and their families on a lap of honour around the outside of Wembley Stadium. Here we are under Bobby Moore's statue. A lovely memory

A great night. The first ever Midnight Walk was the last public event at Millmoor and raised over £80,000 for Rotherham Hospice. I never expected such an amazing response to the idea. Note old and new, the Tivoli End and the half-finished new Main Stand which was never completed *(Sheffield Newspapers)*

With my daughter, Jess, leaving the New York Stadium after a game

17

WHO? PAUL WARNE? NEVER HEARD OF HIM!

The summer of 1998 was important. The time had come for significant signings. Not just any old players to please people or fill in or be part of the squad, but ones that would have an impact; newcomers who would come in and improve us. Ronnie Moore had every right to feel reasonably satisfied with his first season. After all, it was the first full campaign in the Football League for him in terms of getting things shipshape, plotting the course and steering the boat as well. Now, as he'd emphasised on his last-day blast at Notts County, he was looking to step up.

We both knew it meant signing players who would make a difference. We'd now got a first hand idea of what that particular level was about. Lee Glover had backed up our belief he'd get goals with 17 in 37 games, and we reckoned he could repeat that. Ronnie was majoring on midfield and specifically wanted a box-to-box player who would chip in with a few goals as well. But we kept drawing blanks wherever we went and finally Ronnie's patience cracked. "We keep hitting the bar," he said. "If we can't score enough, then we'll stop 'em going in at the other end. We'll keep clean sheets." So a call was put in to Nobby Stiles' son John, an agent who had a goalkeeper we might be interested in.

"I'll call him and bring him over straightaway," John said. "We'll get there as soon as we can." Me and Ronnie stayed in the office and it was about six o'clock when they turned up. I met them at reception and took the prospective signing up to Ronnie's office. The first impression was huge – in more ways than one. "The door opened and he filled the bloody gap, door frame to door frame," Ronnie recalled after he'd gone. "Did you see the size of him? He's a big unit."

The lad agreed to come and what a great signing Mike Pollitt proved to be! Although he had been in the game for almost a decade, he was still seeking to establish himself with any longevity at one club. He'd had a lot of loans and at Sunderland was no more than a back up goalkeeper. This was his big chance, and he certainly took it. Ronnie liked his goalkeepers to have presence and Polly certainly had that, but part of the "big unit" thing was that he was overweight. And well over, too. Credit to him for getting stuck into some really hard work. He had to shed the best part of a stone and a half and Graham Brown, our goalkeeper coach, worked and worked with him. It paid off for Polly and us. Big time!

We had brought Bobby Mimms back to the club a year earlier. He, as with Matt Clarke and Phil Barnes, was another goalkeeper who had brought in good money previously when joining Everton for £150,000 and had adequately filled the experienced 'keeper role in our first year. But Bobby was now almost 35 and we – and probably he – knew we would be looking for someone a bit younger. What a great signing Polly proved from day one. He's actually a big, soft Labrador underneath it all, but he was a big, noisy, funny guy and a massive character in the dressing room for lots of reasons. It was just what we wanted. Polly's presence meant that the biggest dead-end job at the time at Millmoor was reserve team goalkeeper.

He got lured away by a massive money offer at Chesterfield, but, when it all went tits up financially at Saltergate, he was back with us just 12 months after leaving and it wasn't until the April of his fourth season in all for the club that an injury forced him to miss out for the first time – after 204 consecutive appearances in the Millers No.1 jersey. Polly was eventually to play in the Premier League with Wigan Athletic and at one point there was talk he was on the radar of Sven-Goran Eriksson for a possible England call-up. It was great to see him back at the Millers in recent years as goalkeeping coach, assisting his old teammates Paul Warne and Richie Barker, before the lure of joining his home-town club Bolton in the same role in 2019 was too much to resist, later moving to Preston.

Having got his "big" 'keeper, Ronnie wanted to close in on a big striker. We identified one at Lincoln City who had been out injured. The inquiry was made. Yep, we could have him on loan. He came in on the Thursday just after lunch and signed, but all the lads had gone home after training.

We had a game the next day, Friday, at Swansea and, when we assembled that morning ready for the coach trip, it was the first chance we'd got to introduce them to Leo Fortune-West.

He scored to give us a 1-1 draw and in the month on loan he netted four goals in six appearances. Then he went back to Lincoln. Not before we'd tried to get him permanently – only for Brentford, top of the table, to nip in and nab him for £60,000. It was a blow and we had to go down a few other avenues. But then we got lucky – although some might say putting in the hours and the miles wasn't luck. What's the saying ... the harder you work, the luckier you get?

Our weekend game was Brentford at Millmoor. On the Tuesday night they had a game at Swansea. It was a long, arduous, four-hour journey in the depths of winter, but me and Ronnie decided to take ourselves down there on a spying mission on our next opponents. Sitting on the Brentford bench was Leo. This was now February 1999, three months after his loan spell. We were sitting in the directors' box and Ronnie sent me to have a word with Leo to see why he wasn't figuring. Leo looked pleased to see me, and I asked him how it was going.

"Not great. They don't fancy me," he replied.

"Would you come back to us?"

"I'd love to come back," said the big fella.

I reported back to Ronnie and like me, he couldn't believe his luck. "We've got to do something about that sharpish," he said. We did. On the long drive back up the motorway, Ronnie rang Ron Noades, who had the all-embracing title of chairman-manager at Brentford. Because he was the owner as well, you know who was in charge there! Firstly Ronnie put on his Scouse charm. Or was it cheek? "Do I address you as chairman or call you Ron?" he asked. It was Ron. "Ron, we're just making an inquiry about Leo. Would you sell him?" The reply was in the affirmative.

"What would you take?" Ronnie probed. "We're looking to get back what we paid," said the other Ron. That was about £60,000. Cue a sharp intake of breath from the Ronnie at the side of me.

"We can't stretch to that, Ron. How about £30,000?" We agreed on £35,000. But the matter wasn't quite settled. Ronnie asked Noades if we could pay in instalments and he agreed, "as long as it's not 24 monthly payments." We agreed on three, I think. Leo had doubled his money when he moved to West London so we had to offer him a good contract. But he fully repaid us and more, although Noades did make us wait a bit longer. He wasn't parting with him until Brentford had played us a few days later!

Leo wasn't a Monday to Friday player. You'd look at him in training and wonder. But come Saturday at three o'clock ... whoa! He definitely performed all right when it counted. He may not have been Glenn Hoddle during the week – the award for worst player in the five-a-sides was a yellow shirt with "You've had a Leo" on it, which the recipient had to wear the next day. But he was a really awkward handful for opposing defenders when the proper action started on match day and they knew what a tough afternoon they were in for.

Ronnie, with all his experience as a striker, worked a lot with Leo to help him and it paid off. In just 20 appearances he scored 12 times, and he wasn't the only striker to have come in either. Three others had arrived between Leo's loan spell and him returning permanently. At one time or another, in a little more than half-a-season, *nine* different strikers played in the team. But, as Kevin Keegan said to Ronnie when signing one of them: "You can't have too many strikers!"

Two of the signings are at the club now, 23 years on – Paul Warne and Rob Scott – and it was the inquiry about Rob that led to Ronnie dealing with Keegan, who was then in charge of Fulham. Rob was a striker then and we had watched him at Carlisle on loan. Big, strong, good legs; he looked the part. He had an unbelievable long throw which appealed, too. And we knew him from his time at Sheffield United.

So negotiations started with Fulham. Ronnie spoke to Keegan who said they wanted £50,000 for him. Ronnie demurred with a sharp intake of breath, suggesting that it was a bit too much. Keegan never flinched. "I'd rather keep him than let him go for less," he said. "Anyway you can't have enough strikers. I've still got six if I let him go, but I'd rather have seven."

So £50,000 it was. Chairman Ken Booth stumped up the money, but Rob's centre forward career with us lasted just a month before injury at Christmas ended his season. He came back the following campaign with some advice to Ronnie from Keegan still fresh: "Don't be afraid to play him in central defence if you're short there." It proved a handy tip. We tried it, Rob adjusted well to being a defender and served the club brilliantly in whatever defensive role he occupied. His return in 2019 as head of recruitment added to the "old boy" link at the club.

Leo and Scotty certainly proved their worth and were excellent signings, but we could never have envisaged the value of what the next incoming player would bring to the club. Or the impact he would have. When Ronnie and me first clapped eyes on him, giving our defenders the runaround on a cold December night at Millmoor with only 1,200 people there, we looked at each other and said: "Who's this?" And it was nothing to do with the fact we didn't know him or know anything about him. We were impressed. It was the first time I'd ever heard of Paul Warne, let alone seen him play!

He was playing for Wigan in an Auto Windscreens Shield match and ran us ragged, scoring in a 3-0 win and never giving our defenders a minute. A follow-up inquiry the next day was inevitable. Wigan let us have him on loan a few weeks later and his impact was instant – two goals on debut in a 3-1 home win over Leyton Orient and an all-action display that immediately endeared him to the Millers followers.

A decision about an eventual permanent deal soon became a formality and the rest, as they say, is history. But it might have been so different had a Warney wish come true that night. He told me years later that, as the Wigan team coach was travelling over a foggy Pennines, he was half-hoping the game might get called off. I shudder to think of what we and the club would have missed out on had that happened!

Another striker arrived in January although he didn't have the same impact and Millers fans may be excused if this passes them by now – Justin Jackson, on loan from Notts County. Two games, one goal! So, to round up the strikers during that 1998/99 season: Lee Glover, who had a season-ending injury in December, Jason White, Gary Martindale, Gijsbert Bos, Leo Fortune-West, Rob Scott, Paul Warne, Justin Jackson and Richard Tracey, a 19-year-prospect we had signed from Sheffield United the previous summer, but who managed only a handful of appearances.

Appropriately enough, with that number of forwards, we finished joint-top scorers in the division with champions Brentford on 79 goals. Unfortunately we didn't get any when we most needed one in the play-off semi-final against Leyton Orient. We drew 0-0 down there and played well; drew 0-0 at home and played poorly and then lost the penalty shoot-out. It was a shattering blow. One minute we had great hopes of getting through to Wembley and the promotion dream was still alive.

A penalty miss later and your prayers that the opposition will mess up, too, go unanswered. Suddenly your season is over right there and then. Don't get me wrong; the play-offs have been a great addition to the game, but I still think it is one of the cruellest moments in football when you lose in them, particularly on penalties. It's a great game, but so wicked at times.

18

TWO-STAR GUY, FIVE-STAR GENERAL

There was no mistaking what me and Ronnie had to do next – get Rotherham United promoted! The upcoming 1999/2000 season would be our third at Division Three level. A decent first season and a near miss counted for nothing now. We had to deliver this time. And in my opinion a third season is the limit for a promotion return. If you can do it the first time – which is tough whatever the level, so thank you very much, Paul Warne – then great. Preferably do it by the second season, but I think a club certainly needs to do it in the third. If not then, for a number of reasons, the whole dynamic has changed – and probably not in your favour either.

"It was imperative, while we needed to make signings, we had to be mindful of having a stronger squad so that, if we suffered from a few absences – not least at short notice – we would not be noticeably weakening the side. We'd had a perfect example of why we should do this late on in the previous season. Five games from the end we were bang in the fight for the play-offs and things were getting tight as we headed to Shrewsbury. We didn't need to be dropping points. Four key first team players – Mike Pollitt, Alan Knill, Paul Warne and Steve Thompson – were Lancashire-based lads who would travel together daily for training in one car. We didn't want to drag them over to Rotherham just to go on the team coach to Shrewsbury, so they would make their own way to Shropshire and join us for the pre-match meal at the hotel.

We were at the hotel when we got a phone call from Knilly, telling us about a bad accident on the M6. "We're stuck and no one is moving... no idea when we might get going," was the unwelcome message. It was about 12.15pm. There was only one thing for it – keep in touch. And hope. Half-an-hour later Knilly updated us: "We're on the move, but only crawling and we keep stopping." They were in constant contact with us, but it was getting towards two o'clock and time for the teamsheet to go in. Ronnie and me decided we had no choice but to put the names of the four on it, but told no one and instructed the players to keep quiet, too.

Then came another update from Knilly. "We're moving now, but not sure how long it will take," he said. In the meantime we had to make contingency plans. Four players from the five substitutes set to be on the bench would obviously step in. As the minutes ticked down, me and Ronnie were worrying ourselves sick. I took the warm up about 2.30pm and they still hadn't turned up. Fortunately we then got a message: "We're not far away." In the end they arrived 18 minutes before kick-off and were straight in to get changed, being battered with banter by the rest of the lads. They had nothing to eat and no proper warm up. It was hardly ideal preparation. But our biggest sweat and closest shave were over. The outcome? A 3-2 win.

On another occasion injuries meant we signed three defenders who all made their debuts on the same day, so we both knew we didn't want to risk being caught out by an unexpected turn of events in future. Wherever it would take me, I used to enjoy scouting; checking on players and watching potential signings, even at the lowest level. In fact, I loved going where I wasn't known; say, to a non-league ground or even at reserve team games and chatting to spectators. It's amazing what regular fans know about their own players and what they tell you, what you might learn about someone. They'd say how good somebody was, but then let on about his weaknesses as well. It was all done innocently, but you were getting an honest assessment. I wouldn't decide anything on that basis, but I enjoyed it and found it revealing and enlightening at times.

We knew that we had to step up our level of recruitment, that our signings this time would be key. And one we made in that summer of 1999 turned out to be one of the best we made in my opinion. Kevin Watson was perfect for the moment. We didn't know him, but his possible suitability was backed up by the system Ronnie and me used when going to watch potential targets or taking in a game. It was what I called our "star system." Okay, it seems a bit dated in this modern era of video analysis, player statistics and fancy data, but it worked for us and came up trumps on this occasion. Both of us did it. If we went to watch a reserve game, either together or individually, and a player particularly caught our eye for whatever reason, we'd put a star at the side of his name on the teamsheet. If he really did raise an eyebrow, then we'd add another star. Two stars most definitely meant someone worth noting.

During the close season we get a call from the PFA's player agency. We'd told them we were looking for a midfielder and what type. They came back with: "A lad, Kevin Watson, started at Spurs, been at Swindon. He's a footballer." We thanked them, said we would get back to them ASAP and turned to the filing cabinet. We had been to watch Swindon reserves against Southampton reserves that season and I took out the programme from the game. There, next to the name of Kevin Watson, a player I knew nothing about, were two stars. Me and Ronnie never used to know what the other had marked and he looked at the programme he had. *Two stars.*

Seeing that would give us confidence about a player and the fact that both of us had independently noted him made us definitely confident. All looked okay when we did our checks and due diligence on the player, so we rang back. He was on £900 a week at Swindon. We said we couldn't match that. We were assured the lad understood that and, anyway, he realised he wouldn't be getting that "up north." So Kevin agreed to come to Millmoor and meet us. Then came the next part of the plan – to show him round the area, which was my role. His fiancée was with him and, because they'd be moving up, I could indicate possible areas to live and potential homes.

We left Millmoor, went up to Thorpe Hesley and down into Wentworth. I made a little detour to show them Wentworth Woodhouse and then pointed out the two lovely pubs in the village. We ran out through the countryside to Hooton Roberts to see the training ground, made another nice detour to go through Old Ravenfield and came back through Wickersley, noting houses that they could get for about £150,000 – bringing incredulity from the visitors when they compared that with house prices down south – and the nice schools available. Then we went via Brecks into Whiston, noting the Golden Ball, Sitwell and Chequers. By now it was time to head back to Millmoor, so left at Whiston crossroads? No. We went straight up Moorgate and the Breckin spiel was still working.

"A nice part of town, this," I said. They looked impressed. We went past the grammar school, which always gets approval, noted the lovely Minster, mentioned a little market town and finally made our way back to the ground. It's a run I've done many times for prospective signings and their better halves and it never fails. Of course, I offer my apologies to the parts of the borough that I didn't show them!

When we got back into the office, Kevin and his agent asked for a few minutes outside. As his fiancée got up, too, we said: "It's okay; she can stay in here. We can have a chat." I know how important it is that the female half is happy and content with what is a big move for her, too. The player has the final say, but a good impression for both can often be critical. Of course, Kevin signed, taking a big cut in wages in the process. We made him captain and he led us to the back-to-back promotions. He knew the game inside out and was a wonderful passer of the ball as well as a natural talker. It was no surprise to me that he went into management.

***

Not long into the make-or-break season of 1999/2000 it wasn't difficult for me to agree with Ronnie when he said he wanted a big, physical central defender. On our radar we had one we had seen during a loan spell at Colchester and he fitted the bill perfectly – and he was left-sided. The lad who started the season in that role was a youngster, Paul Dillon. Only 20, he had come through the ranks, was fully committed and a real 100 per center. Our target was only 20 years old as well, but had crucial differences – he was bigger, stronger and with a more physical presence. So we made our move for Guy Peter Bromley Branston, to give him his full name, which was eventually shortened to "Psycho" by the fans who came to love him and made him a cult hero.

We initially got him on loan from Leicester City with a view to a permanent move and we won his first four games without conceding a goal. We certainly learned a bit more about him when we went to Hull City and, in one of the most remarkable incidents in my time as assistant manager, I heard a steward shout: "One of your players is dying." A minute from half-time Guy got his first red card for the Millers. He tried to plead his innocence – the first time he did so, but certainly not his last – but it was to no avail. Not 30 seconds later, our plans at reorganising were halted by a frantic steward running down the tunnel and shouting towards us: "Get a doctor, get your physio ... the lad who's just been sent off, he's dying. You'll have to do something ... he's bleeding to death."

Right at that moment the half-time whistle went. We hurried to the away dressing room and, as we looked towards the referee's room, there was blood everywhere. My reaction was like everyone else's: "What on earth has gone off here?" In the dressing room our physio Denis Circuit was tending to Guy. His arm was ripped to shreds and there was blood all over the place. It turned out that Guy had marched down the tunnel and decided to take his anger out on the referee's door. He punched it once, but then had another go for good measure – only this time his arm went through the wood panel and also the wire-reinforced glass behind. As he pulled his arm back out, the damage was done.

It had ripped the guiders in his arm, but he was actually a very, very lucky boy. Had it been an artery or a vein, then it really would have been a life-or-death issue. But this was bad enough. I've never seen so much blood. He went to hospital to have a lot of internal stitches and plenty of external ones and it summed up Guy's attitude when a couple of days later, *The Star and Green 'Un's* Millers reporter Les Payne asked him how the arm was. "Just a scratch, mate, just a scratch," he replied. Some "scratch" with loads of stitches, both internal and external, holding his forearm together.

I think the worst thing for Guy was the thought that, because he was only on loan, we might ditch him and not sign him permanently. That was never going to be the case. We'd seen enough, despite the rush of blood, and signed him at the end of the month's loan for £50,000. He was everything we were looking for and what a character. There was never a dull moment with Guy around, be it on the pitch or off it. The day after he signed permanently, Ronnie and me were having a cup of tea after training when Guy knocked on the door. "Gaffer," he said. "I won't be in training tomorrow ...I'm in court."

"Why? What you up for?" Ronnie asked.

"Grievous bodily harm."

Ronnie almost choked on his cuppa. "GBH? You can go down for that, you could end up in prison. What yer done?"

Guy brushed it off almost nonchalantly. "I'll be okay," he said. "I'll get off. It was self-defence. This bloke tapped me on the shoulder and I only hit him once."

It was some hit. It broke the bloke's jaw! When he'd left the office, we looked at each other. "What have we signed here?" we said. But we never regretted it one bit. And as it turned out, he did get off. Guy didn't always have to be on the pitch to get a red card either. We had a great game at home to Norwich during our Championship years, in the season they ran away with the title. Right on half-time we conceded the softest of penalties when Darren Huckerby went down theatrically. It was never a penalty, Norwich scored to go 3-2 up and Ronnie was fuming as we walked down the tunnel, pulling Huckerby back by the shoulder and unloading some unflattering comments – including the word "cheated".

The pair squared up and Guy jumped in to help his manager, which led to other players getting involved. Some minutes later, as Ronnie was giving his half-time team talk, a linesman knocked on our dressing room door. "Your No.28, Branston, is sent off for his actions coming off the pitch," he told me. I was shocked, but I had to go and let Ronnie know, whispering in his ear. He hit the roof.

"Guy, what have you done now?" he asked. The reply was one we'd heard before. "I've not done owt, gaffer," he said. It turned out that Guy had struck Leon McKenzie, who later became a professional boxer, in the tunnel. "Just a slap" was Guy's description and nothing might have happened if the fourth official hadn't spotted the incident and reported it to the referee. The fourth official that day was Steve Pickavance, who happened to be a big Millers fan and a local referee from Wickersley.

I have a picture in my collection of me with Steve, who was about nine or 10 at the time. I have my arm around him and a little trophy is being presented, although the caption doesn't say whether he's giving it to me or me to him! I would have preferred if Steve turned a blind, red-and-white eye to the incident with Guy, but he was only doing his job. At 3-2 down, with 10 men and Ronnie sent to the stands for his part in it all, it looked a forlorn task. As it turned out we were magnificent in the second half and even went 4-3 up, only to concede an equaliser in the last minute.

We had a great relationship with Guy; the lads loved him and the fans loved him, too. Yes, he had that streak of indiscipline which meant that the red cards in his career climbed into double figures and he did have a few issues at times. In fact, whenever Guy said: "I'm coming to see you later, gaffer," we'd think: "What's he been up to now?" But we loved him to bits. He fitted the bill perfectly and was great for us; a big, big part of our two promotions. I think the world of him and, when I get him back at times as a guest in the sponsors' lounge on a match day, he is always immensely popular. Despite his tendency to get in hot water, he had a heart of gold. He'd help anyone, but once, in trying to do so, it landed him in a police cell.

Every year the club was invited by South Yorkshire Police to a little function at Rotherham Police headquarters. Me and Ronnie would go along and one police officer, a Millers fan, told us about a bit of a do they'd had one night with Guy. We knew absolutely nothing about it, and were eager to learn! The officer said the incident had nothing to do with Guy initially, but he stepped in to try to help a young lad who was being arrested. Guy reckoned the lad had done nothing and he should be let go. He was told it had nothing to do with him and, when Guy persisted with his belief about the lad's innocence, he was warned that unless he desisted, then he would be arrested. Even that didn't settle it.

So, as their patience ran out, the officers decided to arrest Guy. They needed a big effort and a lot of manpower. The officer said it took *seven* officers to overcome him finally and get him in the van. "I was there," he said, "and I've never known anyone as strong and to resist like he did." Again Guy got off, but did spend the night in the cooler. Guy also figured prominently in one of the bonding exercises we used to do with the squad. At some point when things were going well, we'd book a day out doing something different. It might be a day at the races, which was always popular with the lads, or we'd go bowling, to Laser Quest at Kimberworth, go-karting or paintballing near Bawtry. That's where Guy turned into Rambo!

We had two teams with Ronnie and me in one of them and on this occasion we were tipped off by a steward that a member of the other team hunting us down – Guy – had been and bought up extra ammunition, including grenades and bombs. "In fact, he's cleaned us out of ammo and he said that there's no way the gaffer and Breck are going to win," the steward told us. "So I'm warning you." Well, Guy and his team soon captured our village, but they couldn't find Dave Artell – we'd craftily hidden him under a pile of tree branches and leaves. Time ran out, up jumped Dave from his well concealed hiding place – and Rambo Branston had been beaten. These days out relaxed the lads and we found them great for team spirit and bonding, definitely getting benefit from them. Afterwards, depending on where we'd been, we'd often take them for an Italian at Enzo's in Parkgate – he was a big Millers fan.

As with those policemen, Division Three attackers found Guy Branston a tough opponent. To our delight he did what it said on the tin. He chipped in with a few goals as well as we showed the consistency needed for a promotion push. One game that does stand out came on Boxing Day when we played at Peterborough and Ronnie was at home, ill in bed. He went down with flu a couple of days before and, with a few players suffering from it as well and unable to play, we tried to get the game called off. To no avail. It meant that I would be in charge.

Despite the problem of missing players, a couple playing under the weather and Darren Garner spending the entire game laid down on the team coach, we romped to a 5-0 win – and Peterborough made the play-offs that season! It made Ronnie feel a lot better and I could rib him about my 100 per cent record in charge! It certainly gave the lads some ammunition for a bit of banter when he did return a couple of days later. The season's highlight, however, was clinching promotion in the penultimate game with a 2-1 win at Hartlepool. Appropriately two of our key signings, Leo Fortune-West and Guy Branston, got the goals with Guy reprising his famous "Branno stomp" – a distinctive celebration march, on this occasion while carrying about four teammates on his back at the same time!

We celebrated in the dressing room before we all piled on the team coach, but someone was missing! "Anyone seen Leo?" someone asked. There wasn't even an answer on his phone. About five minutes later he was spotted strolling casually towards the coach. Wearing his Rotherham United tracksuit, he'd headed off into Hartlepool town centre to find a store, bringing back some drink and a few goodies for the journey home. And Leo might not have been playing but for his own bravery and willingness.

With eight games left we'd written him off for the season after an eye injury. But on Easter Monday, with just three games left, he volunteered to play, but had to sign a disclaimer because he had suffered a detached retina although we never let on about it. He helped us to win that one and no way was he not going to play in the final games. On the way back from Hartlepool we had a celebration break at Wetherby and directors Ron Hull and Carl Luckock treated us. We had a long and enjoyable night there before heading back to Rotherham – promoted.

It was a pity we couldn't round it all off by taking the title on the last day. Millmoor had its biggest league crowd for 16 years, almost 11,000. We had to win to be champions while Swansea needed only a draw and, when it finished 1-1, the Division Three crown went to Wales. Our equaliser was a stoppage-time penalty from Lee Glover, which proved to be his last kick for the club. After being out more than a year with a serious injury, he had made only a handful of substitute appearances towards the end of that season. But he wouldn't be the only one making way for new signings as we looked forward eagerly to the bigger challenges ahead.

19

IT'S ALL ABOUT GOOD SIGNINGS

When a young manager gets his first promotion, it is inevitable that people take a bit of notice. But it was still a surprise when a caller came on to Ronnie Moore asking if he might be interested in a managerial job elsewhere. Even more surprising was the identity of the club – Chesterfield! We had just swapped places with them because they had finished bottom of Division Two, but they had a new owner – actually a young Rotherham bloke called Darren Brown – and the word was they would be throwing a lot of money at an instant return.

Indeed they had lured our goalkeeper Mike Pollitt across to Saltergate with a very tempting financial inducement so the whisper about money going in appeared to have some credibility on the face of it. Ronnie didn't brush off the inquiry. Instead he indicated he was interested and a meeting was set up. But it was all part of his smart plan. "Let's go across, Breck," he said. "It'll not hurt going for talks – we can pick their brains, see what's what and what might be going off over there." We headed off to a big house in the leafy suburbs of Whirlow, on the south side of Sheffield, to meet the agent who'd called Ronnie. Chesterfield representatives were there, too.

We heard the plans – big, ambitious and costly. We were even asked what we'd do, which players we'd bring in. Ronnie had his questions for them, asking the intimate ones about the wage structure for players and what was their planning. They even told us some of the possible signings they hoped to make. It all sounded really good. After a convivial meeting we shook hands, thanked them for the invitation and said that we'd go and discuss things. We set off back to Rotherham and had been driving only a few minutes when Ronnie piped up. "What's that smell?" he asked.

I sniffed up a couple of times and I couldn't smell anything. "I don't know," I said.

"Can't you smell it?" Ronnie asked again.

"No, what is it?"

"Bullshit. It was all over the place in there," Ronnie concluded. "It must be on my shoes." We laughed. He was right and I'd suspected it, too. We wondered where all this money would be coming from to back up all these extravagant claims. We'd got a proper wealthy man behind us, Ken Booth, but even he wouldn't be throwing money around in the manner of the promises we'd just heard. It just didn't add up, we deduced. It can't be right. When it sounds too good to be true, it usually is.

And so it proved. Although Chesterfield did get promotion that season, it was all built on sand with no substance. The spire wasn't the only thing that was crooked and it all began to collapse very quickly with an FA investigation launched within a year with a Football League tribunal following. Criminal charges were eventually brought by Derbyshire Police against Darren Brown.

The serious fraud office were brought in and Brown did serve a term in prison. Of course, Ronnie had no intention of leaving and joining this fantasy world of lies and deceit. We just went across to see what they were up to and to pick their brains. We returned with some useful information, not least the wages players were on. However, our payments and contracts were all above board, something the Football League tribunal discovered that didn't always apply at Chesterfield under their new ownership!

***

To be honest, the only thing we thought about in assessing the 2000/01 season ahead in Division Two was staying up. Another promotion was the last thing on my mind. It was about consolidating and building a platform so we could spring forward again. We certainly wanted some better players and a stronger squad. You always need to be looking to replace players because, if not, it's you who'll be replaced after a while because things will stagnate.

As it turned out, there were to be some cracking signings, but one thing we did get wrong was our doubts about one player now we'd gone up. It was judgment, I'm glad to say – and Ronnie Moore will admit the same – which proved horrendously wide of the mark. Not only did Paul Hurst prove us wrong, but also went on to become a Millers legend. We based our feelings on one thing and one thing only – his lack of height and physicality.

There was no bigger heart in the club and he was a great professional, never giving less than 100 per cent day in, day out and every match day. A little terrier. A great, dogged man-marker if we needed him to do that. But we were worried that, moving up a level, teams might expose his lack of inches and we might get done too often on the back stick. How wrong we were. In fact, little Hursty had a knack of making it awkward for an opponent to win a header and won his fair share of free kicks in such situations. He was a master at it.

Sometimes you can overlook what you have got and think there's something better out there. He was a prime example of someone you think about replacing and yet you never do. The fact that he didn't start the season probably betrayed our private thoughts on his prospects at the new level. After sitting on the bench for the first four matches, he then got into the left back slot and played every game thereafter. The grass isn't always greener elsewhere, is it? Then he went on and proved us wrong yet again the following season in the Championship when all our worries re-surfaced, once more based on the same feelings. He was to miss only one game in the first season up there and just two the season after that. Just to confirm how wrong me and Ronnie had been!

Another player we were so very close to missing out on proved an invaluable signing. Not that it appeared that would be the case when he limped through his first training session with us, the legacy of a horrendous broken leg which had put him out of action for 10 months and threatened to end his career. Stewart Talbot was a midfielder on our radar. He'd not been kept on by Port Vale, with whom he suffered the injury following a challenge which ended with him successfully suing his assailant. After his time out he'd played just half a dozen times as Vale were relegated from the second tier. When Ronnie made an inquiry, he was told Stewart was joining Carlisle.

"It's all done really," was the message. Undeterred, Ronnie asked what the prospects might be if we matched the two-year deal, suggesting Stewart might prefer playing in League One to playing in the bottom division. The reply was encouraging. We said we'd be back as soon as possible… "And don't let him get on that train to Carlisle." Checks were made with good contacts and one replied: "But for the broken leg, you would not have a chance of getting him. He'd be staying in the division above you." He ticked all the boxes for us and someone who knew him said: "Don't hesitate. Sign him."

Encouraged, and despite the bad injury, we decided to take the plunge. We actually agreed the contract and the terms over the phone. The club matched everything. We knew it was a big gamble. But you might say the vast majority of signings are a gamble. On first sighting I wasn't thinking we'd backed a winner! In the first training session with us in that summer of 2000 Stewart was limping. Noticeably so. Ronnie was genuinely worried. I tried the reassurance bit, but I was sharing Ronnie's worries. As it turned out, there was no need for any concern. What a great signing he proved to be. A leader on the pitch, great in the dressing room, and the perfect foil in midfield for Kevin Watson.

Being out so long and having played so few games since his return, Stewart had still to get up to speed in terms of match fitness and in only the fourth league game that season he actually asked to come off. It was his second game in three days, and there were about 20 minutes to go when I heard: "Breck, get me off. I feel like I'm pulling a caravan here. You need some fresh legs." It was the first time I'd heard that, but he was right. Stewart had realised that a tiring midfielder could well become a liability. He was doing it for the good of the team.

We were leading 1-0 and who knows what the final outcome would have been but for his selfless and sacrificial decision? No player likes to leave the fray, particularly not one as competitive as Stewart, and particularly with a valuable win in sight. It proved right because we won 1-0 and in terms of influential signings, he was right up there with our best. Another one also arrived that summer. With Ronnie abroad on holiday, I took a call from Mark Robins' agent. He'd been released by Walsall, so would we be interested? Most certainly. Now me and Ronnie always took holidays separately and I would never bother him abroad until four o'clock when he'd always be having an hour to himself – that was our arrangement. On this occasion I made a one-off exception.

I just wanted to inform him as soon as possible, not even wait a few hours. I dealt with the move, Robbo came through and it proved a simple deal. And what a signing. He got 26 goals in that first season and 50 in all, at a remarkable strike rate of one every other game. A quality finisher of a type I would show every budding youngster who aspires to score goals. His play oozed the touch of class that backed up his time at a big club in the top flight.

No doubt his first two goals, on debut on the opening day of the season, gave him a little extra pleasure. They were scored against Walsall, the club who had let him go. Unfortunately we ended up losing, but he was to score plenty more which were to secure a lot of points that season. I can't think of a signing I was involved in who was a classier finisher.

A month or so into the season, a different type of player joined us – Alan Lee, the sort of striker who complements someone like Mark Robins. The pathway to signing Alan opened up when interest in Leo Fortune-West was flagged up to us. It was to prove a stunning sale. Ronnie had a phone call very early in that 2000 season. When I got back in his office, he suggested it was time to sell Leo. I agreed. "Would you take £100,000 for him?" he asked.

Now bearing in mind we'd picked up our big striker for just £35,000, you may have thought I'd recommend a hand-snatching job. But I said: No."

"What about £200,000?" Ronnie asked. "Yep," I replied enthusiastically.

"Would you take £300,000?" he said. I suggested he should f*** off because he was surely having me on. He wasn't! Our bargain-priced centre forward was heading off to Cardiff City, who were obviously keen to throw some money around to try to achieve a back-in-one promotion from League Two. Leo had been a great signing and helped us to achieve our first goal – promotion from the bottom division. At that moment he was our best sale. Now for a replacement – and it had to be like-for-like.

One night I went to watch Burnley reserves to check out Alan Lee. He had come on our radar about three years earlier when we hosted an Aston Villa youth side at Millmoor. We marked his name with a couple of stars in our files. He hadn't pushed through at Villa and had moved to Burnley, but wasn't getting a game.

In the first half at Turf Moor I told Sam Ellis, assistant to manager Stan Ternent, that we wanted to take Alan on loan for a month. It was with a view to a permanent deal and we had to pay a £10,000 loan fee, which sort of acted as a deposit. I asked Sam if it would be possible to take Alan off at half-time because we wanted to play him at Stoke on Saturday.

Sam set off at half-time to the dressing rooms, which are behind one goal at Burnley. By the time he got there, the substitutions had been made and Alan had to play the full 90 minutes. Throughout the second half I sat there, cringing at every challenge, wincing at every tackle, wishing he'd stop chasing full pelt after those lost causes. We needed him at Stoke! Fortunately he survived. His impact with us was immediate and everybody knows what a top, top signing he proved to be. Alan became a cult hero among the fans and his overall improvement earned him 10 caps for the Republic of Ireland, the first of which was when still a Rotherham player.

Incidentally three years after "relieving" Cardiff City of £300,000 for Leo, we were accepting a deal initially worth £850,000 rising to £1million from them for Alan. Considering that he cost us just £150,000, he has to go down as one of the best signings Ronnie and me were involved in. Not forgetting the impact he had on the team and not to mention on opposing defenders! Alan's arrival in late September meant we had nine players we had signed in the squad. We were getting together the sort of team me and Ronnie had envisaged. At that early stage I don't think either of us was quite sure how good we would be. Certainly we never reckoned on how good this team would eventually prove to be.

20

THE MIRACLE OF MILLMOOR

There is so often a turning point in a team's season, whether it ends in promotion or relegation. Such a moment came, I have always maintained, very early on in the 2000/01 campaign. We had made a decent enough start in those early days, heightened as they always are for newly-promoted sides by the excitement of a new division and fresh challenges with the touch of trepidation sparked by the largely unknown. We had two wins, both away, two defeats, both at home, and a draw from the first five matches. Then came a disaster and a shock to the system. A 6-1 defeat at Cambridge United – and we'd taken the lead at that!

Ronnie ordered the players to report to Millmoor on Sunday morning. "All in Sunday" the painful demand. Players hate that. It disrupts your day off. And it doesn't go down very well with the missus either because any family plans go out of the window. It was a downbeat group who got on the team coach that Saturday tea time; to a man they would be expecting some "punishment" training next day. Just like their defending that afternoon, they didn't get that one right either.

If there'd been a bad result, me and Ronnie would check the match DVD and make notes. It always looks so different. What you thought you'd seen, you hadn't. Or you'd been convinced about some incident or some player and it turned out to be incorrect. Perhaps you'd handed out a bollocking to a player only to find out he wasn't at fault. On the other hand your belief and understanding can also often be confirmed by the match video.

The players turned up, were filed into a room and, much to their surprise when they expected to be out running, they were handed cans of lager. Ronnie asked a few questions, including to the odd individual. On went the video. At various points he would pause it ... perhaps to ask a player what he thought. To another one: how did you see their second goal? "Well, this is what happened ..." and he'd restart it.

This was repeated a number of times. For sure, rather like the management duo earlier, there was enlightenment for plenty of players during and after a couple of hours or so. There were surprises for them, too. The discussions were good and, I reckoned, healthy. What should we have been doing? Then look what we did do. What can we do better?

It was constructive, but relaxed. It had been a bad result, but there was to be a good outcome. Two days later we had another away game – at Wrexham. What would the response be? Well, it was everything you could ask for – a 3-1 win. In the next 14 games after the Cambridge debacle, we lost only once, at home to Reading. Even by that early part of the campaign that was already our third defeat at home. We never lost another home game all season! We gradually built confidence during an unbeaten run of 10 games after that Reading defeat. Belief grew and a togetherness clearly developed among the players.

We knew we had the character and needed it on an afternoon of teeming rain at Northampton when Guy Branston managed to get his second yellow card inside the first 12 minutes! The 10 men worked so hard and ran so much that day that you could only admire what they poured into their efforts. Never has a 1-0 win been so deserved and I well remember what happened as I waited for the lads, muddy and dripping wet, to walk off after they'd saluted our fans. As I patted each of them on the back I realised that, in the main stand, dozens and dozens of Northampton supporters had stayed behind and were clapping off the away team. To earn such respect from opposition supporters indicates how well we played that afternoon.

We very much knew our best team now; we had a system, basically 3-4-3, that suited us and the players really had grown into the division. Ronnie's early reticence – and mine – had gone. This was typified by a bold statement he made after the last match of that unbeaten run, a win which was one of our best of the season on a pulsating afternoon. We beat the leaders Millwall 3-2 at Millmoor. As darkness descended on that early December afternoon, the noise from the Millers fans seemed to rise the more the winter light faded and the floodlights took over.

They were responding to us going toe-to-toe with the top team and there was a raucous atmosphere typical of the old ground as we came from behind to snatch the win, deservedly so, a couple of minutes from the end.

We had climbed up the table in the previous couple of months into a play-off spot, sitting fourth before that game. With that win we went second. As usual straight after the game we ducked into the coaches' room to catch up with the other results. When our division came through and it showed us second, Ronnie didn't waver. "We've played everybody once now," he said. "We've nowt to fear. Bugger the play-offs, we'll go for the top two, automatic promotion."

It was a bold prediction, but from what we'd seen and experienced and the way we had developed as a team with every prospect of improvement to come, no idle one. Ronnie had to transmit that to the players at some point as a goal that was achievable – because they were good enough and had proved it. He wouldn't be shouting it publicly from the rooftops. But privately and inside the dressing room there was a fresh belief. It was a significant statement of intent.

We actually went top the Friday before Christmas with a 2-0 win at Port Vale, but then had a little wobble. What really got us back on track was a run of five consecutive games at home in mid-winter. We won the lot, delivering constant blows to Reading who were chasing us and hoping we would slip up. We didn't, and we always kept out of their reach. In effect the pressure built on them rather than the team being chased, which is unusual. We had a superb 1-0 win at Wycombe on a night of biting cold and sweeping snow – on March 20th, by the way – to return to the top of the table. Then in the sort of twist football loves, bottom beat top when we somehow lost 4-3 at Oxford United four days later, defending like a relegation side rather than one going for promotion!

We recovered straightaway with a 4-3 win of our own against Swindon Town when Mark Robins produced a finishing masterclass – a classic hat-trick of left foot, right foot and header. It set up the "big one" a week later at Millwall. We were joint top, second on goal difference, but we had a game in hand, so Millwall knew they couldn't afford to lose and really needed to win. And, boy, did we get a reception and a half in south London.

It was an intimidating atmosphere the moment we arrived. Fans were banging on the side of the team coach and there were some ribald comments as the players got off just to leave us all in no doubt. I had no problem with all that. Whether it had been set up or not – and we heard later it had – fans want to do the best for their team and, if unsettling the opposition is part of it, then crack on. Within reason, of course. Pitch-side they had the biggest speakers I'd ever seen, booming out the loud-est mega decibels I'd ever heard as the atmosphere inside the New Den was whipped up to a frenzy. We didn't handle it at all and a 4-0 defeat, with Alan Lee getting sent off, meant a quiet dressing room afterwards. The Millwall captain banged on the door as he walked past and everyone heard him roar mockingly: "Top o' the league?"

In what was a three-horse race for the two automatic places, Read-ing were just two points behind us so the loss of Alan for two of the remaining six matches might have been decisive. But a bit of forward planning helped us right at that moment. Back in January, realising we hadn't a like-for-like replacement for Alan should anything happen to him, we looked for a striker with similar attributes. We alighted on a lad originally from Rotherham, Richie Barker. He'd scored two or three times against the Millers in his career and was now at Maccles-field. Richie jumped at the chance of playing for his home town club, although he would have realised he probably wouldn't be first choice ahead of Alan.

As it turned out, he did make first pick on a couple of occasions. In fact, Richie was quite the perfect signing because, of the seven games he started, we won six and lost only his first one. He was also such a handy guy to have on the bench as well and out of 22 games – call it the second half of the season – he played some part in all but three of them. He was underrated, albeit not by us, and an invaluable signing. Of course, he has been alongside Paul Warne these past few years and they form an excellent and complementary managerial duo at the New York Stadium with Richie well regarded, and rightly so, as an outstanding coach. He also loves cricket and I certainly won't hold that against him. He just needs someone to discuss it with… I think Warney struggles on that one!

Promotion seasons throw up plenty of games that leave you with special memories, but for a variety of different reasons. You wouldn't automatically include a wet Tuesday night in Luton on a heavy pitch and a real scrap of a game against a side fighting for their lives. But it was a huge game for us so close to the end of the season. It represented our game in hand on Reading and there was extra pressure on us to win – doing so would take us second and then, and only then, would it enable us to take control of our destiny in the final two games of the season.

All eyes were on us that night. The incentive was clear, a huge rewarding finger was beckoning and in such circumstances the expectation can overwhelm. The pressure can affect the best. In the end only one thing mattered – to get that win. Because the late winner from Chris Sedgwick happened right in front of the Millers following that night, I guess there are plenty who can still recall it as he stole in at the far post for that precious, priceless goal. It was only Sedgy's second start of the season. Injury had kept him out until December when he became virtually our regular substitute and he wouldn't have started at Luton but for Paul Warne's absence.

There were about 10 minutes left after Sedgy's strike and Luton, who knew that defeat meant relegation, threw everything at us in the final minutes. They were never going to get through! I'm not great at maths, but even I could work out that two wins from our last two games would guarantee a second automatic promotion. What's more, it would even be enough with a win at home to Brentford the following Saturday if Reading were to falter at Colchester. The town was buzzing in the days ahead. The players were too. So, so near ...

***

Every promoted team has certain players who become icons for what they did during a memorable campaign. Often the glory boys – the goalscorers such as Ronnie Moore and Bobby Williamson to name just two, a tricky winger such as Tony Towner and even a prolific midfielder such as Lee Frecklington – tend to get the adulation and probably occupy a bigger part of the memory bank of most fans from success seasons. But behind them are those who provide the ballast, the consistency, produce the performances and the solidity that make a strong foundation; in that category we had such as Guy Branston, Rob Scott, Stewart Talbot; and then those whose roles keep things ticking over. Skipper Kevin Watson certainly did that for us.

But I know also there are the ones – Paul Warne, for example – who are largely unsung, just get on with the job and produce week in, week out. One such player was David Artell and, if there was anyone I was more delighted for than him, the name doesn't immediately spring to mind. Yes, I was absolutely chuffed to bits for two brilliant lads, Paul Hurst and Chris Sedgwick, who I'd been involved with since taking charge of the youth set-up in 1987.

Seeing them come through from 12 or 13 years of age and now this. I was proud of them and for them. But I know what this success would have meant to David Artell and his family. He'd been brought up a Miller from birth. His mum and dad, Jenny and Greg, are massive lifelong Millers, as is his sister Jo and his grandad, too. I think he was registered with the Millers United kids' club when he was about four or five, so to him this would have been the season of his dreams. And make no mistake, he certainly *did* play for the shirt.

In a way it was something of a punt. David was still only 19, with only one brief appearance behind him, when we put him in for what was actually his full debut in the eighth game of the season. He was part of a back three alongside Rob Scott and Guy Branston – not a trio you'd want to meet down a dark alley. In fact, one of the things I loved about that season was when Scotty hurled in those massive long throws – or any set-piece we had for that matter – Messrs Artell and Branston were going to be right in there, full pelt, attacking the aerial stuff full on. If anybody fancied getting in their way, then fine. But at least the opposition knew they'd be coming!

We didn't pick him for his elegance. No one would be asking him to play the ball out from the back. The message was: "Just do your job as outlined" and the fact that he did it superbly week in, week out, in a system that probably suited him, is indicated by the fact that his name was on the teamsheet every week. No ifs, no buts. I can't reckon anyone was happier than he was to have helped *his* club to such a success. It is no criticism of him when I say the step up to the second tier would be, we reckoned, a step too far. David would be the first to admit he would never have got in ahead of Swailes and McIntosh anyway. But he had played his part in Rotherham United history. And I wouldn't have been the only Millers follower delighted when the Crewe Alexandra side he has been managing so capably in recent years, gained promotion from League Two in the 2019/2020 season.

As the big day against Brentford beckoned, I spared a thought, too, for Darren Garner. In what was his sixth season, he was a regular and a key performer until he suffered a broken leg at Reading in March. It was to cause him to miss the whole of the following season as well, which meant he never pulled on a first team shirt again until the start of the 2002/03 campaign. It was worth the wait – I'm certain every Millers fan remembers what he did at Hillsborough in our fourth game that season!

Lots of little factors make up success. It may be the smallest of contributions, but, when you look back, they are so, so important. You wouldn't think a reserve goalkeeper would pop into my thought process, but that's exactly what happened as I pondered the season. The regular No.1 had been Ian Gray, who had big gloves to fill following Mike Pollitt. No.2 was Paul Pettinger, a Barnsley lad who had been at Rotherham for a couple of seasons, not having managed a game at Leeds United and only a small number out on loan. He'd been back up to Polly every week without ever playing and this season was deputy again after we'd signed Ian.

Paul played half a dozen times during the winter and then got in with six games left. It was immediately after the drubbing at Millwall. We went to Swansea a week later and needed to get back on track. We drew 0-0 and how many remember that we did so thanks to a late penalty save by Pettinger? And how many recall a moment understandably overshadowed by what was to follow just minutes later in that final home game with Brentford? It was 1-1 and Lloyd Owusu was bearing down on Pettinger, one-v-one. A goal looked certain, which meant going 2-1 down with not much time left. But Paul denied the Brentford striker and the rest, as they say, is history.

No one will ever forget that last minute winner by Alan Lee even if the game itself was certainly forgettable. It was awful, if I'm perfectly honest, but no one cared a jot. As the minutes ticked down at 1-1, the fans certainly let us know that Reading were losing 2-0 at Colchester. We were nearly there – if only we could get a winner, we would be. Now what made Alan Lee turn and shoot as he did in the last minute, I don't know. I'm not sure I can recall him scoring another goal in exactly that way all the time he was with us. I do know that the ball seemed to travel in slow motion into the far corner at the Railway End before there was an explosion of sound like I'd never heard at Millmoor previously and a pandemonium that I had never experienced.

Of the great moments in Rotherham United's history, that ranks as the favourite one for so many thousands of Millers fans. Perhaps it is the iconic playing moment of the club's modern history. At that precise second, everyone knew what it meant; no fudge, no wondering and no waiting. That was promotion – unlikely, unexpected – right there and then. If you say you could barely believe it and could hardly grasp what an achievement it was from an unheralded group of players given no chance by anybody nine months earlier, then that is understandable and would be feelings shared by everyone else, including me.

There were wild celebrations all over the place. We went daft, running off the bench and hugging each other, and it was all repeated about a minute or so later when the final whistle went to spark a pitch invasion. Heroes were chaired off the pitch to reappear shortly afterwards to take acclaim from the directors' box. Rarely can Millmoor have been a happier place than it was in the immediate aftermath. Strangely enough my celebration that Saturday night was relatively low-key. I did what I often did after a home game; went with Ronnie to the Cavalier pub in Ravenfield on the way home even if we did have a few more than normal.

The club were honoured by a civic reception put on by Rotherham Borough Council shortly afterwards and it's a pity we didn't have the trophy to show off. There had still been a chance on the final day, but I well knew in my heart there was no way Millwall were going to lose at home to lowly Oldham with the title at stake. They didn't, but I was glad we at least got a 1-1 draw from our last game at Peterborough on what turned out to be a carnival day, with plenty of our fans in fancy dress.

I can't recall if there were any looking like clowns. If not, there were plenty of those elsewhere among the so-called experts who would have been aghast at what we'd done. So many tipped us to go down and throughout the second half of the season always seemed to write us off when promotion became a topic. Somehow they never seemed to fancy the Millers to do it. Proving all those wrong just added to the special, happy feelings we all had. In a way it didn't quite seem real. It seemed only two minutes ago that we were scrapping it out in League Two and here we now were pondering a second successive promotion and a move up to the Championship – swapping Halifax, Macclesfield and Torquay for Manchester City, Wolves and West Brom, not to mention the prospect of eagerly renewing rivalries with the Blades and the Owls.

As we travelled back with happiness and joy all around, I recalled something attributed to Bob Paisley, the great Liverpool manager, who said that promotion was often a moment of sadness, too. "Look down the bus," he said, "and some of those lads won't be with you in the future." It is sad, but at that moment our joy and satisfaction were overwhelming. I've heard of managers, their assistants and staff who have been promoted and started planning that same evening for the following season. That favourite saying of mine, about smelling the flowers, came back to me, and we decided that we were going to enjoy the moment. The planning could wait.

21

HOW WE'D SCRAP FOR OUR MONEY

It was now a whole new ball game. The entire football club was somewhere we had never even dreamed it would be just a year earlier when nerves were being shredded at the prospect that a fourth season might be required in football's bottom division. Now we were all contemplating a first season in the Championship, which was then the First Division, and it meant stepping up – not just in quality on the pitch, but also finances off it.

A different world? It certainly was when it came to talking wages and increased player costs if we were to have any hope of bringing in the sort who would give us a fighting chance of staying up. If we were given little chance the previous season, we had absolutely zero of avoiding relegation this time. So everybody said! Rotherham United can rarely have been as popular with the experts right across the football world. When it came to predicting who would go down, every single one of them started with the Millers and then got round to considering two other candidates!

The increased costs put the spotlight very firmly on the chairman Ken Booth, who actually shared the same birthday as me, July 27th. A lifelong fan, he would have been as delighted as anyone with the club's success. But me and Ronnie knew there would be some delicate conversations to be had with him, particularly when the suggestion came round to him dipping his hand into his pocket and paying more – and not just a little bit more – if we were to strengthen, which we had to. Where Ken was concerned, money wasn't an issue. Preferably if he or his company were making it. The company he headed up, CF Booth Ltd., adjacent to Millmoor, was started by his father Clarence back in 1920. To everybody

Ken was a scrapman. But in recent decades it had become a global and international metal recycling company.

He was 65 when he rescued the club in 1987 so here he was, nearing 80 with the prospect of having to shell out extra dough, which was not one of Ken's favourite manoeuvres. In fact, we were warned early in our tenure that, if we wanted to speak to Ken about anything which might involve him spending money, not to do so on a Friday. That was payday at Booth's and Ken wouldn't necessarily be in a good mood as he personally would undertake some payments from his desk in his office. His were old-fashioned ways and, if he'd been in negotiations and then come to an agreement, a spit and a shake – spit on his hand first and then the handshake – meant he'd be as good as his word. I recall we had to reassure a couple of players that they would get agreed payments even though there was nothing in writing. The handshake was as good as a contract in the Ken Booth world.

On one occasion it wasn't about a handshake but an order – and someone forgot to follow a Ken Booth order. When he became club chairman, Ken instructed his men not to 'burn off' in the yard when there was a home game on a Tuesday night. But one home game, the unmistakeable sight and smell of smoke and fumes began to drift over the ground from beyond the Railway End. Ken was apoplectic. He reached into his coat pocket, pulled out the brick-like phone he always carried with him and bent down in front of his seat in the directors' box to give a rollicking to the bloke in charge back in the yard. "What the f*** are you doing? Switch it off now ... you don't burn off when it's a home game."

Ken was no academic, but he was smart and very shrewd where deals and money-making were concerned. You don't get from where he'd come from to where he got to with his company without being so. He knew his business, the scrap world, and I wouldn't like to have dealt with him in that sphere! Having worked with Ken now for two or three years, we knew his character and what made him tick. He did give us an assurance about finances when we started: "While ever I'm in charge, the wages will be there." It was right. Not every football club have been able to ensure that's the case.

Overseeing a multi-million pound company such as CF Booth, we knew that the club was in safe hands – I once saw where the turnover in 2000 was £42million and in a decade it had grown to more than £270million. He was never going to spend a fortune, but I can't really recall us ever being turned down when we did propose making a signing – although, of course, we wouldn't be asking him to shell out ridiculous amounts. It was all about finding a way to get Ken to agree to our requests and we did have a method. Me and Ronnie would fill up our cars at the diesel pumps at Booth's. We had got to know the lads in the yard, some of them Millers fans, and they'd come and chat and want to know what was what.

In fact, one of them told us one day about someone we were trying to sign. How did he know that? He said Ken would come into the yard and ask about a particular player and what they thought. So – light bulb moment – we reckoned we could get them to help at times. We'd drop out who we were trying to sign and usually the blokes would be impressed. In we'd go to see Ken.

He'd ask us all about who we were wanting to sign and the bits and pieces. If he was paying out, Ken wanted to be sure it would be money well spent. "Right, leave it with me," he'd say. "I'll have a think." After we'd gone, he would sidle out into the yard with a piece of paper and speak to one of the workers: "Does tha' know this Vance Warner? Is he any good?" And the bloke in the yard, primed to back us up, would reply: "Hey, he's a good player he is, Ken; it'd be a right signing if you could get him." Having got a favourable reply, he'd go to another one with the same question. Again a similar answer. After his bit of due diligence, Ken would go back to his office and we'd get a call later. "Errr, I've been thinking about that player. We'll take a flier ...offer 'em 25 grand – cash!" That was Ken's way of working and it did happen a few times. We also knew which favourable button to press on other occasions. We'd tell Ken about a player we were after.

The selling club wanted £30,000, but we would inflate the price when telling Ken about the deal, saying they were asking £50,000, but they were struggling a bit and I thought we could get him for £30,000. That was the right button pressed because Ken loved a bargain and he would give us his decision. "Offer 'em £30,000 – cash," he'd say. He believed that offering the cash up front and not paying by instalments might do it for us. In that respect he was right! But had we gone in asking for £30,000, i.e. the seller's price, we might not have ended up with that player. That wasn't a solitary example because we had learned how to deal with Ken.

He was never going to spend fortunes, but a few years earlier in 1995 he had spent £100,000 on a striker, Mike Jeffrey, from Newcastle. He would have been pleased with the profit, doubling the fee when the club sold him on a year later. He did splash out, too, when Archie Gemmill and John McGovern brought in Lee Glover for £150,000 in 1996, equalling the club's record fee for a player. I've noted how we were determined to get Lee a new deal and that Ronnie persuaded Ken to push the boat out to keep him. Lee also got a house, rent-free, in a nice part of Rotherham, courtesy of the chairman owning some properties. One day Lee had reason to phone Ken. "Chairman, I've got a little problem in the house," he said. "We've got mice." The reply was short and succinct. "Get a cat," said Ken before putting the phone down. End of conversation!

Come this particular summer of 2001, Ken knew he would have to pay more for better quality if we were to have a chance of staying up. To be fair, he would come into the office and sit and listen to us, about what we wanted and what it might cost. He was a good listener. He never turned us down, but we knew how far we could go. And by now we knew how to approach him and when to do so. To be fair, he was as good as gold – or whichever expensive metal you wish to mention! He was so shrewd where money was concerned, and particularly making it, and certainly wasn't paying out with the expectation of nothing in return. When I was youth coach, we had a backlog of fixtures and hoped to get in a couple of games during Christmas. We were playing at Wath then but the changing rooms would be shut during the holidays, meaning we couldn't play. I told Ken this and said we really could do with playing. "Come and see me tomorrow; it's bottle time," he said. I didn't know what he meant by "bottle time", but I soon did the next day.

I went to the scrapyard. In his office was a whole load of booze which he was going to hand out as Christmas gifts for the staff and others. He picked up one of the bottles of whisky and wrapped a £20 note round it. "Gi' that to t'groundsman; he'll open up," he said. I went down to see him, proffered the whisky complete with its "wrapping" and asked if there was any chance of him opening up the dressing rooms so we could get in a couple of games during the Christmas holiday shutdown. His face lit up. "Yeah, that'll be all right," he said, "but so long as you sweep out after you've played." I promised we'd do that and we got our games on. That was how Ken's brain worked.

Not long after he'd taken over the club in 1987, Ken got a visit from the boss of the company who had installed the seats on the Millmoor Lane side of the ground. The bloke complained to Ken that they had been put in during Anton Johnson's time as chairman, but the club had never paid him. What was Ken, as the new owner, going to do about it? As he stood in the middle of the pitch looking across at the stand, Ken lifted his trusty flat cap and scratched his head. "Errr, I'll tell thee what," he said. "You can have 'em all back 'cos nobody sits over there. Just let me know when you want to come and take 'em out and I'll make sure t'ground's open for you." It was smart. Ken knew the guy wouldn't go to the trouble and expense of taking out all the seats and he certainly wasn't going to pay what somebody else owed.

He was from another era – probably never better illustrated than on a visit to Watford, who had a rather famous chairman. Not that famous to some! The scene was the Vicarage Road boardroom and Elton John, complete with his trademark huge glasses and rather flamboyant dress sense, was chatting over the other side. Ken made his inquiry of a fellow director: "Who's that then?"

Director: "It's Elton John. Their chairman."

Ken: "What's he do then?"

Director: "He's a singer."

Ken: "Is he any good?"

Director: "Well, he's had No.1s."

Ken was introduced to him. "I'm pleased to meet you, lad," he said. "How's it going? Are tha' making it pay darn 'ere?" Elton's reply is not available!

But that was Ken. Blunt and interested in the money side. There can't have been too many people in the world who didn't recognise Elton John or knew about him. Recognition on another occasion also proved a brief problem for Ken. In an away game during the 1992 promotion season under Phil Henson and me, we took an early lead. Ken looked a bit glum and it was another 10 minutes before he cheered up. "I thought we were losing 1-0," he admitted. "Then I realised the other team were wearing red and white, not us!"

When we secured an FA Cup replay against Kevin Keegan's Newcastle, Ken was as much interested in the size of the crowd at St. James' Park as the game itself because FA Cup receipts are shared. He even inquired if people in the hospitality boxes were included in the attendance figure.

In another FA Cup tie, a third round replay against Northampton Town at Millmoor in 2004, the reward for the winners was a home tie against Sir Alex Ferguson's Manchester United. It would guarantee a full house at Millmoor with added revenue from being live on TV as well. A real money spinner in prospect. Unfortunately we produced one of the worst performances of Ronnie's time at Rotherham and lost 2-1.

Ken always came in after a game, win or lose, to see Ronnie and me and did so this time. It was quiet and we were wondering what he was going to say. Ken broke the awkward silence. "Errr, that's the quickest I've ever lost half-a-million quid," he said in a rather matter-of-fact way before turning on his heels and walking out. Me and Ronnie just looked at each other! Even to someone whose company dealt in multi-millions, that was a fair old blow. We certainly realised it after probably the most disappointing night the pair of us ever had at Millmoor.

We always reckoned Ken would be happy when the club thought they'd be saving him some money over a deal, but I'll always remember his response when it was agreed that a couple of players would be moving out on loan. One was Stewart Evans, who was off to Crewe Alexandra, and a call was made to let Ken know that the moves had gone through. "And it will save us about £1,000 a week, chairman," he was informed. All that came down from the other end of the phone in reply was the sound of a big blow: "Phooo." And nothing else. Ken had hung up. Explanation? An old-fashioned phrase 'Not worth a blow on the rag man's trumpet'. He couldn't get too excited at saving what was, to him, such a piffling little sum.

If Ken lent any money out, he also had his ways of getting it back. One season he loaned Des Hazel £2,000, an arrangement that was all above board. When it came to discussion time about new contracts, Ken had decided that, while wage rises might be agreed, there wouldn't be any signing-on fees paid out. So we went through three or four players and he agreed to another £20 a week here and £25 a week there, adding: "No signing-on fee." Then we got to Des's new deal. Ken agreed he could have an extra £25 and then piped up: "Errr, I think he'd like a signing-on fee – give him £2,000." He was the only player to get one that year, Ken knowing full well that Des would then be in a position to repay the loan.

On another occasion Ken smoothed over a potentially tricky situation. We had spotted a young player in non-league football and, because he wasn't under contract, we put in the required seven days' notice to his club that we intended to approach him with a view to him joining us. What we didn't know, and couldn't have known, is that his club had a contract ready and waiting for him to sign. They were very unhappy at our move, legal and above board though it was, and the chairman and a club official came down to Millmoor to see me.

It was clear they were pretty angry, not least at the prospect that their club had missed out because they would have made something out of the player's departure when the waiting contract was signed. We stated our case, that we hadn't done anything wrong, at which point the air turned a shade darker. "You don't know who you're dealing with here," was the implied threat. It turned out they had involvement in the scrap trade and knew Ken Booth. Off they went to see him. That's the last we heard of it and the player remained with us. How Ken sorted it out, I don't know. But I could have a guess!

Millmoor did need redeveloping at that time, to bring it up to the sort of standard required to be an adequate Championship ground. In fact, the team had moved so quickly with the back-to-back promotions that there'd been no time to make the necessary improvements even if there had been the inclination. Although Ken was delighted for the club to be in the second tier, he would have subsequently known full well that sustaining competitiveness would require the necessary and sustained backing for his manager. In other words Ken would be paying out and, now in his early 80s, he started coming under pressure to pack it in. His backing ensured that Rotherham weren't imperilled when ITV Digital went bust, after many clubs banked on their deal and paid out extravagant sums for players and wages. Although the near-£1million sale of Alan Lee, who had cost just £150,000, won't have dismayed Ken, by then he was definitely seeking to sell the club.

I think he first became brassed off back in 1994 after the opening day 4-0 debacle at home to Shrewsbury. Fans protested afterwards on the pitch and he came in for some abuse, not least with shouts of: "Get some money spent, Boothy." He actually put the club up for sale then, but nothing ever materialised – although there was one occasion when some bloke from down south claimed he would take it on, only for it to prove something of a false promise. An attempt to pull the wool over Ken Booth's eyes was never, ever going to work!

22

THE DIRTY DOZEN – AND DIRTY TRICKS!

In addition to stopping up, there were two priorities to be discussed once the celebrations were finally over following our promotion to the Championship. Mind you, thinking back, I think me and Ronnie discussed them a few times *during* the festivities. We had a few celebrations right across town, and who could blame us? Our first discussion was about players, and specifically the sort we needed to bring in; those who would suit both us and our situation. The second one was pretty callous really – how could we make Millmoor an unwelcome place, one that those high-ranking opponents would not enjoy coming to and having to play at? We were ruthlessly scheming on this last one.

We had a certain way of playing and it had got us back-to-back promotions, so why consider changing it? Ronnie did suggest he was thinking along those lines – not thinking too hard, mind you – when he sat alongside the most famous manager of modern-day football at the end-of-season Northern Football Writers' awards dinner. Ronnie was to be presented with the most prestigious award of the lot – Manager of the Year. It meant he was on the top table of celebrities and he did confide in me beforehand: "I hope I'm not sat next to Fergie… I'm nervous just thinking about having to do that." I went to my table and turned round to see Ronnie sitting down – right next to Sir Alex Ferguson! Ronnie flashed me a knowing glance and I gave one of those smiles that says: "I'm having a little chuckle at your discomfort."

It would be understandable to be a touch nervous about being plonked next to footballing royalty, but, as it turned out, he had an excellent time and got a bit of advice along the way, a story Ronnie loves to tell. Most instructive it is, too; an insight into the mind of the most successful manager English football has known. During the meal Sir Alex congratulated Ronnie on the promotion and said he actually saw Rotherham play twice – both against Wrexham, where his son Darren was playing at the time. "You had a big, strong side," said Sir Alex. "Physical, good on your set plays. I could see why you'd done well." Ronnie thanked him for the compliments and, bearing in mind the Millers were now stepping up another level, told Sir Alex that he was considering "tweaking" things a bit.

"I think we may try to play just a bit more, perhaps play out from the back more than we have done the past couple of seasons," said Ronnie, no doubt hoping the Manchester United boss might approve of this idea to play a bit more football. Sir Alex nudged Ronnie, leaned just a little closer towards him and slightly lowered his voice. "Don't ask your players to do something they can't do," he winked.

What a great bit of sound advice, thought the manager of the year, to get from the "manager of all time." Ronnie just wanted to let Fergie know that the Millers' methods he'd seen were to get us out of League One and that at a better level we would go and play a bit more. By conveying such an idea, he thought it might make a decent impression on his meal companion and get his approval. Of course, Ronnie didn't change and had no real intention of doing so because we played the same way – with support from the top man!

We realised that we needed to strengthen and, in doing so, bring in players who had sampled the Championship, who knew the level and understood what it was about. Experience was important, but so was character. We also knew we couldn't bring in diamonds, but could get some unpolished gems and buff them up. We used to do a lot of due diligence on players we were going to sign and went to so many games that invariably we had actually seen someone we might later consider signing or may even be suggested to us. We were to make three key signings that summer and two more in the early part of the season. I look back now and realise what valuable acquisitions they were.

There was the return of Mike Pollitt after his year's sabbatical at Chesterfield, sorting the goalkeeper situation. But we needed a centre half and we'd had our eye on a real character, a good, traditional, old-fashioned one if you like – Chris Swailes at Bury. He'd been on our radar previously and Ronnie had once been quoted £100,000 for him. Now out of contract he was coming for free. What an asset "Swaz" proved to be.

He was exactly what we needed at that time and had experience of the level at Ipswich and Bury. I once read that he said he had limited ability, but always gave 100 per cent. Well, I can vouch for both. He certainly wasn't a central defender who you'd ask to pass the ball around at the back, but he was someone who loved defending, loved heading it, loved making it as awkward an afternoon as possible for the blokes he was up against. No frills, give your all, stick your head in where it hurts and do your job. And what a bloke to have around the place because he left no one in any doubt about the task ahead.

We didn't arrive in the Championship as a footballing team, the next Barcelona. We did it our way. We got nicknamed The Dirty Dozen. We wanted to make it ugly and I'm not ashamed about that. Opponents soon realised that an afternoon at Millmoor would be slightly different from what they'd experienced in the previous away game. I had to laugh the first time I heard Chris Swailes "introduce" himself in the tunnel, but the fact is that he was right. The two teams were lined up, ready to walk out and towards the back of our lot came the sound of someone imitating a dog barking: "Woof, woof." Naturally all the players looked round. It was Swaz. What came next was in his Geordie accent with the gravelly voice.

"Er, I'll apologise now," he said, sticking his head out of line and addressing no one in particular, but everybody in opposition colours in general, "but it's not going to be pretty out there tonight, lads. So I just thought I'd mention it and get the apology in now." It got the message across and he'd be rubbing his hands together ready for the action which he always enjoyed being at the heart of, no respecter of reputations.

He lived for his Saturday afternoons and Tuesday nights, but on one occasion he appeared to have put himself out of action. No one could believe he could possibly play. On the Saturday he had gashed his head so badly it needed a number of stitches, right on the forehead. We reckoned he'd be out because it would take a couple of weeks to heal properly and no way could he go heading a ball. Chris was having none of it. "I'll be all right for Tuesday night, gaffer," he told Ronnie. We all laughed. "Swaz, you've got stitches in; the first time you head it bang on there, they'll burst open." But he insisted that he could play with his head bandaged. Anyway we trained on the Monday in preparation for Tuesday night's game and Chris was under strict instructions not to head the ball.

We told him that if the ball came towards his head, he was to duck out of the way. That was no problem. He nodded. First thing that happens? A long ball came down the pitch and Swaz headed it. The wound burst open and there was blood everywhere. That was him done for, then. "No, I'll be okay, gaffer," he said. "I'll be okay for tomorrow." He was, and he played. No one would be surprised to know that he looked like Terry Butcher with his blood-soaked bandage. But, such was his attitude, he wasn't going to let a "little cut" stop him from getting out there.

During the week in training you never knew what he might do. One day he picked up a dead rat and was swinging it round, chasing his teammates. Another time he spotted a big fat worm, picked it up, shouted to the lads and then put his head back and popped it in his mouth. It all added to the team spirit and banter that was round the place.

We went to Watford and were getting changed when Swaz spotted Elton John standing outside the Watford dressing room door, talking to the manager Gianluca Vialli. Swaz mentioned to the lads that Elton was just down the corridor and Andy Monkhouse, eager to have a look at the superstar, went to the door to look out. He was only wearing his jock strap and Swaz pushed him out into the corridor, at the same time shouting: "Elton, Elton, look at me!" Elton glanced across to see a near-naked Monkhouse trying desperately to get back in the door, which Swaz was holding shut from the other side!

Talking of Elton John reminds me of my own meeting with superstardom. I'd played at Watford and decided to get his autograph, so went looking for him afterwards. Millers reporter Les Payne had actually been chatting with the Watford chairman and led me to his office – imagine trying to do that in today's secure world! – where Elton was sitting in his black fur coat, checked cap and boots. Somehow he seemed to know who I was! We chatted briefly and he was due to perform at the City Hall in Sheffield not long afterwards. He said he'd send me some tickets and was true to his word. I went along with a couple of teammates and, much to our surprise, we got a name check when he announced: "We've got some Rotherham United players in here tonight."

While completing his move, Chris Swailes led us to another important signing, Nick Daws. As we were signing Chris, he said: "There's a mate of mine here who's out of contract as well; he'll do you a good job." We certainly knew that and Nick did just that for us. He'd played in Bury's Championship years, at one point notching up a remarkable 223 consecutive appearances. We knew what we would be getting; a good professional, a solid character and someone we could rely on. But we hadn't finished there although we had to wait just a bit to bring in Martin McIntosh. Ronnie's son Ian alerted us to him. He was having a football chat one day with Ronnie and mentioned that McIntosh was looking to get back from Scotland where he was playing with Hibs. We were looking for a left-sided central defender and Ian, who had played with him at Stockport, vouched for him, saying: "He'll definitely do you a job." He was spot on. Martin had also had Championship experience in his time with Stockport and again we followed it up, doing our homework. Of course, he came in and I think the Swailes-McIntosh partnership is one fondly remembered by Millers fans. Yes, it was harsh on Guy Branston and nobody thought that more than Guy.

But the brutal truth is that they were the regular pairing because they were better players at that level and that happens in football. A is better at the job than B and so gets in ahead of him. Guy was their stand-in, but that was important, too, because we needed him several times that season. He was a very important part of the squad although those not in the starting XI rarely see it that way. If he was left out, there were times Guy would head for Ronnie's office for an explanation. Sometimes Ronnie might want a one-on-one with a player and I'd go elsewhere and leave him to it. He never saw Guy on his own; I was always in there as well.

The other significant addition was John Mullin. We decided we needed a slightly different type of midfielder from the ones we had such as Kevin Watson, Stewart Talbot and Nick Daws. John was someone who was more attack-minded, probably more of a box-to-box type. He had good energy about the pitch and could add a few goals to our tally, giving us a bit of extra threat from midfield around the opposition's final third. We had to pay for him, mind you. The fee equalled the club record at £150,000 from Burnley, with whom he had played in the Championship. He had played in the Premier League for Sunderland as well. But we didn't get him through the door until the start of October – by which time we had realised what a step up it was.

***

The other priority we had discussed was more a strategy of making life uncomfortable for our illustrious visitors, not just on the field but off it as well. Our view was that playing at Millmoor meant home advantage and we were going to make the most of being in our own backyard. The first thing we did was have a word with our groundsman Bill Corby. He was good at his job; so good Millmoor was named the best pitch to reward his diligence, hard work and expertise. But we had just one message for him that summer: "Bill, you won't be winning groundsman of the year this time." We would train on the pitch on a Friday before a home game and ask Bill not to give it a roll afterwards; just replace any divots to make it look presentable.

We had narrowed the pitch a couple of seasons earlier when we decided to play three central defenders. Me and Ronnie actually went on to the pitch at that time and did the measurements, while acting as defenders; standing here, moving to there. It transpired that we brought in the pitch width to the narrowest allowed under the laws. In the Championship we were going to play with a back four, but decided to leave it narrow. It would make it easier for us to defend. We were going to come up against some good, expansive footballing sides who liked to knock the ball about and were also good at spreading the play. We reckoned that the less space they had, the better it would be for us; the less pristine the playing surface was, then that wouldn't harm us, but it might just affect them a bit. We felt it might just help us to go some way towards our idea to even up the odds. It had its pay off, I'm sure.

Kevin Keegan's Manchester City were romping away with the division and scoring goals for fun – they netted a massive 108 that season – when they came to us in late March. We trained on the pitch every day and told Bill to leave it alone after Friday's session. It had some effect. We got an excellent point in a 1-1 draw and Keegan did have a moan, but rather about the size of the pitch, saying we had brought the touchlines in for that game. No, we hadn't. League rules forbid you from changing your pitch measurements once they are lodged with the EFL pre-season so it was the same small size it had been all season.

Another high profile moan I recall came from Joe Royle. His Ipswich Town side were challenging for a play-off place when they pitched up one Easter Monday. They were a good footballing side, exquisite passers, so we decided we'd train on the pitch a few times, sort of give it that "lived-in" feel. Bill came out to roll the pitch. "No thanks, Bill... leave it alone," we told him. He got ready to water it. "The only water you require, Bill, is for your cup of tea."

He soon realised his services would not be required any more that day. Ipswich actually led for most of the game, but we scored twice in the last six minutes to win 2-1 and so deal a crushing blow to their play-off chances. As Joe came across to shake my hand at the end, I noticed steam coming from his ears. "Where's your fucking groundsman?" the Ipswich boss blasted. "Haven't they heard of water in Rotherham?" Ronnie jumped in before I could reply: "Hey, Joe, I didn't hear you protesting like that at half-time when you were winning." I had to stop myself laughing and not only at the expression on Joe's face. They're nicknamed the Tractor Boys and after the game the pitch looked as if a tractor had been on it. We did tend to do that for the better teams, the top teams who liked a good surface. Our lads just got on with it, but we never got complacent, thinking it might upset the opposition and be enough. We always worked hard. But problems for the opposition had started even before they got on to the pitch.

In the days before sat-navs, if we happened to be asked for the best M1 junction for visiting teams to get off at, we'd always say: "Tinsley," which meant coming in on the less scenic route through Templeborough and past the old steelworks, now Magna. Once at the ground we'd take them down the steps to go under the Main Stand to the dressing room. Lugging those huge, heavy kit containers down those steep, narrow steps was not easy. Certainly much harder than if we'd simply walked them along the front of the enclosure terracing and down the players' tunnel. Once in the dressing room – and this would certainly seem worse on a damp, cold day – the tiled floor would be soaking wet, having just been mopped.

There were only 11 clothes pegs, so some players would have to double up or put their clothes in a pile somewhere. The heater didn't work – we'd taken the fuse out! And what team would bring spare fuses with them? There was only half a toilet roll, so it was more than likely someone would have to come and ask for another – and we'd always blame the apprentices! If it was a cold day, Ronnie would order the doors to be left open so it would be freezing. It was all designed to make opponents moan about going to Millmoor, knowing what it was like – and then coming across reasons for the grumbles when they got here. We didn't want them feeling comfortable; indeed, exactly the opposite.

You may recall West Ham deciding they didn't want to get changed at the ground and doing so at their hotel. Ronnie certainly used that against them in the team talk before the Hammers' 1-0 defeat. It was all part of our efforts to bridge some pretty big gaps. You couldn't do that now anyway, modern grounds are different. Look at the New York Stadium. A nice modern environment, teams then see that brilliant playing surface and look forward to zipping the ball about on it. There is no way that our antics back then could be replicated now and I'm sure by contrast that opponents like coming here to our new home. But, regardless of the "welcome" we laid on back then, what was to happen on the pitch would, above all, be key.

23

A DODGY FAX HELPS AN UNLIKELY SURVIVAL

When you look back now, it seems impossible. If anyone had said at the start of that first season in the Championship in 2001 that newly-promoted Rotherham United wouldn't win any of their first 10 matches and wouldn't win any of their last 10, then I would have reckoned we were bigger certainties for relegation than we actually were. No one gave us an earthly chance anyway, so how would it be possible to stay up with two winless sequences such as those and particularly at such sensitive times?

After all, when you have just been promoted, you like to have a decent start and then, if you are under pressure in the final weeks, you'd hope to get a win or two under the belt. Well, the "no-win" scenario is exactly what did happen – none for the first two months and not one in the last two months either. Yet we defied all the odds, which we seemed to have been doing for a while.

I do recall shortly after the fixtures came out – which is such an exciting time when you've gone up no matter how long you've been in the game – Ronnie was staring at them, a sort of faraway look on his face. He realised I was looking at him and he blinked: "I'm just thinking, Breck ... Have you seen those fixtures in November? Where the bloody hell are we going to get a win from with that little lot?" It was a clump of games that sort of encapsulated what we'd let ourselves in for: Birmingham away – they'd finished fifth the previous season and due to be fifth again; Millwall away – always tough, promoted with us and destined to finish fourth; West Brom at home – sixth last time and destined to be runners-up; Manchester City away – relegated from the Premier League and due to run away with the Championship title. I recall thinking: "Don't know about a win; will we even get a point?"

Well, we did all right. We drew at Birmingham on a Sunday night, were pipped 1-0 at Millwall, beat West Brom with a great performance when Chris Sedgwick was unbelievable and were robbed at Kevin Keegan's Manchester City by a handball goal to rival Maradona's Hand of God job in the 1986 World Cup against England. City were in blistering form, scoring goals for fun with threes, fours and fives littered among their home games. But we played incredibly well and actually led through Chris Swailes.

Then a couple of minutes from half-time Mike Pollitt came out for a cross – only for City's lanky midfielder Christian Negouai to beat him to the punch, as it were, and knock the ball into the net with his hand. The lads protested and we went ballistic on the touchline, but somehow neither referee nor linesman had spotted what, in present day VAR parlance, would be deemed "a clear and obvious error." Ronnie challenged Keegan about it and the City boss claimed he didn't see it. "There's a TV monitor showing it; you can't miss it," said an irate Ronnie. Keegan laughed. The second half was a siege and we looked to have held out until the 89th minute when their little midfield magician Ali Benarbia scored from 25 yards, aided by a looping deflection.

When the team coach arrived back at the ground, me and Ronnie decided to go and have a pint in the Millmoor Hotel alongside the ground. A short time later a coachload of Millers fans arrived back from the game and some came into the little snug where we were sitting. They were full of praise for our performance, saying how brilliant we had been in the first half. And then one of them piped up: "But tell us, Ronnie, why did we change tactics at half-time and sit back in the second half? It just invited them on."

We looked at each other. The answer was simple. We didn't change tactics at all. We simply couldn't get the bloody ball off a side with several internationals, experienced Premier League players, who were bang at the top of their game and in typical Keegan fashion had a modus operandi of swarming on to the attack.

Had we held out and not conceded that fortuitous winner so late on, then it would have been regarded as a great rearguard action. But, as often happens with fans, the perception is that you've "sat back" when in reality you have just come up against by far the best side in the division, against the best players on their own ground and been forced back and back by superior quality. But one thing that game did do – allied to other results that month – is add to the growing confidence that we would be competitive at this level and we had a fighting chance of avoiding going straight back down.

Our belief had grown during that opening 10-game winless run – we drew four – and the first win came on a Friday night at Grimsby when Ronnie, having said during the run he wouldn't shave until we won, stood in front of the Millers following after the game and famously mimed shaving off the beard which had sprouted considerably. I was glad because the beard didn't suit him, but it was a spot of smart management. At the time it switched the focus and took any pressure off the players. Results improved and so, too, our confidence which was boosted by coming back from 2-0 down at Bramall Lane to draw 2-2.

It was further helped, too, by a great 2-1 FA Cup win over Premier League Southampton on a noisy night at Millmoor, courtesy of a superb diving header by Richie Barker. But his most memorable header came a month later in February in what was the eagerly-awaited first visit to Hillsborough for 20 years. Richie had been understudy to Alan Lee, starting a few games but coming on as a sub virtually every week, as in this case.

As the game came to the 90th minute, we'd have been happy with a point, but a free kick gave us an opportunity. Nick Daws put it in and Richie rose to place his header perfectly beyond Kevin Pressman – right in front of a disbelieving Hillsborough Kop as well. We went daft, although not quite matching the delirium at the Leppings Lane End of the ground where our fans were going absolutely potty. I recall looking up there at the funny sight of seeing some fans who seemed to be upside down. They'd obviously fallen over the row in front in their celebrations. Understandably we did milk it a bit on the final whistle, but I was surprised when Ronnie arrived back in a happy dressing room and looked a tad serious. "I think I could be in trouble with the police," he reckoned.

He'd put his fingers up in a 2-1 sign – I'm sure Millers fans remember the picture of it – and then he'd also done it in the direction of the departing, disappointed Wednesday fans on the Kop. Then he repeated it towards the directors' box to Millers representatives in there as he walked towards the players' tunnel. But, of course, loads of disgruntled Wednesday fans were still in that stand as well and might have thought it was meant for them. A police officer at the head of the tunnel pulled him and said his gesture might have constituted incitement and might have led to a breach of the peace. Fortunately no further action was taken but that was Ronnie, revelling in the moment. I decided to wait until I got back to Rotherham!

Having noted earlier that no win in the first 10 and none in the last 10 would have had anyone predicting relegation for us, what about remaining undefeated at home from the end of September until the beginning of March? I would have thought such a run extremely unlikely when we started the season but it happened; sparked by a 3-0 home defeat, when the Wolves goalkeeper was officially named man of the match, and ended five months later when Forest beat us on March 2nd. And, typical of football, it was probably the first time we had really battered the opposition at this level. Yes, we'd had some wins and deserved them, but never quite with the dominance and the sheer number of chances we had against Forest. We felt robbed because they pinched it that day, but it indicated how far we had come. We were also 18th and five points above third bottom with 10 games left. But, as we know, football can be decided by very fine margins. Well, two particular incidents and a huge slice of luck that went our way were most definitely integral contributions towards what was to be our last-day survival.

Stockport were the whipping boys of the division, hopelessly adrift and losing near enough every week, often heavily. In yet another strange footballing twist, they drew at Manchester City and then actually beat them at Edgeley Park. We had a bit of a struggle against Stockport at Millmoor, but were edging it 3-2 as the game entered the fourth minute of stoppage time. Then they were awarded a penalty. At that time, 2002, serious penalty analysis had only really just started, but not in the forensic way they do today with the laptops and footage of every penalty any opposition player has ever taken.

Back then I took out my notepad and pen and had a chat beforehand with Mike Pollitt, refreshing him on discussions with Graham Brown. He was the goalkeeping coach, but, because he doubled up as chief scout, he was usually away on a match day checking on our next opponents! The regular taker for Stockport was Luke Beckett, the ex-Chesterfield striker and future Sheffield United one. The tip to Polly was that the last penalty Beckett took was struck firmly to the goalkeeper's right. Luke didn't let me down, but more importantly neither did Polly, who made a superb save. Yep, low to his right. At the time no one quite realised how important that save might be.

The other close shave was off the field followed by the lucky break on it. We were signing Darren Byfield from Walsall and he and his agent set off for Millmoor on transfer deadline day. But it happened to be Good Friday and holiday traffic meant they got held up and weren't going to make it for the five o'clock deadline. So we told them to go to the nearest hotel and we'd sort it from there. The deal went through two minutes before the deadline and everything from their end was sent through by fax machine. But the Football League refused to ratify it. The paperwork had come through just after the 5pm cut-off. It was strange because it seemed to have been done before it, albeit literally at the last minute. It meant he couldn't play the next day or in the Easter Monday home game. We complained that something wasn't right and contacted BT, who investigated and gave us proof that a dodgy fax machine had been showing the wrong time and that the papers had officially gone through before 5pm – just.

It meant he was then eligible for our final three matches, starting at West Brom the following Sunday in a live TV game with an expectant Hawthorns almost full. A win would put the Baggies into the final automatic promotion place by leaping over their hated neighbours Wolves who had been 10 points ahead of them only a month earlier. Going a goal down against a side who thrived on 1-0 wins and had by far the tightest defence in the division looked ominous.

But Byfield began to pay off the first bit of his £50,000 transfer fee when he equalised early in the second half and we played exceptionally well. Then with about 10 minutes left Lady Luck smiled on us. An Albion corner was hooked towards goal and Chris Sedgwick cleared from well behind the line. Had goalline technology been in use then – and assuming all seven cameras didn't "miss it" as claimed in the infamous incident with Sheffield United at Villa Park on the day of the 2020 Premier League restart during the coronavirus crisis – then the referee's watch would have beeped and we'd have gone 2-1 down and, in all honesty, probably have lost. But we got a vital point.

Things had tightened up at the bottom, but Byfield scored again the following week in our final home game, a 2-2 draw with play-off chasers Birmingham City. And as results came through from elsewhere, we knew that, barring a last-match catastrophe, we would be safe. It was Crewe or us and they were our opponents in what, in theory at least, was a relegation decider at Gresty Road on the last day. But we weren't getting nervous – Crewe had to beat us by 10 clear goals to overtake us because of our vastly superior goal difference, minus 12 against their minus 31. Crewe made a blistering start, we did go 2-0 down on the half-hour mark and it might have been more. But the game actually petered out in the second half and you could say I've never been happier after any 2-0 defeat than on that sunny Sunday afternoon.

Every red-and-white Miller back in August would have settled for fourth bottom, which is where we finished. It was a great achievement to defy the odds, the experts and everybody else. It was a happy team coach that travelled back to Rotherham knowing we had fully earned a second season at this level. We could reflect and enjoy this, but then ask ourselves: "Can we do better next time?"

24

ANOTHER HERO OF HILLSBOROUGH

Football management requires lots of tough decisions. It requires you to take some unpopular ones, too. There are some players in particular who become fans' favourites. If they don't move on themselves, there comes a time when they won't be first choice or are moved on. Equally leave a player out and such a decision may get questioned, challenged and – particularly if you don't win – criticised. Often they are delicate decisions to take. Yes, it is easy for fans to be blinkered when a player they've revered or especially liked isn't in the team. But time waits for no man nor for any player and we had actually thought ahead when bringing in Darren Byfield late the previous season.

It was time to consider our second season in the Championship, 2002/03, and I wonder how many Millers fans can guess the number of new signings we made during that close season of 2002? One? Two? Three? More? The answer is ... None! Yes, between our first and second seasons at the level, and at a time when fans clamoured for new players, we did not make a signing. It was an indication of the faith we had in the squad. We felt that the group of players we had would do better in this second season; me and Ronnie were confident about that so we backed our judgement.

The addition of Byfield meant a direct challenge to Mark Robins as the second striker alongside Alan Lee. As everyone knows, Mark was an exceptional goalscorer. His 24 goals were a major factor in our promotion to this level and he had been top scorer with 15 as we stopped up. He was a natural finisher with such anticipation. The goal instinct he had, you really can't coach. We talk of the "second" six-yard box and he was so good, so deadly in there. His touch was so precise and he didn't blast 'em; he would pass it in. And for a little fella he was good in the air, scoring quite a few headers. So why bring someone in and, as we did, put him in front of our main goalscorer? The answer, above all, was pace.

Darren Byfield had it. We knew he would bring something to our game that Mark didn't have – that speed to get in behind defences if it was knocked over the top. It gave us an alternative, an extra string to our bow, an ability to stretch opposing defences. In addition, we did have a like-for-like, physical replacement should Alan Lee be out, Richie Barker, but we didn't have an additional second striker. The likely candidate was Paul Warne, who was operating on the left with Chris Sedgwick wide right. Also Mark was closing in on 33 so we had to bear that in mind, too, should we have only him and expect 40-odd games a season from him. What no one could possibly have imagined, even in their wildest dreams, was what happened on the opening day of the new season to vindicate our decision.

I grimaced when the fixtures came out. First game: Millwall away. They'd finished fourth the previous season and proved the toughest of nuts in their own Den, be it the New or the atmospheric old one, and were a really good side to boot. It's fair to say that what happened that afternoon made the entire football world sit up and do a double take. After all, teams don't tend to lose 6-0 at home in the Championship. Not good ones either.

The reaction of our chief scout Graham Brown still brings a smile. He was checking up on our next opponents Norwich when almost at the end of the game someone said to him: "Your lads have done well, winning 6-0 at Millwall." Graham was so stunned he dashed straight down to the guest lounge to check the telly, thinking that Millwall must have had two or three players sent off. Of course, the goalscoring hero that day was Darren Byfield.

He scored *four* of them and, if that wasn't memorable enough, the Millwall supporters gave him a standing ovation when we substituted him with about five minutes to go – a considerable accolade from a crowd well known for their partisan support. They had seen a special performance and could not have been more fair-minded in acknowledging it by applauding him off. When we thought that Byfield would give us something extra, we never imagined it would be four goals in a 6-0 away win. It got even better for us all in the next away game even though the margin this time was only one goal. But what a goal it was.

If anyone deserved the glory of a 93rd-minute winner at Hillsborough for Rotherham United, then it was Darren Garner. A broken leg late in our promotion campaign had led to him missing the whole of our first Championship season and it had been a long, long haul back. At one point in his time at the club he worked hard to lose a lot of weight and, come August 2002, almost 18 months after his injury, he was back in the squad and on the bench at Hillsborough.

On he went in the second half and, when he strode forward into the Wednesday half in the 93rd minute, I recall thinking: "Go on, hit it. Even if it lands halfway up the Kop, it'll eat up a bit more time and I'll take a point." After all, we couldn't expect to go and do what we'd done the previous February and get a last minute winner again. Lightning not striking twice and all that! Well, every Millers fan knows what happened next. It was a superb goal, fully 30 yards and more, top corner, one of the best long range strikes I ever had the pleasure of enjoying. I even tell people it was better than my blockbuster against Exeter. Probably!

The laughable thing was Darren's reaction. You'd hardly call him a sprinter and he certainly wasn't among the fastest in the squad, but the way in which he set off on his celebration run, heading back down the pitch with all our lads trying to catch him up, was hilarious. We'd never seen him move that fast! The thousands of delirious Millers fans were probably going dafter than they had done there the previous season. To get one last minute winner was a dream for them, but to do it again with such a goal, well, it almost defied belief. This time Ronnie refrained from giving the Wednesday crowd a 2-1 reminder even though it was the same scoreline. The same copper who pulled him the previous time might have been on tunnel duty again and not been as lenient on this occasion!

We were delighted for Darren after his fight to get back and grateful for such a winner in such a game. I'm sure he was grateful to his manager for looking after him on one occasion. We had a bonus scheme which included an additional payment for every 10th appearance. One season Darren needed to play one more game for his final bonus payment, but there was a snag. He'd just picked up an ankle injury so was out of the reckoning as the season drew to a close. He clearly wasn't fit, we all knew it, but he pleaded and Ronnie put him on the bench with the hope he could get him on right at the end. There were just three minutes of stoppage time left and we told Darren to get ready and go on the next time the ball went out of play.

"Just stand on the wing," was the instruction. But the ball wouldn't go out, and play wouldn't stop. A minute ticked by; then another. All the other lads were laughing as they knew the arrangement and Darren was getting more edgy by the second. Finally the ball did go out and he got on for the final minute, stood on the wing and got his bonus. "Thanks, gaffer."

We were third after the win over Sheffield Wednesday and, as the season unfolded, it was clear that we were more than holding our own. We'd been competitive the previous season, but now we were more than that. Just before Christmas we went to Burnley and won 6-2, following up a 2-1 win at Ipswich. Belief and confidence were rocketing, aided by a handy motivational tool from Ronnie.

Often on the team coach travelling to an away game, there would be clips from previous games featuring all the team members. Alan Lee scoring, Sedgy going past opponents, good saves and defending. It was designed to remind the players what they were capable of, how good they were and how good they could be. It was extremely popular, because it never showed us losing!

I remember Ronnie saying to me after the players had gone out at Watford: "We've got a team here whereby the opposition have to be at, or near, their best to beat us and that's a great feeling to have." He was right that day, too, because we won at Watford. Next up was at home to Coventry – if we could get the game on. We got a helping hand from the best in the business.

Freezing weather in mid-February put the game in doubt, particularly regarding what was always a problem at Millmoor when frost was around – the Railway End penalty area, which didn't get the sun in midwinter. So an inspection was set for the Saturday morning to be carried out by a local official. The best one around turned up – Howard Webb, the future World Cup final referee and a huge Millers fan, of course. We'd heard Coventry had a couple of key players missing and, with us bang in form, we desperately wanted the game to go ahead. It certainly wasn't fit when he arrived first thing so we tugged on Howard's sense of fair play and asked him if he could give us a chance to get it on. The bottom end certainly wasn't fit and he could have called it off there and then, particularly with the rest of the pitch quite hard.

Coventry manager Gary McAllister actually put his boots on when he arrived at about 11 and went out with a ball to test the conditions himself. He wasn't in favour. But Howard said the sun was out and the forecast was for temperatures to rise so he would give it a couple more hours and check again at 1pm. It was a great sense of optimism from Howard because it felt pretty parky out on the pitch, but we had an action plan. We got some huge heaters from chairman Ken Booth's premises next door, set them up under a big tent at the Railway End and hot air blew across the penalty area for two hours. One o'clock came, Howard had another look and gave it the thumbs up. It was still hard, but after our 1-0 win McAllister came in afterwards and was very fair – he said we called it right.

The win actually put us in sixth place in the Championship, leading to Ronnie making a famous quip to me: "If we're not careful, Breck, we'll be going up again." We laughed. Rotherham United challenging for the Premier League with just a quarter of the season left. It showed how far we'd come in such a short time. The feeling I had was one that reminded me very much of what Ian Porterfield, our manager in the 1980/81 promotion season, once told me years later. He said that particular season was the only time he never had sleepless nights on a Friday.

Managers usually do – and assistant managers as well – as they toss and turn, pondering if they have picked the right team. Ian said he could sleep okay because he rarely changed his side and just knew that eight out of the 11 would be on their game. The other three might be on it as well, but he reckoned that, if not, they would always give about a seven or eight out of 10 performance. I could relate to that now as much as at any time and it is certainly a great feeling to have.

Millers fans saw their team sixth in the table in February and, understandably, began to dream. But as often happens in football, big expectations can be hard to live up to. We weren't to know it at the time obviously, but this was to be the peak of our Championship years. The next two fixtures were against the teams fourth – Reading – and third – Sheffield United. We lost both. In the remainder of the season we actually won only twice. We had tried to give the side a boost with our first signing of the season in February; remember, we hadn't signed anybody during the pre-season break. He was a player who actually took a cut in wages to come and play for us – not a common occurrence in my experience.

It was the former Sheffield United midfielder Curtis Woodhouse, then at Premier League Birmingham. We inquired about getting him on loan and asked if we could share the cost of his £4,000 wages, but the Blues' manager Steve Bruce said we'd have to pay the full whack. Usually clubs agree to split a player's wages which helps the club lower down the pyramid while giving him some game time. We were willing to pay £3,000, but Steve stuck to his guns. We told Curtis that we couldn't take him because we could go to only £3,000. He said to forget the other £1,000. "I want to come and play," he said. It was a great gesture to take the drop in wages and come and play for two months. It cost him about £9,000.

That season brought probably the two most surreal games I recall being involved in. It may have been strange in the summer of 2020 when the coronavirus pandemic saw clubs play behind closed doors, but we were extremely close to that when we played Wimbledon at their temporary home of Selhurst Park in front of 849 spectators, the lowest gate for a Championship fixture. We headed back a week later for a League Cup tie and the attendance was even lower – a meagre 664. The second time it was Bonfire Night and at least you could hear fireworks – there was certainly no crowd noise! The late-season run took some of the gloss off things, but also served as a warning that things would be getting only more difficult from now on.

25

THE IPSWICH MYSTERY – AND STAR SIGNINGS

It all began when I accidentally overheard a telephone conversation as I passed through the Millmoor office one Friday afternoon. Chief executive Phil Henson took the call from Ipswich Town chairman David Sheepshanks and it was the prelude to one of the strangest days I can recall of all the many of them I have spent at Rotherham United. I told Ronnie Moore about it before we set off for the gym and we'd no idea why the Ipswich chairman was calling. Perhaps they had an interest in one of our players. Hours later we were to find out the truth – or what we thought was the truth anyway.

An item on BBC's Look North that evening, which said that managerless Ipswich had made an official approach for Ronnie, indicated that news of it had been leaked. The next morning the newspaper headlines were doom-laden as far as stunned Millers fans were concerned. They looked set to lose their idol. Ipswich beckoned. It was the most subdued Millmoor dressing room I had ever experienced on that Saturday afternoon in October 2002 as we prepared for the game with Gillingham. There had been rumours previously that Ronnie might leave, but this time it seemed certain he would. There was an air of resignation about the place and on the terraces.

In the dressing room beforehand there is usually some banter flying about. On this occasion, nothing. When Ronnie walked in the players were looking at him, wanting him to say something about it. He didn't. They probably wanted to ask him questions. No one did.

It was a sombre atmosphere; not the happy, lively place it normally was. It was as hard as I've ever known trying to gee the players up for the forthcoming 90 minutes. It was as if a grey cloud had descended over everyone. Let's just get this game over and done with and then we can all move on.

It was no surprise that the game itself, a pretty poor 1-1 draw, was totally overshadowed. The entire ground was subdued, the fans deflated. After the game, not long after five o'clock, Ronnie was interviewed live on Sky TV. When he said it was a wonderful opportunity, he'd love to talk to Ipswich about it and he'd be sad to leave, then the great adventure looked to be over. Everyone was convinced Ronnie was on his way.

But in the Ipswich boardroom they were watching the same interview live and expressing surprise at it all. No one had made any approach for Ronnie and certainly not David Sheepshanks. He'd never rung Rotherham. Ipswich issued a denial later that evening when asked about the reported interest in Ronnie. The whole thing got more and more curious. The next morning, it appeared that Sheepshanks may have had a change of heart when he was asked about Ronnie in an interview on BBC radio.

He said they had not made any official approach for him or spoken to Rotherham, but young managers with such a record would always be among those on their radar when a vacancy arose. No wonder we were all still a bit confused. Then the next day, Monday, the club who had supposedly made an approach – but, in fact, hadn't – *did* contact Millmoor and make their interest official. The approach was faxed through to the club office, and chairman Ken Booth promptly turned it down. Ronnie was going nowhere, least of all to Suffolk.

The call on the Friday afternoon turned out to be a hoax, seemingly from a fan of Ipswich's big East Anglian rivals, Norwich City. It was a pretty convincing call because Phil Henson has always insisted that the right sort of questions were asked and he had no reason to suspect anything other than Ipswich Town's chairman was on the end of the line. It was certainly an episode we could all have done without and I don't doubt that it did inflict some damage on Ronnie, whose support among the red-and-white faithful at that time was not so much rock-solid as made of granite. It was 100 per cent without a doubt because of the job he'd done. He was idolised.

But the fact he had indicated he would consider leaving and stepping up to a bigger club cost him some backing among the fan base. Even a small percentage, but there was definitely a drop and Ronnie would acknowledge that if asked today. Perhaps the fact this had been all so real, so public, played out in the full glare of a match day and with a typically honest assessment at the end by the man himself, probably left some people feeling that Ronnie was ready to go and that the next club that did come for him would be the one.

Well, most won't be surprised to know that Ipswich were not the only suitors. As his stock rose along with Rotherham's rise, there were at least six other occasions when he was on the radar and might easily have ended up elsewhere. Take Hull City, for example. He went across there to speak to their people and even stood on the pitch, wearing a hard hat when their new KC Stadium was taking shape. Hull even came back again on another occasion. Watford were interested and I drove him to a director's house. It might have happened, but they refused to let him bring in his own assistant manager. "I won't be taking it because I can't take you with me," he told me as we drove back to Rotherham.

His exploits had been noted just up the road. We went to a reserve game at Hillsborough and, not long afterwards, I sat in a hotel on the outskirts of Sheffield for three hours, having driven Ronnie there for him to be collected to go and meet Wednesday chairman Dave Allen. When Ronnie returned he knew a bit more about racing pigeons – Dave's long-time passion – but not quite coming to an agreement about terms. He also met Wigan Athletic representatives just over the Woodhead and there was definite interest from Stoke City.

One club visit he got away with was when Leeds United asked him to pop up to Elland Road. I went with him and, as we were walking across the car park with Peter Lorimer waiting to greet us, a reporter from Sky came running over. It was pure chance because he'd no idea we would be there. We pleaded with him not to put anything out and the fact they hadn't got us filmed as we went in may have helped. Normally such a plea would fall on deaf ears and we anxiously watched the Sky bulletins later that day, mightily relieved nothing was on.

Of course, it's not to say that Ronnie could have had his pick or that he would have got any of those jobs. One or two may just have been inquiries to see if it might be progressed beyond his initial interest in the job. But a few were certainly firmer. No one could blame him if he looked at bettering himself by taking an opportunity at a bigger club and there had been a few rumours flying around, as happens when a manager had the sort of success Ronnie had enjoyed. They really were a strange few days and the irony was that Ronnie probably had the last laugh because a couple of months later he took the Millers to Portman Road, brushed off the jibes from Ipswich fans and enjoyed a 2-1 win, which would have been particularly sweet for him.

***

One of the difficulties for a club such as Rotherham doing well at Championship level is keeping hold of your star players. Alan Lee was a classic case. In his three seasons the big striker had blossomed and improved to such an extent that he was bound to have other clubs sniffing round. He had become a full international with the Republic of Ireland during his time as a Miller and we knew, as the 2003/04 season dawned, that we wouldn't be able to hold on to him. Others knew it, too. During a pre-season trip to the Isle of Man we met Stan Ternent, the Burnley manager who had sold us Alan. He rubbed his hands together. "We've got a nice sell-on," he ribbed us.

Alan made his farewell appearances in the opening week of the 2003/04 season. His last league game was our first of the season on a boiling hot day at home to Cardiff City – the club who were the favourites to sign him, which they did. Before he went, he had the lowest of low-key farewells – less than 3,000 to see him sign off in a Carling Cup tie at home to York City. Next stop was a near £1million move to South Wales, having left an indelible mark in Rotherham's history – not least for *that* goal against Brentford, the one every Millers follower can recall. He's a great lad and I'm glad he went on to have a successful career. Certainly Ken Booth was happy – especially considering that we had to convince him that paying a £10,000 loan fee to get him in initially from Burnley would be good business.

We knew Alan would be leaving and had already been investigating possible replacements. We got a shout from our goalkeeper Gary Montgomery about a young striker he knew at Coventry, Gary McSheffrey. He went on the pre-season Isle of Man trip although he turned up without boots. But he'd no need for them because he was troubled by a hamstring injury. We decided not to pursue that one. A few years later he moved to Birmingham for £4million! Coincidentally in our penultimate away game of the season and still in danger of getting dragged into the bottom four, we drew 1-1 at Coventry when Mike Pollitt made a vital save from a penalty by... Gary McSheffrey.

Another striker we took a look at, but decided not to pursue was Malcolm Christie. We watched him at Nuneaton, who wanted £50,000 for him. We decided not to bother. Derby County did sign him for that figure and a few years later sold him to Middlesbrough for £3million. So, yes, we did miss out a few times. But me and Ronnie certainly put the mileage in wherever it took us. One day we were tipped off about a Scottish striker. His team were in action in Glasgow that night and after training we said: "Are we up for it?"

We were and took the high road to Scotland. On arrival the lad's agent saw us and introduced himself. Twenty minutes in I'd already made my mind up. No, not for me. Not long afterwards Ronnie looked at me and he'd come to the same conclusion. We decided to wait until half-time and then set off back. We got back at 3am and were then in for training the next morning. But that was all part of it and we both loved it and each other's company on those long drives. The number of players we watched was phenomenal. Sometimes it paid off, other times it might be a wild goose chase to Scotland.

The Alan Lee money was burning a hole in our pocket, but at least we had a few quid to play with when we went for a replacement. However, the extra money meant other clubs were alerted and the fee would go up. When they know you've come into some money, some clubs decide they want a bit of it. Ronnie asked me to go and do a final check on a striker we fancied, Dave Kitson at Cambridge United. I went to Rochdale to watch him on the infamous day that West Ham were at Millmoor, but refused to get changed there.

I was sitting there thinking of the £500,000 they wanted for him, which was a heck of a sum for the club. "He's not a patch on Alan Lee," I thought. All the time I couldn't get that half a million out of my head. When I got back I said to Ronnie: "I'm not comfy at £500,000 ... do £200,000, perhaps £250,000." We didn't get him. Six months later he went to Reading for a reported £150,000 and a few years later his value had risen to the £5million Stoke City paid for him. A couple of weeks after ruling out Kitson, we brought in Martin Butler for £150,000 from Reading – a considerable drop on the £750,000 they'd paid for him!

But the fact is we had to move a bit more upmarket now and being in the Championship for a third year also offered opportunities to bring in players we would not normally have got. Certainly not had we been at the level below. A couple of months before the season started, we got a call from an agent. I laughed when he asked if we would be interested in Scott Minto. We were talking Chelsea, Benfica and latterly West Ham; all big names, massive clubs.

Having started at Charlton, he'd always been at London-based clubs apart from his time in Portugal. I said that we'd be interested in a fit Scott Minto, but the last thing we could afford is bringing someone in who may be injury prone. He wasn't, but either way, we couldn't afford him considering the clubs he'd been at. But we were absolutely assured, 100 per cent, that it wasn't about money and Scott wanted a couple more years, wanted to enjoy it and give a bit back at a club where he would be appreciated.

We pondered and were still a little doubtful, but were told: "He'll come and prove his fitness in training and in a friendly." I think that tells you plenty about the guy himself. He played 90 minutes, looked class – as you'd expect – and told us it wasn't about the money. Which was a good job! He was a very clever guy. He even moved to the area and bought a house in Rotherham. In fact, he volunteered to help out at Rotherham Hospice and used to taxi patients to their homes – and never charged a penny. When you bring someone such as Scott Minto into the dressing room and introduce him to his new teammates, then the message it sends out is: "We mean business." Then other players respond to such a signing.

A few games in and, apart from the win over West Ham which precipitated Glenn Roeder's departure as manager the next day, we'd had a poor start. Midfield was identified as an area we needed to strengthen. We noticed that Carl Robinson, a player we'd seen and liked at Birmingham, was not in the side at Portsmouth. So me and chief scout Graham Brown headed south to check him out in a reserve game – he was going to cost us, even on loan, so we needed to see him with our own eyes.

When we arrived the first person we saw was Jim Smith, Harry Redknapp's assistant at Fratton Park. "What you doing down here?" he queried. We said we were looking at Carl Robinson and fancied him if they'd consider letting him out. Jim said he'd have a word with Harry. "For sure, for sure," said Harry, who was brilliant. We watched the first half and Robinson was different class. Just what we needed. My hands were together. I was praying.

Jim, in agreement with Harry, ensured that Carl was taken off at half-time. "Look," Jim said, "get yourselves off; you've come a long way. We'll get in touch; you'll get a call." So me and Browny headed off back north and there was a call from Kevin Bond, Redknapp's first team coach. "Yeah, we've spoken to Robbo, no problem... he'll come. Do you want him at the training ground or the football club in the morning?" We thanked Kevin profusely, asked him to thank Harry on our behalf and rang off. As we continued the journey, Browny said suddenly: "How much is he on, Breck?" I'd completely forgotten to ask!

So I had to ring Kevin back. "I forgot to ask about money and what he's on?" He handed the phone to Harry. Carl was on £6,000 a week. I told Harry – nay, pleaded with Harry – that we couldn't get anywhere near that. I asked if they would halve it with us – our top man was on £1,500 and at double that we'd have to get it past the chairman. "For sure, for sure," said Harry. We told him that we were sure, too – that we could get this one through with the chairman.

I told Ronnie it was £3,000 a week and that we had to push the boat out on this one. What a player. He agreed and we went to Ken Booth. "It's only a loan, is it? Errr, go on then, we'll take a flier," said Ken. Phew. Thanks, chairman. He was on loan for three months and was a star for us. Real quality. Any club, such as ours, which brings in a player like Carl, who was a current Welsh international, raises eyebrows and improves their playing level. Who wouldn't want to do that? Incidentally it wasn't the only time Harry Redknapp helped us out. He let us have striker Mark Burchill on loan. Mark was on £10,000 a week at Pompey and we got him for £3,000 a week. Unfortunately that one didn't quite work out for us although Mark was a very good player.

But Carl Robinson wasn't the end of the "star" signings. Later that season we got a call – often I'd take the calls, but Ronnie took this one. "Are you looking for a midfielder because I've someone who might be of interest to you?" The reply was obvious, but then Ronnie grimaced in disbelief. We were being offered Jody Morris. Another class act. But bearing in mind he was on about £16,000 a week and our top earners were the loan stars on £3,000, it was a non-starter. "No," we were assured, "it's not about money. He just needs to get his career going again."

Rotherham had been picked out because they were among the lower gates in the Championship and he didn't want to be at a high profile club.

We actually thought it was a wind-up. I rang Scott Minto about Jody. Scott was dead enthusiastic about it: "What a player," was his remark. So for £3,000 a week we got Jody and in the final couple of months he helped us to stay away from the relegation zone. We were cheeky enough to try to get him to stay up here, but he is a London lad and headed back down to the capital. He later played for Millwall and became assistant to Frank Lampard at Chelsea. I have seen Jody since – he gave me a great welcome – and I do know that he was genuinely grateful to Rotherham for that late-season return to the game.

Sometimes when making a signing, you can get lucky and that's what happened with Jamal Campbell-Ryce. I went to Saltergate to watch Chesterfield reserves one night and sitting right behind me was Roy McFarland, then their manager. He was chatting with Frank Barlow, who was doing some scouting, and I heard Roy say that Campbell-Ryce was travelling up from Charlton the next day to join Chesterfield. Now Glynn Snodin was at Charlton at that time, who I knew from my time at Doncaster Rovers and when he had a month with us at Millmoor.

I rang Glynn, a lovely guy, and he said he was sure Jamal would prefer to play in the Championship rather than League One, promising to have a word with him. He persuaded Jamal to head to Rotherham next day and speak to us first. Thanks to Glynn's massive help we got him – with a bit of ear wigging on my behalf. If I'd have been sitting anywhere else in Saltergate's old wooden stand that night, we'd have missed out.

To bring in such as Minto, Morris and Robinson meant we had stepped up with our signings and at that level, we had to. But the loss of Alan Lee was huge. We also lost Darren Byfield mid-season to Sunderland. He was swapped for Michael Proctor who made an early impact but, it's fair to say, wasn't able to live up to it afterwards. Other key players were now no longer as influential as they had been. The successful side was slowly breaking up. The warning signs were flashing.

26

THE LONG GOODBYE

It's going to happen one day. As a football manager, you know it's inevitable. The sack. Parting of the ways. Leaving by mutual consent. A goodbye. Whatever you want to call it, it's the end and you are shown the door one way or another. Unless, that is, you are fortunate to go out on your own terms, having got the chance to move elsewhere, almost certainly to a bigger club and earning more in the process. And who can blame someone for taking the opportunity to better himself? Particularly in such a precarious profession. Many of the best have suffered the moment when they are pointed towards the exit for whatever reason, usually linked to results. As they say, it's all about results, which means there have been some poor ones if the departure is not of your own free will. Rather like when you are born, you know your end will come some time. You're just not sure when.

When it did come for Ronnie Moore, I was gobsmacked. It led to my leaving as well and was the most painful thing to happen to me in all my years in football. Although time moves on, it still hurts when I look back at it and how it all unfolded. People say that in view of the disastrous results in the first half of the 2004/05 season, his crown askew somewhat, Ronnie might easily have gone earlier. It was only because of his reputation, his popularity among the fans and what he had given them in recent years, that they weren't calling for him to be sacked. The irony is that a group of fans, who we called the Famous Five, were to dethrone the king.

To be honest, things were changing at Rotherham United. Owner and chairman Ken Booth was now in his 80s and looking to get out. Criticism from fans had turned into abuse for his failure to make the necessary investment needed to strengthen the side and also modernise the ground. This lack of ambition, in the fans' eyes – and mine, too – affected the club when we stood sixth with only 14 games left a little more than 18 months earlier in 2003. Alan Lee's subsequent £1million departure, while inevitable, was seen by many as clawing back some of the money the chairman had spent and they couldn't now see the club moving forward under the octogenarian; hence the calls for him to step aside.

Dear old antiquated Millmoor desperately needed bringing up to date, but, if Ken was getting out, no way would he be spending money on the ground – nor, one suspects, paying off a sacked manager and hiring a new one. Yes, new blood was needed. But those leaving – including Chris Sedgwick, who went to Preston for £400,000 – were being replaced by lesser players. It all added up to fans becoming increasingly disgruntled at the sense of a club stagnating.

At one point, with talk of potential new owners, there was some ridiculous idea about Paul Gascoigne coming in to replace Ronnie. In fact, I was with him outside the ground one day when a fan came up and actually said: "Nar then, Ronnie, I see Gazza's goin' to tek thi' job then." This was actually the first we'd heard about it and we laughed it off. Word spread that the prospective new owners, who shortly afterwards pulled out, had lined Gazza up to come to a home game although that fell through after Millers fans reacted vociferously to such a possibility. They were still backing Ronnie despite results going badly in the opening months of the 2004/05 campaign. In fact, those results indicated changes were happening on the pitch, too, and, as the disastrous first few months showed, not for the better.

The winless run in the league went on and on and although we weren't ever getting hammered – losing a lot of games by the odd goal – we couldn't get a win. Not until the 21st game did the first one come and, when it did, I'm still not sure how! Leeds United pitched up on a freezing November night for a game live on Sky and I have another reason for specifically recalling it. I had returned to the training ground that week for the first time in two months after a hip replacement, which meant an artificial hip on each side. I'd been around only because Ronnie picked me up from home every day when I wasn't able to drive. I worked in the office doing all the calls, making various arrangements and lots of necessary stuff. So that week it had been great to get my boots on again and be back where I really belonged; out on the training ground and working with the lads.

Leeds managed to hit the post four times in the opening 15 minutes so luck was definitely on our side. Somehow we held on and ended up getting a late winner from Martin McIntosh for that first win, which our fans celebrated as if we'd won the cup. By then a group of five fans, including businessmen and professional people successful in their own spheres, were involved in talks with Ken Booth about a takeover. All of them had been part of the Rotherham United Supporters' Trust set up a few years earlier and RUST's influence had increased because in a way they became an official voice of the fans. The idea now was for a take-over led by supporters; so the Millers 05 group was formed and, after what were known to be difficult negotiations, they became the club's new owners at Christmas 2004. In fact, they must have celebrated their first game heartily – we won 1-0 at Leicester City on Boxing Day.

We then drew with promotion-bound West Ham, lost to Coventry and won at Millwall to give the new board a pretty good start. A massive blow, however, was then losing at home in the third round of the FA Cup to Yeovil. The new men in charge, with huge financial issues to sort, would have been banking on some money from a cup run and this defeat would have hit them hard. A week later Wigan Athletic, who were to finish second on their way to the Premier League for the first time, came and beat us 2-0. After that game there were significant meetings for the manager and me.

Things had been bubbling under before then. At his first meeting with the new board in early January, Ronnie had been told that talks about renewing his contract would be put on hold for a couple of months because there were a number of issues that required urgency. I remember he wasn't pleased about that and specifically recall his words to me: "They said: 'We need to get to know you.' Well, I've been manager for nearly eight years; they've seen what I've done. What did they really need to get to know?" He was fuming and I actually had to calm him down. I had an idea what might happen eventually and was fearing the worst.

Now at times we all need an arm round the shoulder, particularly when life is hard or difficult. Me and Ronnie had been doing that to people for years – and to each other. He'd been having a tough time in his personal life. His marriage had been breaking up, naturally it affected him and, we've agreed on this since, it did cause him to lose focus at times and had an effect on the way he did the job on occasions. With the side he'd put together breaking up and results going downwards, the empire was crumbling. He expected some support and he needed it – an arm or two around him. But he got the feeling he might not get it from the new people and was left alone – apart from his old mate, Breck.

So after the Wigan game on January 15th, more than a week after his initial meeting sparked the doubts about his future, Ronnie was called in to see the new chairman Peter Ruchniewicz – who, as with all the other directors, was and still is a big, long-time Millers fan. I went into another office to meet another director, John Harrison. He told me they wouldn't be renewing Ronnie's contract, which was up at the end of the season, so would be moving him out, but wanted me to remain part of the club.

He showed empathy in sympathising about the situation with my wife, then seriously ill, but they saw me as part of the club and hoped I would stay and take on a role identifying younger players elsewhere, at under-21 level, whom the club may be able to bring in. I was gobsmacked. "The king is dead," I thought. It was a stunned manager and his assistant who met up after their respective meetings that Saturday evening and went for a drink to discuss matters.

Ronnie was seething. He'd been told that his contract wouldn't be renewed at the end of the season, but he was expected to stay on and "fulfil his contractual obligations." In other words he would still be the manager, but would be a dead man walking. I don't know – and have never asked – but it seemed to me as if someone hoped he would walk away from the job there and then. A cash-strapped club could then avoid a pay off. He was never going to do that because he said over a pint of lager that night: "I'm not walking. If they're going to sack me, then they can sack me."

A week later we took the team to Crewe. What was strange was that Alan Knill and Mark Robins, two of our coaching staff, were in the Main Stand and we didn't know they'd be there. What I reflected on later was that the hierarchy must have been preparing the ground, knowing we would be on our way very shortly, because Knilly later became caretaker manager with Robbo helping him. The following week we were in a sort of limbo because there was no game on the Saturday after the draw at Crewe. I do recall at some stage chief executive Phil Henson coming into Ronnie's office and asking: "Do you want me to force the issue with the contract situation?" Ronnie said: "Yes." The portents seemed clear.

I was told by Phil that it would be okay not to come in on the following Monday, January 31st, and to have a few days off, but I insisted I would come in. Although the club wanted me to stay on, I reckoned I didn't want to give anyone an opportunity to say I hadn't turned up for work with the possibility it might be regarded as breaching my contract. I'm sure it wouldn't have come to that, but I wasn't going to risk it.

On Friday, January 28th, the club officially announced that Ronnie would not be offered a new contract, but would remain *in situ* until the end of the season. All hell broke loose among the fans, both in the media and on the phone-in on *Radio Sheffield*. In the previous couple of weeks Ronnie had made his feelings known publicly about talks stalling over a new contract so the pressure had mounted and mounted for something to get sorted. It was. The following Monday I went to the training ground and afterwards to Millmoor. I walked into Ronnie's office and sitting at my desk was one of the new directors, Trevor Smallwood – another big, lifelong Millers fan and as an extremely successful businessman the wealthiest of the new group.

In fact, he was to exercise extreme personal generosity towards the club during the trying times of the next two years and even after the demise of Millers 05, he volunteered to pay more than £200,000 when the next board took over. That payment ensured the club met Football League requirements and without it may well have gone under. Following a subsequent administration, he was one of the major creditors who lost out, having been owed amounts totalling £860,000. With the club so close to his heart, I imagine now he wouldn't have enjoyed the job he sat in my chair to do ... although that wouldn't have made me feel any better!

I sat down opposite Ronnie. "I've come down this morning to move Ronnie out and sort out yourself smoothly," said Trevor quite calmly. So this was it. A short time later things were sorted and the club officially announced that day that Ronnie Moore was no longer the manager. The phrase used was "left by mutual consent." It meant they had agreed a severance package. The strange thing was that I was no longer assistant manager, but hadn't left! I was still officially a club employee, but not quite sure what my role would be. It was a bit of a farce really, but there you are! Alan Knill was named caretaker manager later that day with Mark Robins assisting him.

One thing we were clear headed about was that we were going to say an official goodbye to the players. At the training ground at Hooton Roberts we said our thanks and Ronnie said: "Me, Breck and Browny are off to the Earl of Strafford up the road and we want you to come and join us over a coffee." Everybody laughed. They'd never seen him drinking coffee in a pub. It wasn't going to cost them a penny either because Ronnie put his credit card behind the bar, and we were proud that all the players turned up. Even Chris Sedgwick came over from Preston and Alan Lee rang from Cardiff, saying he wished he was a bit nearer because he would have loved to be there. Some players stayed a bit, some for longer, others stayed on for quite a while as we reminisced, had a laugh and talked over the good times and the great times.

In one way it was a good finish, but in another very sad, too. An era had come to an end. Many would look back on it as a golden era. Everybody would certainly look back on it as a memorable one. If all good things come to an end, this one just had. But one good thing certainly wasn't going to end – my partnership with Ronnie. That evening on the radio, when asked about his future, he said: "Me and Breck will have to go and do a similar job elsewhere." That was interesting because I was still a Rotherham United employee!

I felt for him. His departure hurt me. We'd helped each through some tough times and not all football-related. He'd given me great support during my wife's illness in the early years of the century and amid his own personal crisis I was there for him too, supporting him. We were like brothers. The club did give me a few days off; some thinking time to decide what I was going to do. Yes, I could have stayed, but in a lesser role. Did I really want that? I felt in view of everything I would be loyal to Ronnie. It wasn't long before he had contact about the Oldham Athletic job. As one door closes ...

People subsequently asked if I was bitter. It would have been easy to feel that way, particularly at the depth of my pain, but my overall feelings were of deep sadness and immense disappointment at the way the ending all unfolded. Asking me to stay on in a lesser role, as the new board did, may have denoted an appreciation of my value and service to the club, but would I really want to drop down and be a bit part player after years in such an influential role as assistant manager?

Of course not and that probably indicated a naivety at the heart of things. I acknowledge they were all genuine Millers fans who had the club's best interests at heart, but, successful though they were in their own spheres of business and work, running a football club is a different game completely.

Taking on what they did, with all the financial implications and problems, was a massive task and to start building a new Main Stand – still standing, half-finished to this day – may indicate that their vision was naive rather than futuristic. They did their best, but perhaps "naïve" was about right. I just think they got out of their depth, biting off more than they could chew albeit with the best of intentions and probably never realising the sheer enormity of it all until they were actually at the heart of it. I took no pleasure whatsoever in the demise of Millers 05. In their year I followed every move, always hoping they would be successful. I was the last person who wanted to see them fail and the club go out of business.

When we arrived in the Championship, not only were me and Ronnie punching above our weight on the pitch, but trying to do it with a completely dysfunctional support system, understated and inexperienced at this level and struggling to cope. Ken Booth was unfairly criticised because he'd saved the club from extinction and provided the finances to help them to survive, but I would at best describe him as a reluctant hero who lacked the ambition of the management team and the supporters, but spent the money when he needed to. But the end was coming and, when it did, I didn't enjoy it one little bit!

27

IT'S NOT MORE IMPORTANT THAN LIFE AND DEATH

Criticism. Stick. Abuse. Call it what you will, but it is all part of a footballer's life. And a manager's life as well at some point. Even a chairman can come in for it. As a footballer, you come to accept it. Not to like it obviously. Nobody likes being criticised and particularly so publicly. I had my fair share during an early part of my Rotherham United career and it wasn't nice. I have seen players become badly affected by it, become cowed, become apprehensive. I have even known instances when individuals didn't want to go out and perform, so fearful were they of knowing that one mistake meant the crowd would be getting on to them.

The abuse for current players also takes on a different, additional and often sinister method – something not dreamt of when I played – on social media. Some of what goes on there aimed at players is, quite frankly, an utter disgrace. It's a wonder they are motivated to go out and play when fans of their own club are posting some of the abuse they do. Always, of course, anonymously. Hiding behind a nickname, afraid to put their real names to it. In my eyes they are cowards, skulking behind anonymity and making hurtful, abusive comments which they wouldn't have the guts to say to a player's face. But it's easy when no one knows who you are.

Yes, fans pay their money and are entitled to have a go when things aren't right. Get behind your team, whoever you support, during the 90 minutes and whatever the situation. But, if you've lost 3-0 and played rubbish, then I wouldn't expect a standing ovation walking off. I recall the difficult time I had in my early years. There were my mother and dad sitting in the Main Stand with people calling out their son and rubbishing him: "Tha' rubbish, Breckin. Gerrim off." It hurt them, I know that, and that's inevitable. Like parents, wives and, yes, even some kids, they have to sit and suffer in silence when it happens. It's horrible for them.

Of course, we're seen as just footballers. But we are also human beings, ordinary people with feelings and emotions like everyone else. We suffer the same difficulties in life as those who come through the turnstiles and help to pay the wages. I can only reckon that the pain, the suffering, the traumas I have gone through, mirror what will have happened to so many other people out there – divorce, losing a loved one after a brave battle with cancer and the heartache it all brings. In my case it might be ecstasy at work, but agony at home.

In one respect, I do consider myself fortunate. When so many marriages dissolve in acrimony and anger, the split irreparable, me and my first wife Elaine remain good friends to this day. It was actually through football that we met. Or rather through a football injury! During the close season in 1978 I went to Rotherham Hospital for an X-ray. My life was to take an unexpected turn as a result. After the X-ray, the radiographer – I'd spotted her name badge, Elaine – took me to see the doctor who was a big Rotherham United fan. You can imagine how delighted he was to tell one of the players at his favourite club that the X-ray was clear and an operation wasn't necessary. We had a chat about the team and prospects for next season and I left. On the way out I went to thank the radiographer for her help, but with an ulterior motive. I asked Elaine if she fancied coming out one night for a shandy.

She said: "Yes" and actually turned up for the date as well. So far, so good. We then struck up a steady relationship and, although she wasn't into football, she subsequently would come to all my games and give me her support. Inside a couple of years the relationship developed and we got married in the spring of 1980. We were together for 14 years and never actually fell out – we just sort of drifted apart, a situation that isn't, I know, unfamiliar in a lot of marriages. In 1994 I moved out, but we remained friends and kept in touch. We would chat on the phone and indeed we never got round to actually getting divorced until another development in my personal life a couple of years later.

One evening I was at a pie-and-pea fundraising event for the Millers School of Excellence and I met Denise and her son Adam. We hit it off instantly. After a few dates both of us were comfortable in the relationship, so she moved in with me at Ravenfield. Neither of us had actually been looking for a partner; Denise had been through a divorce and I was still technically married. This situation continued for a couple of years when Denise became pregnant. It was unexpected but we were both delighted. I did now need to sort out a divorce because I intended to marry Denise. Elaine was understanding and wholly accommodating. Yes, it helped me to move on with the next stage in my life and I was happy to do so, but the actual day the divorce came through wasn't quite one to pop the champagne when reflecting on the original happiness of the wedding day.

We were thrilled when baby Jessica arrived in 1998. It was fantastic to have a daughter and I actually felt more relaxed about that than if it had been a boy because being the son of a professional footballer might have put unnecessary pressure on him from an early age and he would have been expected to follow in certain footsteps. Jess has certainly made me proud of her and to be her dad, you can imagine how I felt when she graduated with a degree from York University in 2019.

Just two years after having Jess, Denise discovered a lump in her breast. She wasted no time at all in getting it checked out and acted immediately; it is something I would advise any woman to do in a similar position – act straightaway. Unbelievably the doctor diagnosed breast cancer. It didn't seem real. It was what happened to someone else. But no, here it was happening to my wife and me. Who did I call? My ex-wife. She was a diamond. Elaine took Denise under her wing at the hospital in the X-ray unit and was a great help to us both, keeping us informed of the situation.

Denise was determined to fight the cancer and she battled all she could. Treatment of such a condition is determined by how aggressive the disease is. In her case it was a very aggressive form and she had a very tough time. She had a lumpectomy at Rotherham District General Hospital and then I accompanied her to every one of the chemotherapy and radiography sessions at Weston Park Hospital in Sheffield. While she was having treatment and losing her hair in the process, I'd take Jess, who was only two when this started, across the road to Weston Park on the swings and roundabouts. Then we would pop to Uncle Sam's up Ecclesall Road for a burger, which was her little treat.

Finally Denise got the all-clear after months of suffering and treatment. We looked forward to rebuilding our life again with some sort of normality. However, not long afterwards a problem developed with her hip. We didn't relate it to the cancer, but any other subsequent symptoms have to be checked by a specialist. The doctor who had given her the all-clear confirmed that the cancer had returned. We were devastated. Apparently, with breast cancer there is a chance it can spread to the bone, brain, liver or lungs. For Denise it had spread to the bone and a new course of radiotherapy would be required, which she then underwent and completed.

A few months later we went out to the pub to celebrate Denise's birthday. It was only a modest one, with nothing much at all to drink, and we were home fairly early. During the night I was woken up by what I thought was Denise having a bad dream. Then I realised she was actually having a fit. I knew this because it was something I had seen during my football career and I knew how to deal with it. I didn't panic and stayed up with her for the rest of the night while she slept. First thing next morning I got in touch with Matthew Hatton, oncologist at Rotherham Hospital and a Tranmere Rovers fan – a happy coincidence in view of what was to happen two years later. I'd struck up a relationship with Matthew when the original condition occurred and he was a great help. He checked out Denise and left me a message to ring him on the Saturday morning.

I don't recall who we were playing that day because my mind went into a fog after Matthew told me it was more bad news. Denise now had a brain tumour. And just think, you reckon it's bad when your team concede a goal in the last minute to lose! Well ... something such as terminal illness puts everything in perspective. I felt for Denise and for Adam and also for little Jess, who had been great and taking everything in her stride. In a way she helped me to cope at that time. Matthew wasted no time in getting Denise admitted to Hallamshire Hospital where the tumour was removed. The operation was a success and Denise gained strength, but another setback was around the corner. Even before she could be checked to see if she was clear, she had further problems, this time with her liver. By now it was March 2004 and again, for the third time in four years, Denise had to undergo a course of chemotherapy.

It brought back memories of my parents. I'd lost my mum at 66 to breast cancer just three months after losing my dad, who was 69, to stomach cancer. He'd been taken ill after sitting down at the table for dinner one Christmas Day. My mum had suffered with her breast cancer and I could not believe the condition could be worse than what she had. But I realised it was not like Denise's condition. When losing both parents so quickly, I remember thinking that I had got to battle on. Perhaps being younger helped. I've always been one of those who try to get up and go again, keep moving forward. Perhaps that comes from experiencing the highs and lows of being a professional footballer; you have to learn to be resilient.

But this latest experience with Denise was a situation I had not faced before. Witnessing someone you love suffering beyond belief and feeling so helpless because you aren't able to help them very much or how you'd want to, is a very draining experience. I certainly didn't want anyone feeling sorry for me. After all, there were people in far worse positions. I just wanted, just hoped and prayed that Denise would get better. It had all started about 2000, a time of great success at Rotherham with Ronnie and me right in the midst of the back-to-back promotions. So I was having a successful time at work and thankfully it took me away from all the problems with my wife. But then, when I got home, there were the harsh realities of life and potential death with a wife and a young daughter who both needed my full attention. In fact, as time went on, I became Denise's carer at home. All I could do was juggle it all the best I could, giving my best at work and my best at home.

At the time of my departure from Millmoor after Ronnie's sacking at the start of 2005, Denise was very ill, having undergone more chemotherapy. But she did improve and I went with Ronnie to Oldham as they battled against relegation. Battle? Now there's a word I had been experiencing for some time now. But I must say that at that time, when we could have both been really low after the nature of the departure from Rotherham, Ronnie was so upbeat and it kept me going with him being that way. If I was asked who I would want on a desert island with me, I'd say Ronnie Moore – although I'm not sure about his cooking!

After winning the relegation battle, Ronnie was asked to stay on by Oldham for the 2005/06 season. Denise actually improved and encouraged me to stay with him. A promotion push faltered at the last and, with Oldham fans never really taking to Ronnie and voting with their feet, he was fired at the end of that season. In fact, he was sacked while on holiday sunning himself abroad. I could have stayed on. Oldham owner Simon Corney had been brilliant with me throughout, knowing the situation with my wife, and now he asked me to take on a scouting role. I thanked him, but said I couldn't. I had to hand in the club car, which meant I didn't have one.

What did Simon do? He gave me his own, a Mercedes-Benz, for about a month. With a petrol card thrown in as well. It was wonderfully compassionate behaviour by him and, at such a difficult time, it was outstanding how he helped me. I want to thank him a hell of a lot.

But Denise was my priority now and by July 2006 things had got so bad that the doctor advised that she should be moved into Rotherham Hospice, that shining jewel in the town's often-tarnished crown. Ronnie called me from Spain to say he'd been sounded out about manager's jobs at Notts County, Hartlepool and his old club Tranmere Rovers. I knew he'd want to take me with him, but my total priority now was Denise. I had become overwhelmed by her condition; I was getting very little sleep and it was all so stressful I couldn't think straight.

Ronnie called again and said he was leaving the family holiday and flying to Manchester. Could I pick him up at the airport? Denise was comfortable for the first time in months as she received wonderful nursing in the hospice. I told her I needed to be here for her but she told me to go and pick up my old mate; she'd be okay and anyway the break would do me good. So I picked Ronnie up and took him to Birkenhead for an interview at the club I knew would be closest to his heart of the three interested in him in view of his time there as a player and as assistant manager.

Of course, he got the job and didn't so much ask me to go with him, but told me in as many words. "You're coming with me," he said. "Do what you've got to do, but you're going to be my No.2." I was in no position to agree, but, almost in a state of shock and, as I said, not thinking straight, I said: "Yes." But I most certainly had more important business back at the hospice because by then I knew Denise would not be coming out. How on earth could I tell my eight-year-old daughter? That was causing me sleepless nights, too. And that was when the quite magnificent people at Rotherham Hospice stepped in – in the most unbelievable way imaginable.

28

THE SHINING JEWEL IN ROTHERHAM'S CROWN

There are so many worthy good causes out there which deserve our support. The top one as far as I'm concerned is Rotherham Hospice. I have reason to be so very grateful and mere words can hardly express my gratitude. I will forever treasure for the rest of my life what a fantastic place it is and what wonderful people work there. It is more than likely, if it hasn't already done so, that this amazing place will touch the lives of just about everybody in this town. Mum or dad, grandma, grandad, brother or sister, relative, friends ... I'll wager that somebody somewhere across our town has had one of those family members in there or has had a friend as a patient. Or simply just knows someone who has been cared for. If not, the chances are your life will probably be touched at some point in some way by this wondrous place.

The idea of a hospice in the town originated in 1988 with an appeal to launch £1million. The building on Broom Road was completed in 1996 and Rotherham Hospice took its first day-patients later that year. An in-patient unit of four rooms was opened in September 1997 and was subsequently extended and modernised in 2010 with 14 single, en-suite rooms. The care and comfort it provides – physically, emotionally and spiritually – is legendary among those who experience it as a patient or as a relative.

A celebrity match at Millmoor in 1990 was an early fundraiser while also aimed at raising the profile of the hospice and its financial necessity during the early construction. Two directors at the hospice, Steve Burns, the club doctor at Millmoor, and Brian Chapple, well known as the Millers' commentator on *BBC Radio Sheffield*, originated the idea of a game and, with volunteer Mike Wild, did a great job overall. They roped me in to help to pull a few strings to get two sides together and the biggest footballing name of the lot was Sir Alex Ferguson – then plain Alex – who turned out and played with his assistant Archie Knox. I wonder how many of the several thousand there recall Alex scoring, doing so in a Millers shirt too. His appearance was down to Billy McEwan – who used to babysit for Alex back in his Glasgow days. Billy contacted him, explained what it was all about and Alex agreed. This same month in 1990 he won his first trophy as Manchester United manager, the FA Cup, and I recall that on behalf of the hospice we sent a telegram – yes, a telegram, no mobiles or e-mails then – to Wembley, wishing him good luck in the final against Crystal Palace.

There were actually two matches – three if you count Monkwood beating Greasbrough on penalties in a primary schools' game. A John Breckin XI, including Millers stars past and some present, beat a Rotherham Sunday League XI 2-1 with goals from Bobby Williamson and Ronnie Moore. Then came a Millers All-Star XI, including Fergie, Paul Hart, Emlyn Hughes and ex-Millers such as Dick Habbin, Trevor Phillips, Trev Womble with a playing appearance from Barry Chuckle. As you'd guess, he raised a few laughs with a "to me, to you" passing sequence and when he went down injured and needed "treatment." They played Johnny Quinn's All-Stars who won 3-2 with the Millers goals from Alex Ferguson and Billy McEwan. And I was standing with Alex when he was blown away by the quality of the star of the afternoon – Rotherham's Olympic athlete and Millers fan, Peter Elliott. He wasn't the only one. I was too.

A "track" had been set up around the Millmoor pitch and Peter was to race against several of the fastest Millers youngsters who would get half a lap start over the four lap, one mile race. Peter turned up well beforehand and I recall seeing him do a 45-minute warm up in the gym. He'd already had a training run that Sunday morning, too. That warm up itself, the intensity of it, was a real eye opener, showing his professionalism and how seriously he was taking it. When the race got underway, Fergie was in awe and actually puffed out his cheeks at the sheer pace of Peter. "You don't realise how fast they are actually moving until you experience it as close up as that," Alex said to me. "It was worth coming just to watch this."

Peter seemed to be gliding over the surface, barely touching it. It was almost like poetry in motion. To see and experience a professional athlete at the top of his sport, so close up, was amazing and pretty special. We thought our youth players were fast – and there was a particularly quick one – but needless to say they got blown away even with the big start. Peter had overhauled them by the time of the last lap. This whole event was a great success – about 3,000 turned out to give their support in the end – and I recall even going round pubs across Rotherham selling programmes for it.

Afterwards we all went into the Tivoli Club and Alex came in and stayed some time, chatting with people and wanting to know all about the hospice and the plans for it. So did we all and little did I realise then how much it would come into my life years later. Quite simply I could not have coped without it. When Denise's condition worsened, I had virtually become her carer at home during the final 18 months. I tried to keep life as normal as possible and Denise was positive about things, an outlook I could only admire.

But then came the time, at the start of the summer of 2006, when the doctors said her condition had deteriorated to the extent she should go into the hospice. For the first time in months she was comfortable. Straightaway the level of care and caring in there I saw and experienced gave me comfort as well. Quite how I had juggled the 2005/06 season at Oldham Athletic with Ronnie and my home situation, the very ill wife and a young daughter, I don't know. At Tranmere, it was even more difficult and I can hardly now comprehend when I look back, except it would not have been possible without the amazing help of a number of great people.

For a start I had to be setting off at 7am for the drive to Birkenhead. Yet Jess needed to get to school. I was living in Ravenfield and had actually been put in touch with a childminder there, Paula Troop. I went and knocked on her door and made the inquiry. But she didn't start taking kids in until 8am. I couldn't leave it so late. But Paula, with wonderful compassion, made an incredible gesture. I could take Jess there for 7am. Talk about above and beyond the call of duty. It saved me. Travelling to Oldham, just a hop over the Pennines, hadn't been too bad. Going to Tranmere was two and a half hours at best at that time in a morning – it might be three hours and more on a bad day.

I had to be off at seven. Then there was picking Jess up from school. No chance of me doing that. Paula did that as well. She took her home, gave her some tea. I would get back as soon as I could, usually about five o'clock, and then we'd go home and be able to spend a bit of time together – even let her stay up a bit later. It was certainly a hectic four days a week – we usually had a Wednesday off – but football helped me to get through it.

But as I was starting at Tranmere in July 2006, I knew that Denise was not coming out. The hospice had already stepped up once. It was now to do so again because I was being tortured by the thought I would have to tell my eight-year-old daughter that her mummy was going to die. I had no idea how I was going to bring myself to do that and also not a clue how I was going to go about telling her or what to actually say. Step in Cath Todd; another angel, although the hospice seems full of them.

I didn't know Cath, but she knew of me from Rotherham because the family are huge Millers fans and Sam Todd, later to become the head of media at the club, is her son. I sat down with Cath and unloaded my fears to her about Jess. I actually said to her: "I can't tell Jess, so how do I do it? How do I bring it up and then get the right words to tell my eight-year-old that her mum's going to die? I don't know how to approach that." She then said the most comforting, reassuring words. "We'll take care of that. You bring Jess down here tomorrow."

I did that along with Kay Wassell, Jess's godmother and a big friend of Denise, and also another big friend, district nurse Debbie Rowbottom, whose son was in Jess's class. Cath and another nurse, Lesley Knight from the hospice, took us all in a quiet room. You can imagine what the atmosphere felt like for me. I knew what was coming. Cath started. "You know why your mummy is in the hospice, don't you, Jess?"

"Yes, she's poorly."

"She is Jess; she's very poorly. Your mummy has been so very brave while she has been in here. But now there is no medicine that can make her better. There's nothing now. So she won't be coming home and will be staying in here."

We are all starting to sob by this time. Jess suddenly realised what it meant and yelled out in that piercing tone kids have, hugging me tightly as she did so. It was one of the worst moments of my life. Just as I was wondering what to do next, how to handle the next bit, Cath stepped in again. Cath and Lesley took Jess out into the garden. They looked at flowers, talked about birds and lots of things. It calmed her down. We went home; it wasn't the best night I've ever had and poor Jess cried herself to sleep. But they did say not to worry about her, that kids are more resilient and stronger than you think, particularly under nine. They focus on one thing – and next day she was off to school in her pretty normal manner!

I knew Denise hadn't got long. In fact, it was suggested at one point she might not live more than a fortnight. When that came and went, a doctor said to me: "She's very strong; is there anything she's hanging on for?" I could think only of my birthday on July 27th. I went in on my birthday and also in the room were Denise's mum and dad, Kay Wassell again and a couple of friends. Then the door opened and in came the nurses, with a birthday cake and a spread. Denise knew what was going off that afternoon. Three days later, on the Sunday, the nurses had another surprise for me. Another cake and more sandwiches. This time it was just close family. But it is that sort of place. They weren't just doing this for me; they do it for other families as well. And they cater for you in more ways than just food. If Jess was being a bit noisy, as eight-year-olds are inclined to be, I'd be shushing her and the nurses would be saying: "Leave her. She's okay. It's fine. It's the hospice."

But the end for Denise was ever closer and she slipped into a coma. I was asked if I'd told her that she could go. I hadn't. "Well, you can do that," I was told. So I went and sat with Denise. I held her hand and told her not to worry; that Jess was okay, that Adam was okay. "You are in so much pain," I said. "You can go. They'll be all right."

Cath Todd said: "Go home and get a good night's sleep. Come back in the morning." The next evening Cath said the same: "Get off home and get a few hours' sleep." But the day after Cath's advice had changed. "Don't go home tonight," she said. "Sleep here." I stayed in Denise's room, her mum and dad stayed in the chapel and Adam and her good friend Kay were also provided with somewhere to sleep. As you might imagine, I had a fitful night. For some reason, and I don't know why, I woke up at 3am. Perhaps it's like something stops and it wakes you up. I looked at Denise and she had stopped breathing. Two nurses on duty – yes, like the two angels they are – came in. They nodded. Denise had just gone.

I went out to see Adam and Denise's mum and dad and we consoled each other. A short time later I was taken back in the room to see Denise after they had prepared her. A red rose had been placed at the side of her, which was a nice touch. She looked at peace. There was a feeling in me of relief that her suffering was over.

I have heard a lot of people say that they are happy when it is finally over as your loved one doesn't have to suffer any more; happy that the pain has ended. I can understand that feeling. I knew a while ago there was no magic wand; there was no way back. I had come to terms with it a short time before, with the inevitable loss at some point, to be followed by a different kind of pain, but manageable, for me and others.

I headed back off home later that morning and, because it was the school holidays, I picked Jess up from a friend's house. This next bit was now up to me. Angel Cath wasn't there this time. Breathe in. I took Jess into the garden. I told her that her mum had died. She screamed and jumped into my arms. Then the tears came again – from both of us. A few hours later there was further evidence of that ability of young kids to put something to one side and focus on what is happening in front of them – she was out playing with her friends.

That difficult time led to the development of Sunbeams, a children's club at the hospice which acts as a bereavement support service specifically for children. Cath had the idea after dealing with Jess and me and another family back then in 2006. She realised it was something that would be an important and necessary addition to what the hospice was already providing and Trudy Perkins, manager at the time, said: "Make it happen." I was really proud when Cath told me subsequently that, when dealing with me at the time, she realised something so helpful needed implementing and that it was important to offer holistic support to children as well as patients and adult family members.

Sunbeams is still going strong, working with children who are recently or soon to be bereaved; helping them with special support go through the stages of bereavement and doing so in a positive and helpful way. Sunbeams meets twice a month with small groups of children, incorporating valuable activities and chats. At the time I realised the value of what Cath and the hospice had done for me and Jess, but I didn't know then there wasn't anything specifically aimed at children in operation there. When Cath did tell me she realised what a valuable asset it could be and that she had this idea, I told her to go for it and felt really proud when she later told me my subsequent encouragement helped to push her on with it and get it started.

Cath is not a one-off. She is just one of a whole group of marvellous people who work at the hospice at all levels. Those who provide the specialist palliative care are so professional, so caring and I wanted to give something back afterwards, which is how the sponsored midnight walk came about when people set off from Millmoor at midnight to walk a given number of miles. The inaugural one was so well supported that it raised £80,000 for the hospice. They still have an annual walk event, now called "Glow with the Flow", and over the years thousands across Rotherham – either individually, as community groups or businesses – have raised money or contributed towards the upkeep of the hospice. And with more than £2.5million needing to be raised every year, every pound is vital. It is a place close to my soul. I'll never forget how it helped me and my daughter. It deserves all our support. Thank you, Rotherham Hospice, from the bottom of my heart.

29

THE HARDEST JOURNEY AND THE EASIEST RETURN

As I pondered life after death and how I would deal with things going forward, a conversation with the famous boxing coach Brendan Ingle came to mind. Brendan did such great things for so many people, particularly youngsters from deprived or difficult backgrounds down at his internationally-acclaimed boxing gym in the Wincobank area of Sheffield, just beyond the Rotherham boundary. It produced many stars, among them world champions such as Naseem Hamed and Johnny Nelson, and Brendan certainly knew about people having troubled times and difficulties in their lives.

Many people in that part of Sheffield have Brendan to thank for straightening them out. One day I well recall him saying in his Irish brogue: "We've all got problems, so here's a plan. We'll all write down our worst problem on a piece of paper, then roll it up and pop it in a pile on the table with the others. We'll mix them up and each of us will pick one out. And I'll tell you what will happen – the first two who pick up a piece of paper and read it, will roll it up and say: 'Can I have my problem back, please?'"

Perhaps that can put things in perspective. Here I was, worrying now about ensuring my young daughter was going to be looked after while I headed off to Tranmere every day. Losing her mum in those circumstances must have been extremely difficult for her and for someone so young really to be able to grasp and understand. But it did focus my mind and meant I had another important matter to deal with. It wouldn't now be just about work – important to me though football was. Being someone who always enjoyed playing cards on the team coach as a player, I looked at life at that moment – and as it had been in the preceding months and years – as like being dealt a bad hand. It was now about how I played that hand.

I feel lucky to have had lots of friends and acquaintances and also family who rallied round and helped. Stepson Adam, then 21, had already moved in with his grandparents and Jess would stay there most Saturday nights while I travelled back from games. Even home matches at Tranmere meant I wouldn't be back until about eight o'clock and Friday nights were difficult if we needed an overnight stay for an away game. In fact, without friends and family it would have been impossible. Her grandparents, Denise's mum and dad, were a great help, as were my nephew Ian and his wife Leanne.

Kay Wassell was again so supportive and a big strength and I mustn't forget childminder Paula Troop, without whom a morning start at the right time would not have been possible. Friends rallied round and a couple in particular, Carole Bramham and Jayne Wagstaff, who were both big friends of Denise, stepped up. They both had children – Victoria and Leah, who were schoolmates of Jess – and many times during the six-year period she would be invited over to one or the other's house. It was fantastic support, particularly when the illness was really taking its toll.

Women, particularly mums, do rally round when friends are in need. I can't thank them enough for stepping up as they did. Yes, I grew up in an era when men were classed as dominant and women generally did as they were told. But the battle of women in the modern world for equivalent status is absolutely right; we are all equal. Put me down as a feminist by all means, but I know one thing – without the many caring women who helped in the way they did, I could not possibly have got through that most difficult period and certainly not at its most traumatic. Thanks, ladies.

My old pal Ronnie was such a fantastic help and support, standing beside me like only really true friends do. In fact, the people at Tranmere Rovers were brilliant and the chairwoman Lorraine Rogers was especially sympathetic to my situation all the way through and was always eager to help in any way. I even took Jess through with me to some matches and Jason McAteer's mum looked after her in the main stand. One time she took Jess on the ferry across the Mersey as a treat. She remembered that and talked about it more than she ever did about the football. On one occasion Jason, the former Liverpool and Republic of Ireland international, gave me his keys and let me stay overnight in his own house. What a place that was, by the way!

Just two days after Denise had died, I was on the touchline with Ronnie. He'd persuaded me to join him – "Get yourself across and just sit on the bench, nowt else," he said – and that's what I did, reckoning in a way it might help. Ironically it was against Oldham, the club that sacked us a few months before. Yes, people may think it was only two days after losing my wife, but I think that getting back that way so quickly helped me to start coping with what was now the next stage of my life. My new normality.

Would it have helped me to spend that Saturday afternoon at home grieving? I suppose, in the way I had always done as a professional footballer, you get on with things and deal with the situation in front of you. For me, that meant being at work, being somewhere I was required. However, as the weeks and months rolled by, it was becoming increasingly harder every day to juggle life around Jess, the childminder, the commuting and the demands of the job. As usual Ronnie and me worked well together and we were having a good season – and were top at one point.

But I knew when it came to the end of that season, May 2007, I had a decision to make. The daily travelling to Birkenhead was becoming a huge strain and, allied to everything else, not great for my health. People may question why I didn't move over to the North West, but that was never an option in my mind for several reasons. With all the uncertainty of football management, there was the possibility of buying a house over there and then getting the sack not long afterwards.

Then there was Jess's situation. It was hard enough having to leave her all day and have other people look after her, but at least she was close to family and her friends in Rotherham. Taking her over there would have meant no family, no friends or familiar surroundings. That was always a non-starter. Then a phone call out of the blue, a month from the season's end, changed things again. Rescued me, you might say.

It was from Mark Robins, who had been in caretaker charge of the Millers for a month after the departure of Alan Knill. Ronnie had brought Mark in as a player and, as Millers fans know, he was a great goalscorer with us and an integral part of our success at the turn of the century. We always had a great relationship, it was a pleasure to get him started on his coaching badges as his playing days began drawing to a close, and now he was stepping up.

Mark said there was a good chance he would be appointed manager and, if so, he wanted someone experienced in the game alongside him. It was no surprise to me to see him moving into management; he is one of football's thinkers and here he was, carefully planning ahead. He couldn't have picked a better time to ask me although he wasn't to know that. But then I had a dilemma. It would mean splitting up with my great pal Ronnie, and having a very difficult and painful conversation with him. And there would be no hospice angel to do this one for me!

When Mark was confirmed in the Rotherham job in early April, the assistant manager's job was mine if I wanted it. I did. But I did not want to desert Ronnie and Tranmere because we were still in with a great chance of promotion. One game I well recall was New Year's Day at home to Rotherham – would you believe it? – when our only fit goalkeeper got injured the day before. We asked Manchester City if we could borrow their promising young goalkeeper Kasper Schmeichel. They said: "No" but had another promising one a year younger, Joe Hart.

He didn't come in until the morning of the Millers game and nobody knew who he was, but his professionalism at only 19 was of the highest order. He wanted me to go through everything, all aspects of what we did and how we did it. Then after the game – which Tranmere won 2-1 – there was a knock on the manager's door. Joe came in and asked for the DVD of the game so he could take it back to his goalkeeping coach and go through everything with him. Most impressive.

The Rotherham job offer was still a few months away, but it hung over me after Robbo's approach and I decided to wait until the end of the season. On the day I intended telling Ronnie, I didn't realise that what lay ahead was the hardest journey of my life. In fact, after it, I couldn't recall anything about that journey across the Pennines to Prenton Park because my mind was buzzing so much. I was preparing for one of the most difficult conversations I've ever had. Telling someone you are parting with them when you have had such a close and successful partnership is never easy. Ronnie was shocked and, despite our great relationship, I don't think he took it too well. I think it rather saddened him and I certainly don't blame him feeling that way, perhaps a little bit let down.

But deep down I'd like to think he understood. Ironically a few months earlier Ronnie and me had been offered the chance of coming back to Rotherham – yes, two years after the sack.

But it was a different regime by this time, early 2007, and the chairman Denis Coleman rang to inquire if Ronnie would be interested in coming back to Rotherham. With the club poised to go under after the difficulties encountered by the 05 board, Denis had stepped in to save it with Dino Maccio in March 2006 amid a plethora of well-documented financial problems. Had that intervention not happened, I believe the club would have become another Accrington Stanley or more recently a Bury. A meeting was arranged and me and Ronnie met Denis and fellow director Dave Costin at a pub on the Lancashire side of the Woodhead.

We had a good couple of hours with them and could see they were keen to make a go of it at Millmoor after their rescue act. In my heart I was wanting Ronnie to take it. He was flattered by the approach. But this was midway through his first season back at Tranmere and, what's more, he had moved his family over there. Had he been still living here, I think he would have taken over again.

So, a few months later in 2007, chairman Coleman got half of the package, although I'm sure he would have preferred the other half! There was no contract issue at Tranmere either, because I didn't have one! I told Ronnie on a Saturday and on the Monday was back once more at Millmoor, now as assistant manager to Mark Robins. The team had been relegated from League One that season, having had the first lot of 10 points deducted for problems concerning administration – although the team wouldn't have got enough points to stay up even with those missing 10. It meant being back in League Two with another deduction, so we started the 2007/08 season bottom of the table on minus 10. But we viewed that as a challenge, one to be overcome.

Mark's plans and ambitions were underpinned by his experience in a wonderful playing career, especially the disciplined apprenticeship at Manchester United. And if you can't learn from Sir Alex Ferguson, then there's not much hope! The way Mark spoke about the way forward was a good indication of why he had been given the opportunity in management at this relatively early stage. He was 37. He spoke passionately, but with a considered, realistic assessment of the challenges ahead. In the early days of working with him, my first impressions were confirmed.

He had the right ingredients, an enviable playing experience – always handy if required to chuck your medals on the table – and his coaching was good.

He was very ambitious and nothing fazed him. He wasn't perfect and we had regular, healthy arguments – which, I hope, was one of the reasons he recruited me. But generally we got on very well and it was a joy to go to work. Nick Daws, another former Miller, was on board as the conditioning coach and, although I didn't know goalkeeping coach Simon Tracey, I was obviously aware of his Sheffield United background.

Mark brought in Steve Taylor, a coach who had been at Derby County and was well respected, and the five of us made a good team. We soon gelled. Mark impressed me by the way he focused on performances and results as if there was no points reduction. He just took everything in his stride. It was the right approach. We had cleared off the deficit by the seventh game and were only another couple of wins away from overhauling the clubs genuinely at the bottom. Then a run of seven straight league wins ended at home to Rochdale – so, yeah, they were bugging us and beating us back then as well! We actually finished ninth, but what no one knew was that it would be the final season at Millmoor, the club's home for 101 years.

There were financial difficulties again and, hard though Coleman and his fellow directors tried, with Maccio no longer on board, the financial burden was too great and new ownership was sought. But the club also went into administration for the second time in two years in March 2008 and the third time in all. Mark told the coaching staff about it at training one morning and called a meeting of everyone for the afternoon when a representative from the PFA came in and spoke.

The players agreed to a wage deferral – all except one, striker Chris O'Grady. At a difficult time, when you're all in it together, players expect all their teammates to stay side-by-side, shoulder-to-shoulder. O'Grady's decision, primarily looking after himself and not sticking with his mates, was not popular. They made him an outcast and Mark Robins had no other choice but eventually to remove him from normal involvement with the squad. He trained on his own and didn't play in the final half-a-dozen matches. Not surprisingly he was sold at the end of the season to Oldham – and for less than the £65,000 the Millers had shelled out to sign him just 18 months before.

Administration would mean another points deduction the following season. If there was a football club still there to deduct points from, that was! Yes, it became that serious. That was the moment for the arrival of Tony Stewart, galloping in on his white horse you might say. Thankfully. Whatever mode of transport he arrived in – most probably a pretty impressive car – he was certainly riding to the rescue. I didn't know him and to be perfectly honest had never heard of him or his company, ASD Lighting. I was just grateful he was going to save my football club. Like everyone else, I hadn't a clue either what a pivotal figure he would become in the club's modern history. I did know, though, that when confirmation came through that the club had a new owner, chairman and a future, you could feel the sigh of relief across the town – whether someone was a football follower or not.

From the start Tony led from the front. He came to the final game of the season, in May 2008, on what proved to be the club's farewell to Millmoor. With the sort of panache he has displayed since, he took to the microphone on the pitch beforehand to introduce himself and address the crowd. All 4,834 present that day were witnesses to two pieces of Rotherham United history. An end and a beginning.

The prospect of staying at or re-developing Millmoor was killed off by demands never likely to be met by the new owner and we had to decamp just across the border to the Don Valley Stadium, which had been built for athletics and once had 25,000 in there for an international meeting in which Peter Elliott memorably beat Steve Cram.

There were Millers fans who vowed never to go and watch the team in Sheffield and even stories of some who went to away matches but couldn't bring themselves to go to "home" games. But it wasn't just the footballers who had to move. The whole caboodle had to shift; the administration and the commercial side all needed a new base. In the close season the offices and the entire contents were moved to Tony's ASD Lighting company premises on the Barbot Hall industrial estate. I was sure it would take a month to relocate everything. But it was sorted in a week with bricklayers, joiners, plasterers, painters, electricians and the whole job lot ensuring it was sorted in double-quick time. The new man obviously got things done and wasn't one to sit on his hands.

The deduction for the 2008/09 season was even harsher than the previous one. Minus 17 points this time. But we weren't the only ones.

Bournemouth had the same, Luton's was a massive 30 points and Darlington had 10 taken off them. We had to tackle our own situation in a stadium as alien to us as to the opposition. But Mark again met the challenge head on. With no chance of promotion, a battle to ensure we stayed in the Football League was on the cards and was hardly an attractive proposition for potential signings. We also had to train out of town, the chairman hiring facilities at the Keepmoat Stadium in Doncaster. But Mark did well to bring players in, including Nick Fenton, Reuben Reid and Micky Cummins. It was important to get off to a good start and we did that, clearing off the 17-point deficit after only nine games, which was promotion form.

I don't think teams liked coming to the Don Valley Stadium and I know many Millers didn't like it either, because of what seemed like a permanent wind that always made it seem cold and primarily because of the lack of atmosphere. There were times when you could stand in the dugout, close your eyes and wonder if there was anybody in the ground! The players were so far away from the stands because of the eight-lane running track and the whole environment was unsettling for them. But that part soon seemed to work in our favour because our lads quickly appeared to get used to their new surroundings and began to relax and play with confidence. In contrast some opponents seemed confused by the setting. In some cases you could tell by their body language.

We actually posted some good memories in the opening months, beating Wolves – the eventual Championship title winners – on penalties and Premier League Southampton 3-1 in the Carling Cup to follow spot-kick success against Sheffield Wednesday at Hillsborough. We also beat two big names in League One at that time, Leeds United and eventual champions Leicester, in the Johnstone's Paint Trophy.

It wasn't bad for a League Two side and, with confidence boosted and momentum gathering in the league, we showed by the turn of the year that we were good enough to dismiss any thoughts of the dreaded relegation. Even though we were still fourth bottom, our form was equal to being in the top half. In the end our points tally of 58 would, with the deduction added on, have been 75 – comfortably enough to finish in the play-offs.

It meant hopes were raised among the fans ahead of the 2009/10 season with Mark pulling off arguably the most popular signing of all those he made – Adam Le Fondre for £100,000 from Rochdale. "Alf" was an instant hit and scored in each of his first four appearances. But Mark Robins wasn't to be his manager any longer than that! Barnsley were without a manager at the time and rumours grew that Mark was their target. The interest might have been sparked well before. The previous April, Mark and me were at the *Sheffield Star and Green 'Un* Football Awards in Sheffield and we happened to be sitting alongside the Barnsley chairman Patrick Cryne. He and Mark appeared to get on famously during the evening. Perhaps a seed was sown then.

Mark was indeed their target and after an approach through the official channels, club to club, I got a call from him. "I've got the Barnsley job," he said. "What do you think?" I was stunned by the call, but it seemed a great opportunity for him and we had a long chat although I didn't attempt to persuade him either way. It was for him to make his mind up and, even if I had tried to persuade him, I think he would have still decided to take it. He was given permission to go to Oakwell on the Wednesday evening to meet the Barnsley directors. If he hadn't already made up his mind – and he probably had – he certainly did so there and then. The next day, the Thursday, Mark was put on gardening leave so the end was nigh. But what did that mean for me?

30

IF ONLY I'D WAITED!

Ever made a decision you later regret? I'm sure most people have. I certainly did in September 2009 although it wasn't because I didn't enjoy what was to follow. Just that I wished I'd known what was coming next at Rotherham United. Had I done so, I would not have left my club again – although it was of my own volition this time. After Mark Robins had been put on gardening leave, I was asked by the chairman to take charge of the team for the home game with Chesterfield two days later. But my Friday night relaxation before the game was interrupted by a phone call – from the soon-to-be Barnsley manager.

Mark wanted me to go with him. How long had I got to think about it? "A minute" was the earnest reply. "While ever I'm in football," he added, "there's a job for you." As I reckoned he would be having a career of some longevity in management, then that seemed a pretty secure future for me albeit wherever that might be. Yes, I'd come back to my club and thought that was it. That I'd be here for good. Hopefully. But you never know in football. So I decided I would go with him. Yes, I can understand some Millers fans who questioned my loyalty at the time and how they felt about my leaving after coming back only a couple of years earlier. I did get one or two remarks for sure. But football doesn't really work that way.

The game can change for those in it very quickly. A new manager would be coming in at some point, perhaps someone I didn't know. If he decided he didn't want John Breckin because he is bringing in his own trusted staff, I'd be out – and the boat to Barnsley had just sailed. The cabin set aside for me has been filled. With the uncertainty nagging at me if I stayed, my loyalty in this instance went to Mark Robins. He'd given me the chance to come back and we'd worked well together. He was relying on me to recreate that partnership and support him in this new opportunity in his career. I felt I owed him the move. But in hindsight it was the wrong decision.

Not because I didn't enjoy it at Barnsley. I did. But had I known then what I learned a few weeks later, I most certainly would not have left. That's because Ronnie Moore was going to be the next Rotherham manager! Ronnie actually let me know. He rang me to say he had got an interview with the new chairman Tony Stewart. I told him I didn't even know he was in the running and the night before the interview he picked my brains over a drink in my lounge. He took out his notepad and a pen and I filled him in, ensuring he was nicely primed ahead of meeting Mr Stewart.

Of course, he rang me subsequently to say he had got the job and thanked me very much for all the information. We weren't going to reprise our partnership though, much as I would have liked to. I could hardly go back on my word to Robbo after just a couple of weeks at Oakwell. Ronnie knew that too and had lined up Jimmy Mullen, captain of our 1980/81 promotion side, as his right hand man. He had booked Jimmy to join him a few months earlier at Tranmere. He'd gone in to see the Tranmere chairman, leaving Jimmy sitting outside the office waiting to be called in and introduced as his new assistant. Ronnie came out and had news for Jimmy: "I've been sacked." Jimmy's reply was: "Well, that's the quickest I've ever lost a job."

After Mark's call on the Friday night I took charge of the team against Chesterfield knowing I was going to Barnsley. We gave a great performance that afternoon against a Spireites side who included my nephew Ian Breckin and were managed by John Sheridan, a big friend, who had been on the coaching staff at Oldham with Ronnie and me and had taken over as manager when we left Boundary Park. I was delighted with the 3-1 win, but knew it would be my last one.

I was aware that Barnsley would make an official approach for my services after the game. Exhausted and stressed after a long day, I asked Nick Daws if he fancied a pint to relax so we took ourselves off to the Sitwell Arms at Whiston on our way home. The quietness in the bar was soon pierced by my phone ringing. It was Paul Douglas, Rotherham's chief operating officer. "I've had Barnsley's chief executive Don Rowing on the phone and he's asked if you want to talk to them." I said that out of courtesy I would. His reply was: "Right, in that case you are on gardening leave." As I related that to Nick, his phone rang. "It'll be Paul Douglas," I said. It was and Paul couldn't possibly have known we were sitting side by side.

There was the same conversation and Nick, the fitness coach, was put on gardening leave as well. A couple of minutes later my phone rang again. It was our coach Steve Taylor. He was on gardening leave, too. Simon Tracey had received the same call. Was I doing cartwheels? No, even though I had swapped League Two at a temporary ground and crowds of 3,000 for the Championship, fine stadia and crowds of more than 25,000, as there was for my second Barnsley game at Pride Park.

It was disappointing to not be able to savour the Millers victory that weekend, which sent them top of League Two. Sunday was a very busy telephone day and the outcome was an interview for us all at Oakwell the following day. I'd told Rotherham's kitman Steve McVann, a long-time friend from our schooldays and a really top bloke, what was going on. I had cause to ring him again on the Sunday night and he inadvertently coined a phrase – the first thing he said was: "How are the Barnsley Five doing?" The events on the Monday morning went from the ridiculous to the sublime for us five!

We met at the Cavalier in Ravenfield and all set off in one car, me navigating a back way to Barnsley. We thought we might get spotted if we went the busy route! But within minutes of setting off, Mark's phone rang. There were rumours spreading that something was about to happen at Oakwell and suddenly there were lots of prying eyes at the ground, not least the media. We were asked to delay our journey for an hour. "What are we going to do now?" came the query from one of the three hunched up in the back seat. I had the answer. "Let's go for a coffee; I know a place."

They had no idea where we were going, but I headed for the lovely village of Wentworth and took them to Wentworth Garden Centre, one of the biggest in the north of England and extremely popular across the region. It's a super place and I knew we'd be safe there. I knew Sandra Airey, the owner with husband Tony, from our schooldays. Many moons ago her dad had played with my dad in the same team, Wilton FC. But I wonder what she thought when she saw me and four others turning up there first thing on a Monday morning, all dressed in suits and ties. Rather strange attire to be visiting a garden centre!

Sandra looked after us and there were a few puzzled looks. We waited and waited and after loads of coffee and several toilet visits, finally the call came through we could carry on to Oakwell. Perhaps "carry on" was the right phrase! We had our interviews and terms were agreed. The Barnsley Five were given a tour of the ground and I realised how much the club had improved its facilities. I'd been many times as an opposing player and assistant manager, but wasn't aware of the full extent of the progress made in recent times.

Still, it looked like a big challenge. Barnsley were bottom of the Championship with one point from the opening five games. We all started at Oakwell on the Tuesday and there was no need for clandestine car journeys and coffees this time. I was genuinely sad about leaving Rotherham, but the decision had been made easier by Mark's initial invite which brought me back to the club and his continued faith in me. It was a wrench closing the door on my Rotherham career – for what I thought would be the last time. A comfort was that I received some nice letters from a number of Millers fans – with a couple of not very nice ones. The good, supportive ones were really appreciated.

Suddenly my personal life became a lot easier, too, travelling to Barnsley and not Birkenhead. But I still needed help and childminder Paula, not forgetting her husband Craig, helped me a great deal. The Barnsley fans were very welcoming and, of course, very much like the folk of Rotherham, so we were on the same wavelength whenever I met any. I couldn't quite say the same about all the players, particularly the foreign lads in the dressing room, of whom there were quite a few. I don't think they could quite understand me when I started talking in my Rotherham accent!

There was another difference, too. At Rotherham and elsewhere I'd been used to all the squad, or nearly all, being on the team coach at the ground when we set off for an away game. I recall once getting on the coach at Oakwell, looking round when we set off and seeing just four players on board. The rest would be getting on at various pick-up points. After all, we had three lads who lived near Liverpool.

The fans were similar to most others. They were ambitious and wanted to get there tomorrow. After all, their solitary Premier League season a decade earlier was still fairly fresh in the memory. But so, too, were the four recent seasons in League One. They wanted signings and wanted the chairman to spend money. But I felt the club was run properly and Patrick Cryne, the chairman, ran a tight ship, but also understood the demands of the supporters. After all, he was a Barnsley supporter himself. An improvement meant that relegation fears were seen off reasonably comfortably and the chairman seemed keen to listen to Mark's ideas.

It was a happy working environment with the fellow members of the Barnsley Five group and I was privileged to be involved with them. It was enjoyable working with good players at the second tier again and I must mention Darren Moore, who was different class. What a thorough professional he was in the way he trained, looked after himself and his general attitude towards all aspects of his job as a footballer. A top bloke and one of the nicest I've met, something he was to reinforce when our paths crossed a few years later. Being at Barnsley was slightly unusual in one respect, though. In Rotherham everyone knew Breck. Here the fans certainly knew Mark Robins – but not JB.

Fifteen players were released at the end of that first season when we managed to keep the club up and, on what was a relatively low budget for the Championship, we had to work the transfer and loan market quite skilfully. The following season was a minimal improvement, 18th to 17th. That's when the problems began. Mark was unhappy with the size of the budget for playing staff. He met Patrick Cryne, armed with his "homework."

In the whole of the Championship, only Scunthorpe United's budget was lower than Barnsley's. He had decided to propose a modest increase to the chairman, feeling this would give the club a reasonable chance of making real progress in the division. The alternative, he felt, was to be a team of perennial strugglers. In fact, in the five seasons since getting out of League One, they had never finished higher than 17th.

The chairman did not share Mark's view. In fact, he told him he was looking to reduce the spending. No agreement could be reached and Mark made it clear that he couldn't work with either the existing budget or a reduced one. The term "gardening leave" appeared again and Mark

Robins was the one put on it – with, it seemed, no sort of timescale. It seemed like mind games. It would probably have been better from Mark's point of view if he'd been sacked. I knew Mark would not put up with this for long; he's not that type of character.

So it came as no surprise to me that, soon after the imposition of the suspension, he chose to resign. While on gardening leave it meant he could neither manage the Reds – unless he compromised his position – or look for another job. Shortly after the end of the season, Barnsley put out a statement that Mark Robins had resigned his position as manager because of differences with the board. He'd been in charge less than two full seasons – and my position was unclear once again.

31

THE CALL THAT NEVER CAME

It was strange that my phone stayed silent in the days after the big decision had been announced by Barnsley midway through May 2011. I was expecting a call from Oakwell, explaining where I stood and what they wanted me to do after Mark Robins' departure as manager was finally confirmed. After all, I was the assistant manager. When the phone did ring, it was never Barnsley Football Club. I had a gut feeling they may have been waiting for a call from me, either resigning in solidarity with Mark or because I had been offered another job.

If Mark got another job and took his bunch of merry men with him, then there'd be no compensation to pay out. We would have resigned. Even better if Mark did get another job and the other club were prepared to pay some compensation for our release. Anyway I decided to sit tight although not idle, not with a daughter who was coming up to 13 to look after. As girls hit their teens, that can be an awkward age, as many a mum may tell you!

Anyway Barnsley's wish – if it was as such, that is – was almost granted when Mark nearly ended up at Bramall Lane. Sheffield United had parted company with Micky Adams as manager and Mark was on the shortlist, then in the final two to be his replacement. We'd spoken during the interview process and he sounded pretty convinced he would get the job and told me of his plans to have all the Barnsley Five at Bramall Lane. It was obviously a great opportunity. So when the announcement was made that Danny Wilson was the new manager, a subdued Mark called me. He sounded down. He'd hit the crossbar.

I was disappointed for him. I genuinely thought he could take Sheffield United forward despite his relative inexperience in management.

What I didn't know was that the decision would affect my own future. It seemed only a matter of time before Mark landed another job. If nothing else, his work at Rotherham United and Barnsley had shown great potential. But days turned into weeks and nothing happened although he was linked with jobs and vacancies elsewhere.

I had still not received any communication from Barnsley and as a precaution I contacted the League Managers Association, who told me that if the wall of silence was to continue or I was sacked, then I would have a good case for compensation. That situation moved on quickly when the club appointed a new manager and an assistant, which was strange. I was still assistant manager – no one had told me otherwise – and yet they had appointed another one. Perhaps he was sitting in "my" chair. I contacted the LMA again, they spoke to the club and matters unsurprisingly came to a head rather sharpish. I was compensated and left the club with no hard feelings. I was now officially unemployed and the starting pistol was poised for another run to somewhere.

Mark kept in touch with regular calls, but now the weeks turned into months. Not working wasn't a problem, though. Throughout Denise's illness I had worked continuously and now, stepping off the treadmill, the break was probably doing me good. I was spending more time at home and able to think more radically about the circumstances of Jess and me. I hadn't planned to sell my house in Ravenfield, but I began to think a change would do us good. Perhaps a fresh start might help to erase some painful memories. The more I thought about it the more it appealed, so I decided to downsize from a detached house to a nice apartment in Wickersley. It suited my needs perfectly and Jess was in walking distance of her school.

With a desire to make a new start, I started to dispose of most of my furniture – much of it lovely, but not really suitable for my new place. I got a second-hand dealer to give me a price for it all, but he made such an insulting offer I told him I was going to give it to Rotherham Hospice for them to raise funds. He suddenly upped his offer considerably. It gave me a lot of satisfaction to tell him that I wouldn't reconsider. It felt right, after all, to give a bit back to the hospice. I didn't move in straightaway because of alterations to the kitchen and bathroom at the new place, which wasn't the only significant addition to my life. One night at the Courtyard in Wickersley I bumped into Gill, who I had known for a few years through her serving me at my bank in Rotherham. We found ourselves in similar situations because I had lost my wife and her husband had died suddenly.

We chatted and went our own way. She later texted me, asked how I was and suggested meeting for a coffee. And that was it. We hit it off and some time later she even proposed that me and Jess should stay at her place in Braithwell until the renovations to my new apartment had been completed. Not long after I'd moved to Wickersley, I was able to return the favour by helping her to move into a new place, conveniently in Wickersley, and also help her with some work on a little holiday home at Scarborough. I've now moved in with her after selling my apartment while in 2020 Jess got what a young woman dreams about – her own house.

In the late summer of 2012, Mark Robins was appointed manager of Coventry City, but because of financial restrictions he had to work with what was already there and was unable to offer me anything in the short term. I wasn't entirely disappointed by that news because the apartment was almost ready and a fairly lengthy commute to the Midlands every day wouldn't have been ideal. However, he did ask me to undertake a couple of scouting trips for him – one of which involved my first "official" visit to the New York Stadium. My brief was to check out a promising 19-year-old striker who was on loan at Southend, Britt Assombalonga. He scored twice in their 3-0 win and I told Mark he was definitely one with a future. Incidentally he came off near the end to be replaced by another young striker on loan… 18-year-old Jonson Clarke-Harris!

Then in 2013 two things impacted on my future. It was the year I turned 60 and I'd always looked at considering finishing working when getting to that particular milestone. But when the prospect comes around, there are many people who aren't so sure about finishing after all. They feel they'd like to go on. But a few months before that Mark had been appointed manager at Huddersfield Town. Now I hadn't worked with Mark for more than 18 months, but I didn't hear a word from him when he got this new job just up the road. He'd said to me previously that there would always be a role for me with him, which was reassuring. So I was a bit surprised to not get a call and, in a way, it was a bit disappointing. I had been waiting and hadn't been putting myself in the shop window for any other football position elsewhere.

But I did have an opportunity to get back into the game just weeks before Mark was appointed at Huddersfield. Simon Corney, Oldham's chairman, had been excellent with me in my time there with Ronnie and asked if I'd be interested in going over there and giving a helping hand to his manager, Paul Dickov. They'd been having a bad time in the league, without a win in 10, yet ironically had done well in the FA Cup and had beaten Liverpool. But Paul was working without three of his coaching staff who had been removed from their posts a month or so earlier. I said I wasn't really looking for a job, but he asked if I'd pop over and see him.

So I had a chat with Paul and Tony Philliskirk, who was then youth coach, and Simon asked me if I'd watch their next match at Walsall on Saturday and give my opinion. Oldham lost 3-1, but I tend to remember the day more for the fact I drove straight up to Liverpool for Ronnie Moore's 60th birthday party after the game. He was manager at Tranmere at the time and he'd led them to the top of League One, so there was plenty to celebrate there as well. They'd won six out of their previous seven games, but lost on the day of his party, 1-0 at home to Carlisle. The next day Paul Dickov departed as Oldham manager!

With no role for me at Huddersfield, it was decision time. My 60th birthday was just a few months away and my pension fund was due to mature. I gave it some thought and it occurred to me that I was quite enjoying having less pressure and certainly didn't miss the inconvenient parts of the travel round the country that involvement in football entails. I decided to take the pension and see what happened during the next few months.

I had been fortunate enough to invest in some property during my best earning years and although I was never in danger of becoming mega-rich, I did pay off my mortgage early. Another summer rolled by and for a second year I wasn't involved in the excitement and anticipation of a pre-season build up. Perhaps I wouldn't be getting back in the game after all, and I was coming to terms with that. Then the phone rang.

32

NOT TOO SURE – NOW IT'S JUST THE JOB

Just when I thought I'd done everything I could do and was qualified for at Rotherham United, the offer to return to the club was to do something I didn't think I could do and wasn't qualified for. I am so glad now that the doubts didn't stop me. The call in 2013 came from the club's commercial director Steve Coakley. He wanted to meet me to discuss an idea the club were considering for the New York Stadium which had just celebrated its first birthday.

It was based on something a growing number of clubs were doing, namely, offering a corporate match day package in the main lounge hosted by a club legend. My job would be to take the microphone and guide the guests through their pre-match lunch, interview a personality and then do a bit on stage afterwards with the Millers man of the match. I wasn't sure. I didn't think it was me. But Steve felt I could do it and said he'd be happy to take it on a match-by-match basis to begin with.

That seemed the fairest way and then nobody would be upset if it didn't quite work out. However, I had another slight doubt. "You'd better check with the chairman and make sure he's happy with it," I said. I simply didn't know if Tony Stewart would welcome me back. Rightly and understandably he had been upset when I left as part of the Barnsley Five in 2009. After all, I didn't know him and he didn't know John Breckin when he came in and saved the club in 2008. Then only a year later there I was walking out to go elsewhere. Steve checked. Fortunately the chairman had no issue with it at all and I'd be welcomed back. That made me feel great. I decided to give it a go.

So in September 2013 I donned a smart suit and tie and, like all newcomers, would have loved a winning first game. But after a good start to the season we lost 1-0 to Peterborough. Even so the event in the room went well despite my novice attempts and the guests seemed pleased with this addition to their Saturday afternoon's entertainment. I enjoyed the experience and despite some teething troubles in the early weeks I got more of a feel for it, got some valuable help along the way in those early days and with the lounge full or near enough for every game, it started to go down well. Rather like my efforts as host, the team picked up after my first game loss to Posh and were promoted to the Championship.

Had I done well enough to be kept on? It seems I had and have continued to be the match day host for the sponsors, corporate guests and others enjoying the bonhomie. I've got to know some great people, including many business people who have importantly invested in this town and also invaluably for Rotherham United in the football club. I am delighted to have made some great friends among them. As a player and in the dugout, fans would let you know in no uncertain terms when it wasn't going right.

In the lounge, because they are friends, they will come and tell you personally what's what, give their views and opinions. We share our thoughts. That's great and all part of the game. Of course, there are always those who pick the team they thought should have been picked, but that's usually after a defeat and at about five o'clock! I do tend to point out that the manager had to pick his team before two o'clock and hand in the teamsheet and, if he had known what he knew now – that so-and-so wasn't going to play too well that afternoon – then he wouldn't have picked him!

There have been some great guests along the way, including many legendary names and some of my playing heroes such as Dave Watson, Albert Bennett, Pete Madden – sadly taken from us during 2020 – and a number of the crack 1960s generation. It was great to get Tommy Docherty back, 50 years after his astounding time in Rotherham in 1967 and 1968. He was 89 then but still sharp as a tack, still wisecracking, and made a big fuss of Johnny Quinn, even serenading him with a rendition of *'Mighty Quinn'.* Tommy was a real character and he loved being interviewed on stage that day. It was sad hear of his death, at the age of 92, as we were about to turn into 2021.

Another special guest of mine was one Neil Warnock, and I just wonder if his day in the lounge played a part in his return to save the club from relegation in 2016. Often the idea is to invite someone who has a link with both clubs playing here. So, when we played Neil's former club QPR right at the start of 2016, I contacted him and he said he'd love to come. I was a youngster in the reserves when Neil was a player here – I used to clean his boots – and towards the end of my playing career he signed me at Burton Albion, so obviously held no grudges even though he does remember me kicking him when he was at Chesterfield.

He was extremely well received in the lounge; then he went down on the pitch at half-time. He acknowledged the QPR fans who cheered him in recognition of his success with them and then he turned towards the home supporters. I think the reception genuinely surprised him. He got a fantastic ovation and many stood up to applaud him. It was no surprise really, just added appreciation for his support for the club when he was manager at Sheffield United, loaning players to boost us when we desperately needed it during the difficult, financially stricken days of early 2006.

He was a dream to interview and went down really well. I took him to the boardroom to meet the chairman and he loved his day. In fact, when he finally left, he leaned aside to me and said: "It's a pity the New York Stadium is a long way from Cornwall, isn't it?" But the seeds had been sown. He was soon making that long journey to come back as manager and the rest, as they say, is history. Certainly, as he has said many times since with genuine affection, he looks back on that miracle escape from relegation in the Championship in 2016 as one of his best achievements in football, which is saying something considering he has had more promotions than any other manager. At one stage we looked doomed and I'm sure Neil was having his doubts at one point before he oversaw what was the ultimate great escape – a feat in football that season bettered only by Leicester City winning the Premier League.

The role is certainly different for me and, instead of mulling over plans for the next coaching session, I find I'm considering who might be my next guest in the lounge. Certainly I have loved being involved on match days again and in a role I find enjoyable. It was also nice to have involvement on occasions with *BBC Radio Sheffield* as co-commentator. Again that was something I wasn't sure about doing – it can mean a long away day at times.

But I have enjoyed doing it when invited and got some good feedback on my style as summariser, in which I have tried to include a bit of a coach's insight combined with, where possible, a little humour. I've done the same with the Millers' iFollow commentary and I was astounded at the various places all over the world where fans listen in to follow the fortunes of their club – from the Cayman Islands to New Zealand, Australia to America and all sorts of places in between.

Me and Ronnie Moore were were summarisers at the Wembley play-off final against Leyton Orient in 2014, backing up *Radio Sheffield's* Andy Giddings and Paul Walker who were doing the commentary. I got to London on the Saturday before the final the next day and met up with Ronnie in a hotel bar near Wembley. It was immediately like old times. We'd done the same many a time during our management days on those Friday overnight stops. What hadn't changed either was our attitude towards a spot of frugal living and we'd certainly noted the London prices at the bar. We did what all good Yorkshiremen do – Ronnie is an honorary one – and called at the little supermarket nearby to stock up with a selection of beers. Back in the bar we ordered a pint of shandy each and mysteriously it lasted us all evening.

Wembley on the day of a big final is always a wonderful place and it was great to see all the red and white down Wembley Way. At first I thought we were going to fill the stadium until I remembered that Orient are red and white as well! At 2-0 down it looked ominous, but we all know the fightback that followed and, whether we were on radio or not, we both jumped to our feet like excited kids and shouted out when Alex Revell's stunning equaliser went in. When the penalty shoot-out was on, the adrenalin was pumping like it did in the old days together and we were both delighted that our back-to-back promotions had been emulated by the 2014 squad.

It meant stepping up to the Championship – an excellent division that in some ways has become more exciting and unpredictable than the Premier League. It was a great achievement by Paul Warne to take the team on another "back-in-one" promotion in 2020 as he had done in 2018 and with some big-name clubs playing in the game's second tier, there is an attractive name on the opposition board more often than not. And I've noticed, too, that on a number of occasions sponsors or companies have invited clients or friends connected with the away side. It all helps with the banter and the atmosphere of the pre-match build up. Long may it continue!

33

BRECK ON RONNIE... RONNIE ON BRECK

My introduction to Ronnie Moore was a painful one. In fact, I met his elbow before I met him! We were playing Tranmere Rovers, I went up for a header and someone smashed me. It was Ronnie. He always said he put chalk on his elbow. No yellow card back then and certainly not a red. I was young and naive and had played about a dozen games at that time. Welcome to first team football. When someone does something such as that, then you tend to remember them. And Ronnie, with his blond hair, wasn't easily forgettable. But I never realised that we would one day go on to have the great relationship and friendship that we have had and which endures to this day. My biggest friend in football. I love him to bits and we really have had some memorable and unforgettable times together.

A big money move from Tranmere to Cardiff City didn't work out for him unfortunately. That's when Rotherham stepped in back in 1980 so our paths crossed again but this time on the same side. However not, initially, on the same wavelength. In one of the first games, I knocked a lovely ball into the 'tramlines' expecting Ronnie to run out wide and chase it down. Ronnie just shook his head. At half-time I complained to him and said it was a great ball. He looked at me... "I've just done that for two years at Cardiff," he said. "Chased balls into channels all the time. It's why I didn't get many goals for them. I'm going to be in that penalty area, in that six yard box. Get that ball in there and I'm going to score goals for you."

As any Millers fan will tell you, he was dead right. I knew that, if I got down the line and crossed it, the big fella would be in there and he certainly thrived on those crosses from such as me, Gerry Forrest and Tony

Towner. He proved as good as his word, finishing as top scorer in the promotion season with 25 goals and then winning the Golden Boot as top scorer in the whole of the Championship, which was then Division Two, the season after that with 24. He wasn't just a hero to the fans, he was a hero to me as well – and I was playing with him!

We actually hit it off as mates straightaway, rooming together for away games. We would go out to old haunts such as the Millmoor pub or Cavalier and with our wives and families for a meal to Sir Jack's, King William or the Golden Ball at Whiston. Together we arranged to have a players' lounge at Millmoor; there wasn't one before. All the players chipped in and me and Ronnie ran it, sorting out the drinks etc. After training on the Friday before a home game, we'd go to the cash and carry and get some beers and lager in.

We'd get good lager for our lads and cheaper stuff for the away team. We'd tell Joyce, who ran the bar for us, to pour the other stuff for the away teams. Players would buy it and we'd charge the London teams a bit more because they were usually on better money than us. We'd make a profit and that would be ploughed back in, helping with the supply of soft drinks, crisps, etc. It certainly helped to add to our team spirit because teammates were now staying behind after a game to have a drink and a chat and some of the wives and girlfriends would be there, too. At the end of the season we divvied up whatever money was left over between the lads and gave Joyce a bit, too. Not that there was too much left. After the opposition had gone, Ronnie would order a Happy Hour which meant a free bar!

We had a bond as players and as people and we got on great but when he moved on, to Charlton early in the fourth season at Rotherham, we actually didn't stay in touch. It happens. Careers take people elsewhere. We had become mere passing acquaintances by the time our relationship resumed 14 years later on his return to Rotherham in 1997. Neither of us could ever have envisaged what a very special time we were due to have. When Ronnie got the Millers manager's job and asked me to be his assistant, I vividly remember him saying: "We had great success on the pitch as teammates, so let's make a success of it and have a real good go and repeat it on the management side."

It was the start of an unbelievable journey in management for us both and it developed nicely as a partnership. We'd work things out, but we didn't always agree and we could talk about it. And that's a good relationship. But when we came out of the office, we worked on the understanding that his was the final decision and I would back him all the way. If he got something wrong, he would always say: "You got it right, I was wrong on that one." But I always backed him and that's what an assistant does. We complemented each other nicely. Sometimes we could just look at each other, a glance, and we'd know what the other was thinking. Ronnie would generally get into the players when they needed it. Sometimes a player might have his head down after Ronnie had had a pop. I'd follow the player and pick him up. On occasions I would have a go, but we worked well together. It was teamwork between the two of us.

Nearly all players and managers have their superstitions and I know a lot of managers who had a wardrobe full of losing suits – not to be worn again. To a match anyway! Ronnie was one of those and he certainly had a lot of superstitious ways. On the way to Brighton, we passed a wedding party outside a church and Ronnie said: "I've seen the bride, that's good luck. We'll win today." We did. For the next away game, he ordered Syd, the coach driver, to detour and go past as many churches as he could, hoping we'd see another wedding!

Another time, at a funeral, Ronnie sneaked off and I saw him dipping his gold crucifix in the font. His explanation? "It's holy water, it'll see us okay." We then went on a long, unbeaten run of about 14 matches. When it ended Ronnie said: "Can you take me back to that church, Breck?" Unfortunately, and much to his frustration, I couldn't remember where it was! Closer to home his superstitious mind kicked in. Early in our partnership, when he'd more points on his licence than the team had got, I noticed one Friday that his driving skills were perfect. He kept to the speed limit, drove carefully, let people out at junctions. His explanation? "Driving like that might just get us three points tomorrow, Breck." For the rest of the week it was a white knuckle ride!

He was a great support to me at my most difficult time when Denise was ill and that's what great friends do. He was always there for me and I've always appreciated the support he gave me. I always say we are like brothers and that buzz is still there whenever we get together, whatever the situation. Frankly, as a friendship it was a partnership made in heaven – and I hope we meet up when we get up there.

RONNIE ON BRECK

Breck claims that the first time I met him, he got an elbow from me. Is he sure? Mind you, I accidentally caught a lot of defenders, so remembering everyone individually would be a bit difficult. I do remember the first time I did come across him. I'd signed from Cardiff, went in the dressing room at Millmoor and this blond-haired bloke seemed to be the loudest, telling stories. He seemed a character and took my eye among all the others. I'm not sure when they say first impressions always count, but this one did.

It was clear that he was well liked by the other lads; he always seemed to be telling jokes and was always involved. There were things I saw in him and saw a little bit of myself in there. He was the one I took to straightaway. We hit it off, were on the same wavelength and, off the field, we started knocking about together. Certainly we had a great dressing room then and Breck was a big part of it, taking the mickey out of the lads and winding people up. We bounced off each other. Importantly he was a very good player – which is important, because there are a lot of jokers who can't play. He could and his record proves it.

Soon it got to the stage – and subsequently continued – whereby we'd know what the other one was thinking. Although we had gone our separate ways after I'd left as a player, as happens in football, I was clear about what he would bring if I made him my assistant. We worked well as a pair. He was very solid, very bright on the coaching side, good at planning set-plays and always well prepared. He also assured me that he didn't want to be a manager, and that I wouldn't be stabbed in the back. I've seen plenty jump into the hot seat when the manager has left.

Breck even came up with a very smart idea which stemmed from spying on the opposition. You note their corners and set-plays and plan in the week how you are going to cope defensively. But one day he said: "This is how they do their corners; this is what they do – why don't we copy that and do their own attacking set-plays against them? They won't expect it, they will have watched us and set up to combat our set plays. So we'll pinch theirs and surprise 'em." It was clever thinking.

We'd sit in the office, reflect on how the last game had gone and plan for the next one, discuss how we'd do something or the way we'd play. If there was a problem, he wouldn't hide it. He might say: "I don't think we should do this or play this formation" and he'd plant a seed. I'd understand where he was coming from, but I'd decide to stick with what I thought and he'd back me. Then, we'd start 3-5-2, it wasn't going too well and he might say: "I think we should go this way" – which was a diplomatic way of saying: "I think we've fucked this up." We'd change and get better.

But he never expected to take the credit for that. I was the one who took the plaudits, got the glory. He was never one to seek the limelight, even when he deserved it, but I'd thank him. It was a sort of good cop, bad cop relationship whereby I would have a pop at someone and a couple of minutes later he would speak to the player with an explanation and reasoning. We dovetailed nicely in that respect. But one thing he didn't like was going in the boardroom after games. He hated it.

"I don't know how you do it," he'd say. He asked if I would allow him to stay away and not go in. He feared that he might say something he'd regret when someone was expressing an opinion he disagreed with or he knew to be inaccurate or wrong and would prefer not to get embroiled in such a conversation. I think that indicated how passionate he was and how he might have struggled to keep that passion in check as he defended the team.

Such a working relationship as we had is once in a lifetime really. We loved to go out for a beer together and did so as families. We have always been there for each other when there were difficult times for us in our personal and domestic lives. He went through hell when Denise was ill and I think it was fantastic how he coped with that, bringing up Jess during that pain and agony. So many ups and downs he had then, having to deal with an awful lot. Denise would be proud of how he brought Jess up.

I've only admiration for how he coped so well then. It was a very sad day when he couldn't continue at Tranmere with me, but I had seen the strain it had put on him and understood his explanation and decision not to continue travelling over. Such a friendship as we have had happens only once in a lifetime, too. I know he says we're like brothers and I think he's right on that. We've had many a laugh; we've had differences of opinion, but he's never one to hold a grudge. Yes, we've had a few tears along the way too but, above all, we've had a great time and have forged an unbreakable bond of friendship. Long may it continue.

To me and everyone else he is Mr Rotherham United. A true legend.

34

AN HONOUR AND A PRIVILEGE

I feel honoured to have been invited back to be part of the modern history of Rotherham United, albeit not on the grass or in the dug-out this time. In fact, it's a new era at the football club we all love and there is no doubt who has been responsible – not only for rewriting this modern history, but also for driving this new era forward from a standing start. As mentioned before, I didn't know who Tony Stewart was when he came to the fore in 2008. At the time, like thousands of others, I was just so relieved and grateful that he did what he did and saved the club.

As chairman, Tony has led from the front right from the start. He promised a new ground – "an iconic stadium" was his phrase – and, as the many initial doubters among the pessimists melted away, he most certainly delivered on that. A lot of thought and work went into the design and various aspects. He did his due diligence, as they say, and even had his brother Terry checking out other new grounds to see what ideas Rotherham United might benefit from and if there were any mistakes they had made, so that we wouldn't repeat them.

What we have ended up with is a stadium to be enormously proud of. One that serves not just football, but also the community. Local pubs and businesses will tell you it has galvanised the town on match days. He even alighted on a perfectly appropriate name, the New York Stadium, considering it adjoins and is part of the old New York district. By now everyone will know that fire hydrants exported to New York were made at Guest and Chrimes, the former brass foundry on the site, where the screw tap was invented.

It is a super stadium – is there a better one of its size in the country?

I think not. The Football Association certainly like it, considering the number of England women's internationals and age-group internationals played there. In addition, UEFA staged their Euro Under-17 Championship tournament at the venue in 2018, including the final, and must have been impressed because it has been named as a venue for the UEFA Women's European Championships in 2022. I call it the town's shining light – a bright, red ruby there for all to see from road and rail and testimony to Tony's vision and positivity. It will remain a huge part of his legacy – not only to this football club, but also to the town.

As the head of his own very successful company, ASD Lighting based in Rotherham, it means he is that rarity among many football club owners – someone who lives in the town and employs a lot of people in it. As he proved with the football club, thriving businessmen get things done either by their own efforts or by proper delegation and I had an example of this a few years ago at Rotherham Hospice. They had a big, stainless-steel sculpture made in the shape of a tree – the Tree of Life, they call it, with people adorning the leaves with names of loved ones. There was a strong Millers connection with it. Sandra Robinson donated a large sum towards it in memory of her husband Chas, who died in the hospice.

"It just needs some lights to finish off our Tree of Life nicely," they said. "We'll get a quote," they said. I suggested that I knew someone who might just want to help. I rang Tony, explained what it was about and to see if he could help. He could. "There will be someone from here at the hospice tomorrow morning to sort it; let me know how it went," he said. For me that summed him up – when he says he is going to do it, he does it.

He fully deserved his OBE in the 2019 New Year honours' list for services to business and the community – the latter with a nod to "his" stadium, I guess, which he once described as his finest achievement. He's certainly enjoyed times of success at the club, but, as many a successful businessman has learned after coming into football, it's not all sweetness and light. If after a dozen or so years in football he hasn't had any disappointments, suffered even a touch of disillusionment at times or made a few mistakes, then he'll have been the only chairman in the game who hasn't!

We can all dream, can't we, perhaps of winning the lottery? In football we can all dream of "our" club getting into the Premier League. But the way football is going, the reality makes it appear increasingly difficult for the smaller clubs to attain that dream. The vast budgets of the many big clubs who inhabit the Championship are making it far harder for those smaller clubs on a lesser budget to produce that one-off season. People liken us in size to Bournemouth and say they did it, even after a deduction of minus 17 points in League Two at the same time as we got ours in 2008. But a Russian multi-millionaire moved in there and a massive injection of funds followed. They did get to the Premier League in 2015, but a year later were found to have violated EFL fair play regulations and were fined heavily.

The list of club owners and their net worth shows billionaires and multi-millionaires. And lots of their clubs haven't either made it into, or in many cases back into, the Premier League, which shows how extremely hard it has become for a club such as ours. I think being in the Championship, managing to stay in it, adding some seasons on to that – any, some or all of those – should be regarded as success for a club such as ours. A lot of people should think about that. And should consolidation occur, then you can build from there. As many bigger clubs discover, it ain't cheap. But one of the things about this great game is that you never do stop dreaming.

I did dream of becoming a footballer for Rotherham United one day. I never did dream I might become president of the club. When Tony Stewart bestowed on me the title of Honorary Life President of Rotherham United, it was a mighty honour and a privilege. I don't mind admitting I got emotional and had a lump in my throat, certainly when I thought about my mum and dad looking down and remembering when they took that eager little lad down to Millmoor to stand transfixed by the boundary wall. I thank Tony and the football club for that accolade and I would like to think I will represent the football club in a manner befitting the role.

I was honoured, too, by another gesture. Now, if we should all be grateful for Tony Stewart's involvement, then we should consider ourselves very fortunate indeed that Paul Warne became the manager of our club in 2016. All football teams win and lose and all chairmen get managerial choices right and wrong. So have we. The choice of someone whose longevity at the club, whose personality as a player and in whatever role since his playing retirement had already earned him legendary status, certainly proved inspired. But there were those who doubted the decision at the start, amid accusations he was a cheap option after some costly failures.

Well, I for one wasn't among the doubters. I felt that here was a very clever, highly intelligent, humble human being with an empathy and duty of care that would stimulate and bring out the best in those working for him and under him, all allied to a fantastic work ethic. My feeling was that he could do any job in football and certainly could tackle management and make a success of it. That feeling was strengthened from further personal experience after receiving a call from him, which gave an indication of the sort of person he is.

As Millers fans will well remember, Kenny Jackett walked out on the club back in 2016 after just five games in charge and Paul Warne was left holding the baby. It wasn't blissfully asleep either. It was screaming its head off because it was hungry, had a wet nappy and was teething as well. In other words what a job he had on! He rang me one Sunday morning and asked if I would consider coming to the training ground and act as a sounding board. "I don't want you to be my assistant, just an experienced body and additional mind," he said. "I don't know how long I'll be in the job and I didn't want to ask someone else to leave their job to join me and then they find themselves out of work later." That is the sort of bloke he is. He was urgently in need of additional help and assistance, but was not wishing to put anyone else's job in jeopardy to get it. I went up to the training ground and we quickly agreed I'd operate in a sort of consultancy role at all times if required, but as and when necessary.

It was a sort of role reversal really. Here he was signing me – albeit temporarily – after I'd had a hand in signing him three times when he was a player. After teaming up with Paul in that winter of 2016/17, it meant being on the inside again and it wasn't long before I realised what a thankless task he'd taken on. The team was relegation-bound even from a long way out. It was a sinking ship and the bucket he'd been handed to bale it out had holes in it. There was some talent in the dressing room, but the shirt was not producing it. There were question marks against two or three whether they even wanted to produce it! One game, on a cheerless, freezing day, I was in the dugout and looked at Warney, standing out there in the technical area, all alone, with this doomed team losing. In such a moment you can capture the utter loneliness of the football manager and I actually felt sorry for the guy.

He turned and beckoned me to his side. "What about making changes?" he asked. I turned round and looked to the dugout. Not one substitute gave me eye contact and I could name a couple who definitely looked the other way. They were wrapped up and no one fancied having to get warmed up. "This bench won't help you," I said. "Leave it as it is." He did, but it was an indication of the uphill battle he faced in those first six months. But even in that difficult spell, which would have tested even the most experienced of managers, I saw him grow into the job. It didn't take long at all to confirm and strengthen my view that there was a manager in there. He had all the attributes to make a go of it and be a success at it. If he wanted it. In fact, in those opening six months and even beyond for a while, I don't think he had enough belief in himself to do the job. He underestimated himself. I stayed alongside him until the end of the season before getting back to the warmth of the corporate lounge and by then I was even more convinced that he had what it takes. For me he's proved it.

Certainly it has been a pleasure to see him develop as a manager and definitely pleasing to note his growing maturity in the job after the initial doubts and blaming himself a lot. I used to say: "Don't blame yourself; you inherited this. Yes, it's your problem, but it's not your team." So it delights me that he has risen to the top of the "Breckin Beliefometer". The faith and patience shown in him has been rewarded to the benefit of all, particularly in the way he has developed a structure and established a culture at the club; a way things will operate, not least in terms of hard work and fitness. He is clever, very intelligent and could do any job in football. I can see him only getting better as a manager.

What I like, too, is his ability to "sell" the club to others – that's to other clubs and to potential signings. On the latter he does a tremendous amount of homework. For example, when endeavouring to bring in a loan signing, Paul has visited top Premier League clubs and put on a presentation – described by one major club representative as "quite outstanding" – about how things operate at Rotherham United and how they see the player fitting in. The club will receive regular reports on his fitness, how he is in training, his performance overall and playing performance. It shows the other club that their player will come on loan to help to further his football education, but be looked after at the same time.

A potential signing will be told: "This is what we expect of you, this is what we do and how we do it and how and where you fit in." He sells the club to them. I know of one player who had other clubs wanting him when he came to Rotherham, and he made up his mind after an hour with Warney. And not because it was more money, either. I often meet new signings in their early days and I will tell them: "You will leave here a better player and a better person."

The football club has, above all, got a good human being leading them as their manager. He has blossomed and I feel he will go down as one of the best managers this football club has ever had – and may even come to be regarded as the best. His whole philosophy impresses me and I like that he has got a relaxed side to him. Be sure, too, that he knows the game inside out and in a short time he has become very popular in the football world. Long may he reign, hopefully at Rotherham United, but the rarity of two back-in-one promotions alerts others and does not go unnoticed elsewhere. Cards will have been marked.

Of course, managers need a good staff around them and I have seen at first hand that Paul has surrounded himself with a very good crew and has got the right people alongside him. Richie Barker is an outstanding coach – he was called into the England set-up a few years ago, which tells you something – and, having seen his sessions, he could work at a Premier League club. His preparation is first class and the two of them complement each other perfectly with their different types of skill sets.

Then you have Matt Hamshaw, a young, up-and-coming coach who I have seen develop and grow into his role from his time as academy head coach. He'll be delighted buds of promise from there are starting to blossom, notably Ben Wiles who has made a first team mark. We now have Andy Warrington, a popular former Rotherham player as goalkeeping coach after replacing Mike Pollitt. And the head of player recruitment is another promotion winner in the red and white, Rob Scott.

Note the connection between all of them. Rotherham United. Five of them as ex-players, most as teammates and, although Hammy didn't play for the club, he's a Rotherham lad through and through, from Rawmarsh and part of a family who are all big Millers fans. In fact, during his playing days, including several years at Sheffield Wednesday, he would often get a Millers reminder from his dad Phil who would say "Yeah, you've played well today ... but you'll never be as good as Tony Towner." You can guarantee there are no issues about commitment to the job with all those guys.

It has always been a privilege to have been in the team talks and to have seen how they prepare for a game. The most memorable was seeing what they did and what went into their preparation for the 2018 League One play-off final at Wembley, when we beat Shrewsbury Town – managed by a certain Paul Hurst. I feel honoured and privileged to have experienced it all first hand. Warney was up first with his talk to the players, then Richie and Matt stepped in with thoroughness and clarity on various aspects, including set-plays. "This is great," I thought. Everyone would go out there so well prepared, aware of the opposition's strengths and weaknesses, and knowing their jobs. Shrewsbury, I said to myself, would have to be at their best to beat us.

As the meeting ended and we started to get up to leave for the short trip to the stadium, Warney told everyone to sit back down. What happened next sent an emotional shiver through every one in that room. I sat there and got goose pimples – and it wasn't through being cold because it was red hot. Warney started up a film he had commissioned from the club's analysts, having arranged for all the players' families or partners to send supportive messages to each individual player. There were lots of: "Good luck, Dad" and "C'mon Dad" in there from young sons and daughters; you had mums and dads on there and wives and partners, all backing their sons and blokes. Wherever families were, they'd been tracked down; there was even a message from Australia for Will Vaulks from his folks. It was inevitable that some of the players got emotional. It even tugged at me. It was all magnificent.

When the video finished, the gaffer had his final message. "They're the people who love you and mean so much to you and you to them," he said. "Whatever the result, everyone on there will still love you, no matter what happens. But let's get on that bus now, have no fear and we're going out there to do a job." After all that, even I was ready to get the old boots out again and play! Even something as simple as what the lads were allowed to wear pre-match showed the thoroughness of preparation. It was a boiling hot day, you may remember, and the lads wore T-shirts and shorts on the team coach and for their pre-match wander on to the pitch. Shrewsbury may have looked smarter in their three piece suits, shirts and ties. But they also looked considerably hotter by the time they had baked for a bit in that cauldron.

Did I jump up and go mad when we scored, like in 2014? Have a guess! And I eventually laughed along at the madcap sprint of Richard Wood after his winning goal in extra time. Where he got that speed from, I'll never know, but he's never moved anywhere near as fast before or since. That day Woody became the first defender ever to score twice in any Wembley or Cardiff play-off final, which is a nice statistic to tell his grandchildren one day.

We had great celebrations that night and for Warney, who lifted his first managerial trophy, it was a very emotional time. His dad, Russell, was very ill and unable to attend the game and Paul knew he would be losing him at some point. He died in June 2019. Emerging from our hotel opposite the ground the morning after the final, Paul, his staff and their families, me and Jess, did a "lap of honour" right around the outside of Wembley Stadium; strolling along, sort of taking it all in, basking in the moment and reflecting on the success and the memories of the great day. It was a nice way to round off the weekend.

If I have a vision beyond 2021 for Rotherham United, it is that Paul Warne is the type of guy I want in charge of my football club. What's more I think he will get better and better at the job because he is someone who will learn and learn and continue to learn. And is eager to. He represents the football club so superbly and the town itself so well. If I had a fear, it is that we could lose him at some point. He has proved the perfect catalyst for what has rightly become the template under Tony Stewart – stability, continuity and the establishment of a culture at the club. There are, and always will be, bigger clubs than Rotherham. We have had good players taken from us, and that us likely to continue.

But the present-day Rotherham United has a vision of where it stands and how it should move forward in this third decade of the 21st century. I believe our fans have bought into it and patience from everyone – from right at the top to those fanatics behind the goal on the North End – is very much a key part in helping the Millers move forward. I love my football club, have been proud to support it, play for it and serve it.

I hope, as my favourite saying goes: *I have smelled the flowers as I've passed them by.*

ACKNOWLEDGEMENTS

There are so many people I would dearly like to acknowledge and thank for their help and contribution to this book, but there isn't the space to mention everyone. So to all those who have assisted in whatever way, be it large, medium or small, please accept my heartfelt gratitude. Be assured, it has been greatly appreciated.

However, may I express my deep and sincere thanks in a number of directions. To Rotherham United and all the wonderful staff, with a special mention to Sam Todd for his patience and particular help. To Paul Warne for providing the foreword; to him, his staff and the players for their support; to Tony Stewart for not only bestowing on me the honour of Life President, but also for ensuring there is a club to be president of; to Steve Coakley for bringing me back to my beloved club.

To Ronnie Moore for always being there and without whom ... and to those other former colleagues for their stories and reminiscences, notably Seamus, Lengy, Crawf, Fin, Branno, Carl Luckock and the rest who chipped in. To Rotherham Hospice and especially to Cath Todd for her invaluable contribution. And special thoughts and thanks to those no longer with us, such as Alan Archer, Micky Hukin and dear old Derek Dalton. I look upwards to you all with gratitude.

A word for Gerry Somerton who sparked off a book idea many years ago; to Stuart Clarkson, sincere thanks for all the effort you put in. And to Dean Andrews for an eventual push. I am grateful to publisher Danny Hall and Vertical Editions for all his help, to David Bond for his proofreading work and to the *Rotherham Advertiser* and *Sheffield Star* for use of their pictures. Massive thanks to Les Payne for all his time, effort, patience, exhaustive research and guidance and for knocking my many tales into shape. It has been a thoroughly enjoyable time doing it, whether meeting up or during four-hour phone calls – I even got a word in at times! Or was it the other way round?

Finally thanks to the subscribers who supported me – their names are included in the Roll of Honour – and all those who have bought the book. You will all be contributing to a very worthy cause. I hope you enjoy it.

- John Breckin, Rotherham, 2021

THANKS, DAD...FOR EVERYTHING

Dear Dad,

I don't even know where to begin. Maybe I will start by saying I am forever grateful for all you have done and are continuing to do for me. I cannot express how so very thankful I am for everything. I don't think I can ever really thank you enough for the things you have done for me. There are so many good times and memories and I can't possibly write about them all. But here's a few... Baking Victoria sponge cakes and taking me on bike rides on Saturday mornings before every home game. Taking me to the training ground or the football club admin office on days when you didn't have childcare or times when mum was at hospital or too poorly to look after me.

For looking after me throughout the hardest times of our lives with losing mum, throughout the times of travelling to Tranmere every day and the 6am get-ups, then driving two hours or more to get to work and dashing home as fast as you can to look after me. To this day, just thinking about it all, I still cannot imagine how you have done some of the things with all the stresses of work and personal life and still being the man you are. I will never forget the time when you told me in the back garden that you were coming home to Rotherham United and we were both so happy. At the time I probably didn't understand the relief that coming home was for you. As I'm growing older, I now have a better understanding of how much it will have meant to you and how much Rotherham United and football means to you now.

I will always love the stories you tell me about your playing career, funny background ones of football life and playing pranks on each other – putting honey in other people's shampoo bottles and people messing up the things in your office because you have a tidy OCD streak. I think you may have inherited that from Grandma Breckin! From the bottom of my heart, and forever, I am so proud of everything you have achieved in life. I am so proud to call you my dad. You will forever be a legend in my eyes. I know that this is very much a cliché, but you are literally the best father a girl could ever wish for. You are incredible. As you always say to me and just like your friend Derek Dalton – Up the Millers.

- Lots of love, Jessica Grace. xxx

APPEARANCES, GOALS, HONOURS

John Breckin's total of 467 is third on the all-time list of appearances for Rotherham United, behind Danny Williams (500 plus another 97 wartime games, which don't count in official records) and Paul Hurst (494). Ironically, John was responsible for ensuring Hurst stayed at the club as a 12-year-old on returning in 1987 to reorganise the youth system.

Appearances (substitute appearances in brackets) -

ROTHERHAM UNITED
Football League: 409 (4)
FA Cup: 27 (1)
League Cup: 31
Total: 467

DONCASTER ROVERS
Football League: 18
League Cup: 3
FA Cup: 1
Total: 22

DARLINGTON (Loan)
Football League: 4

BURY
Football League: 17

Career total: 510

The No.3 was synonymous with John Breckin. But he wore the No.6 shirt on 18 occasions from the start of the 1979/80 season when playing in central defence, the No.12 shirt on five occasions when he went on from the substitutes' bench and on just one occasion the No.11 shirt. That was when Alan Crawford missed the game and John was asked to play as a left winger at home to Carlisle United – 0-0 – in September 1977.

He scored 12 goals, all for Rotherham United – eight in the Football League, three in the FA Cup and one in the League Cup. Here are John's dozen with his own description from memory. For the one he couldn't remember, a newspaper description of the time will suffice.

League goals

January 13th, 1973 v. Brentford (A) 1-1: A corner from the right, a run to the near post and a header. It was my first goal, so it was a special feeling.

September 7th, 1974 v. Lincoln City (H) 2-2: Picked ball up near halfway, Lincoln's Sam Ellis was shouting: "Show him down the line," but I

dropped my shoulder, came inside, swung my lamb chop – my right foot – at it and it flew in the bottom corner.
November 5th, 1974 v. Stockport County (H) 3-0: A Trev Phillips shot came off the goalkeeper and I smashed in the rebound.
November 16th, 1974 v. Exeter City (H) 1-1: The best goal I ever scored. With a couple of minutes left, I moved forward and decided to have a go even though I was a long way out. I struck it as sweet as anything and never felt a thing which means I must have caught it right. I had my head down and looked up to see it in the top corner. That one really sticks with me. Also the point it gained meant reaching an accumulated points target by a stipulated time so a £2,000 bonus in the players' pool.
August 23rd, 1975 v. Hereford United (H) 1-1: Alan Crawford played me in, I hit it really well and it flew past the goalkeeper into the far corner.
October 1st, 1977 v. Bradford City (H) 2-1: Richard Finney crossed from the right, big Dave Gwyther headed on and I arrived at the far post, took a touch for control and fired into the roof of the net.
August 26th, 1978 v. Blackpool (H) 2-1: A free kick was touched aside by Mark Rhodes and I struck a shot past the wall into the far corner.
October 31st, 1981 v. Chelsea (H) 6-0: The opener. Attack built down the right, it was worked across towards the left and the ball was laid into my path by Rod Fern. Struck it from about 18 yards, not the sweetest of strikes, and the goalkeeper, Petar Borota, got his hands to it, but the ball looped behind him and dropped into the net. My last goal and the only time I scored in the same game as Ronnie Moore.

FA Cup goals
November 20th, 1977: first round v. Altrincham (H) 5-0: Low shot from outside the penalty area.
November 25th, 1978: first round v. Workington (H) 3-0: Couldn't remember this one! Described in *The Advertiser* as a "20 yard grass-cutter." John was quoted after the match – with tongue in cheek – as saying: "I was a little closer in than usual."
January 17th, 1978: third round replay v. Manchester City (H) 2-4: Won the ball off Gary Owen about 35 yards out, moved forward, thought: "I'll have a crack here" and it went past the 'keeper's left hand into the far top corner.

League Cup goals

October 27th, 1981: second round, second leg v. Sunderland (H) 3-3: A weird one in a way. Phil Henson, who played in front of me on the left, popped up on the right for some reason, crossed to the far post and I arrived on cue to head in.

John's club honours at Rotherham United include five promotions.

As a player ...

In 1974/75 from Division Four – now League Two.

In 1980/81 as champions of Division Three – now League One.

As assistant manager ...

In 1991/92 with Phil Henson from Division Four – now League Two – as runners-up

In 1999/2000 with Ronnie Moore from Division Three – now League Two – as runners-up

In 2000/2001 with Ronnie Moore from Division Two – now League One – as runners-up

In addition, he was coach of the Millers youth side who won the Northern Intermediate League Cup in 1990 and manager of the reserves who gained promotion to the Central League First Division in 1991.

In 1983/84 he was a player in the Doncaster Rovers side who gained promotion as runners-up in Division Four – now League Two.

John was chosen three times by his fellow professionals for the PFA Team of the Year: In 1974/75 in Division Four – now League Two; in 1978/79 in Division Three – now League One – and in 1980/81 in Division Three – now League One.

ROLL OF HONOUR

John Abbott
Michael Abbott
John Abell
Dave Abrahams
Stephen Adams
Fred Adamson
Harry Adshead
Lee Agus
Thomas Peter Aitchison
Geoff Albiston
Tim Albiston
Jonny Allan
Linda Allott
John Anderson
Chris Andrews
Johnathan Andrews
Mark Andrews
Scott T. Ansley
Paul Appleby
John Appleyard
Joanne Archer
Sue Archer
John Arrowsmith
Greg Artell
Michael Asbridge
Andrew Ashmall-Liversidge
Dave Askew
Jon Atherton
Chris Badger
Richard Badger
Mick Bagnall
Neil Bagnall
Glenn Bagshaw
Tim Balcon
Allison Ball
Shaun Bamford
Martin & Sue Barber
Kevin Barker
Richie Barker
Dan Barlaser
Eric Barlow
Matthew Barlow
Peter Barlow
Graham Barnes
Robbie Barron
David Bartholomew
Gary Barthrop
Nathan Barthrop
Maurice Bartley
Dawn Bates
Ian Bates
Peter Bates
John Baxter
Christopher Beaumont
John Beaven
Eric Beeley
Darren Beesley
Bill Bell
Michael Bell
Dan Bennett
Wayne Bennett
James Bent
Graham Benton
Keith Beresford
David Bester
Andy Bierton
Graham Billups
Tony Bingham
Ian Birch
Isaac & Jacob Birch
John Birch
Frank Bird
Anne Bisby
Ashley Bisby
Gary Bisby
Lisa Bisby
Marlene Bisby
Stephen Bisby
Richard Blackburn
Terry Blackburn
Jamal Blackman
Tom Blake
Ian Bool
Ben Borkowski
Stephen Borkowski
Marie Boston
Roy Bott
Matthew Boulton
Chris Bowden
Matt Bower
Stephen Boyce
Chris Bradford
Caroline Bradley
Jemma Brailsford
Jim Brailsford
Roger Brailsford
Stephen Braithwaite
Debbie Brashaw
Garry Bray
Charles Edward Breckin
Elaine Breckin
Jessica Breckin

John Breckin
Charlie Brittain
Ian Brittain, *1956-2012*
Craig Brown
Paula Brown
William Benjamin Bryan
Dennis Bulleyment
Ross Burbeary
Ray Burcham
Martin Burrell
Barry Burrows
Chris Burrows
Glenn Burrows
David Burton
Paul Burton
Ryan Buxton
Duncan Bye
Ross Byers
Mary Cainey
Joy Calladine
Josh Cardwell
Lee Cardwell
Matthew Carnall
Andrew Carpenter
Michael Carr
Luke Carroll
Paul Carter
Alan Cawkwell
Shaun Cawkwell
Gavin Chadwick
David Chamberlain
Geoff Chapman
Natalie Chapman
Brian Chapple
Paul Chapple
Ras Chauhan
Joshua Chettleburgh
Tony Childs
Stephen Clarke
Trevor Clarke
Peter Clarkson
Rachael Clayton
Steve Coakley
Colin Colburn
Denis Coleman
Steve Colton
Jordan Concannon
David Congreave
David Conway
Leonard Cook
Paul Cook
Simon Cook
Paula Cooke
Jake Cooper
Paul Cooper
Stephen Cope
Ben Corns
Gerald Corns
Gary Coughlan
Karl Coughlan
Phil Cowley
Brian & Linda Cox
Malcolm Cox
Jack Coy
Ian Cranmer
Graham Crompton
Andrew Crook
Matt Crooks
Philip Crutchley
Martin Cuckson
Geoff Cutts
Robert Cutts
Steven Dack
Barrie Dalby
Tony Dalton
Will Daniels
David Darby
Paul Daughtry
Jordan Davenport
Ian Davies
Chris & Andy Davies
Edward John Davis
Paul Davis
Margaret Davison
Mick Dawes
Geoff Deakin
Zachary Dearden
Marie Delaney
Martin Dent
Tiffany & Alfie Dickens
Christopher Dixon
Matt Douglas
Paul Douglas
Charlotte Down
Mark Downey
Paul Dransfield
Karen Ducker
Stephen Duty
Bob Earnshaw
Alan Eastwood
David Ede
Michael Edwards
Richard Elderkin
Alison Elliott
Tony Ellis
John Elvidge
Chris Elvin
Philip Evans

Peter Every
Steve Exley
Dave Eyre
Stephen Farr
Steve Fells
Terence W. Fenby
D.J. Ferguson
David Finnie
Rob Fletcher
Trevor Fletcher
Martin Ford
Michael Ford
Trevor Ford
Anthony E Foster
John Foster
Malcolm Foster
Mark Foster
Neil Fox
Derek France
Jordan France
Pip France
Christopher Frier
Karl Frier
Iain Frost
Mark Frost
Michael Frost
Stephen Garnett
Burt Garnham
Katie Garrity
James Garrow
Don Gartside
Sean Gavin
Mark Gee
Rupert Genge
Martin Gibbins
Paul Gibson

Mary Gilbert
Tony Gillott
JC Godfrey
Rian Godfrey
Matt Goodwin
Alan Gordon
Jacob Gratton
Billy Gray
Amber Greasby
Matthew Greasby
Jerome Greaves
Paul Greaves
Helen Green
Philip Grove
Barry Guest
Patrick Guest
Dick Habbin
Michael Hadfield
Michael Hague
Gareth Haigh
Jonathan Hale
Robert Hale
Danny Hall
Jake Hall
Raymond John Hall
Ricky Hall
Simon Hall
Eric Hambleton
Marie Hamby
Dee Hamilton
Matt Hamshaw
Phil Hamshaw
Mark Hanby
Rachel Harding
Wes Harding
Carl Harris

John Harrison
Damien Harry
Doreen Hartland
Trevor Hartland
Debbie Harvey
Will Haywood
Jayne Heald
Steve Heathcote
Eddie Helliwell
Rona & Graham Helliwell
Tom Helliwell
Ray Hemingway
Marie Hepburn
Michael Heppenstall
Andrew Hercock
Suzanne High
Andy Hill
Anton Hill
Gill Hill
Max Hill
Barrie Himsworth
George Hirst
Kelham Hilton
Dan Hodgkinson
Alyn Hodgson
Phil Hollinger
Derek Holmes
Richard Holyhead
Robert Holyman
Kevin Hood
Staceyleigh Hopkins
Jack Hopkinson
Edna Hopson
John Hopson
Shane Horne
Daniel Horner

Susan Horner
Thomas Horner
Michael Hornsby
Jack Horton
Richard Horton
Phillip Howdle
Chris Howis
Mark Hoy
Martin Hudson
Anne-Marie Hughes
John Hughes
Peter Hughes
Jake Hull
Alan Humphries
Andrew Hunn
George Hunton
Gary Hurlstone
John Hutchinson
Kevin Igoe
Michael Ihiekwe
Ken Ingram
Richard Izdebski
Chris Jackson
Martin Jackson
Harry Jamieson
John Jenkinson
Shaun Jennison
Maureen Jewison
Eric Job
Viktor Johansson
Darrell Johnson
Kev Johnson
Mike Jolly
Billy Jones
Carol Jones
Neil Jones
Philip Jones
Paul Jordan
Florian Jozefzoon
Paul Jubb
John Kay
Steve Kay
Joshua Kayode
Darrell Keeling
Paul Keeling
Reece Kellock
Darren Kelsall
Lisa Kelsall
John Kerr
Chris Kerry
Claire Ketton
David Ketton
Tim King
Michael Kingham
Alan Kirk
Andy Knight
Gillian Knight
Dave Knott
Nicky P Krakowski
Freddie Ladapo
Andrew Lait
Toni Lakin
Joan Lally
Mick Lambert
Alan Langstaff
Paul Latham
Geoff Launders
Brian Lee
Graham Leese
Elaine Leesley
Andrew Leng
Susan Levick
David Lewis
Zac, Ella & Steve Liles
Robert Lilley
M.E.J. Lindley
Jamie Linsday
Michael Longden
Ben Longden
Thomas Longden
Chris Lord-Tyrer
Richard Lovell
Matt Lowndes
Carl Luckock
Daniel Luckock
Steve Lyles
Dan Lyne
Shirley MacCormac
Angus MacDonald
Shaun MacDonald
Monty Mack
Sarah & Freddie Mack
John Makin
Sean Makin
Doug Manning
Roy Markham
Jonathan Marshall
Malcolm Marshall
Mandy Marshall
Keith Martin
Riegan Martin
David Matthews
Joe Mattock
John Mawson
Geoff McDonald
Tom McHale
Robert McKernan
Gordon McVann

Stephen McVann
Lewis Meadows
Ashley Meakin
Robert Mercer
Andy Miller
Mickel Miller
The Bournemouth Miller
Kenneth Millns
Christopher Millward
Ian Milne
David Mirfin
Joseph Jesse Christian Mirfin
Margaret Mirfin-Chapman
Samuel David Kane Mirfin
Kathleen Moffatt
James Moore
Joe Moore
Ronnie Moore
Nick Morgan
John Morley
David Morris
Mark Morris
Peter Morris
Stuart Morte
Antony Morton
Ashley Morton
David Moxon
Nick Mulkeen
Andrew Mullett
Graham Murphy
Val Murray
John Myers
Susan (Rudram) Naylor
Alan Neal
Arthur Neale
Geoff Needham
Lynne Nelson
Clare Newby
John Newey
Nick Newsum
Mick Newton
Maxwell Nicklin
Matthew Norcliffe
John Norris
Richard North
Jonathan Nugent
Jonathan O'Boyle
Chiedozie Ogbene
Danny Ogden-Glaves
Lewis Oldham
Michael Oldham
Matt Olosunde
Winnifred Olosunde
Philip O'Nion
Steve Orton
Kenneth Oxley
Kevin Oxley
Matthew Parker
Kev Parkin
Michael Parkinson
Barry Payling
Les Payne
Stephen Payne
Dawn Peacock
Nigel Pease
David Peers
Brian Perch
Geoff Peters
Howard Pierpoint
Gill Pierpoint
Angela Plummer
Colin Precious
Ian Prescott
Lewis Price
Wesley Prince
Gary Pritchard
Jamie Proctor
Steve Pursglove
John Pycroft
Brian Quinn
Terry Quinn
Patrick Ramskill
Jim Ransford
Philip Rawlinson
Margaret Reading
Shaun Reed
Matthew Reeves
Adam Richards
Stephen Richards
Charlotte Richardson
Ian Richardson
Julian Richardson
Paul Richmond
Mark Rigby
Sue & Ray Roberts
Clark Robertson
Ashley Robinson
In memory of Chas Robinson
Sandra Robinson
Dawn Rockley
John & Brenda Roddis
Keith Roddis
Katharine Roddis
James Roddison
Helen, Peter & Neil Rodger
Paul Rodgers
Richard Roebuck
Stephen Roebuck

Brian Rosling
Lee Rowbotham
Rob Rowbotham
Sam Rowbotham
Oliver Rowett
Thomas Edward Rowley
Mark Rowling
Peter Ruchniewicz
Paul Rudge
Liam Rusling
Stuart Ryan
Kieran Sadlier
Nick Sanders
Christopher Sanderson
Joshua Sanderson
Pete Sanderson
David Savage
Chris Sawford
Jill Schofield
John Scott
Paul Scott
Darren Seddons
Mick Seddons
Maurice Sellars
Madeline Selwood
Raymond Senior
Adam Senior
David Senior
Paul Senior
Jamie Sewell
Martyn Sharpe
Stephen Shaw
Jamie Sheldon
Stephen Shephard
Chris Shepherd
John Shepherd
Olivia Shipman
Archie Shore
Peter Short
Kevin Simmonds
M.L. Simmons
Trevor Simpson
Alan Simpson
Ian Simpson
Adrian Skalycz
Beverley Skidmore
Michael Slater
Ralph Sliwa
Jack Smallwood
Paul Smallwood
Brenda Smith
Alan Smith
Chris Smith
Howard Smith
Ian Differ Smith
John Stephen Smith
Lee Smith
Michael Smith
Peter Smith
Roger Smith
Stuart Smith
Tom Smith
Wilf Smith
Gerry Somerton
Alan Soper
Alison Sorsby
Paul Spenceley
Craige Spencer
Keith Spencer
Allen W Squires
Colin G Squires
Matt Squires
Roy Squires
Angela Staley
John Stanton
Tom Steers
Laura Stevens
Richard Stewart
Terry Stewart
Tony Stewart
David Lee Stockdale
Carol & Melvyn Storey
Phillip Storey
Colin Stride
Keith Stride
John Stubbings
Ann Styring
Bev Sugden
Ann Swallow
Terry Swift
Martin Sykes
Adele Taft
Margaret Talbot
Ashley Taylor
Dave Taylor
Ian David Taylor
John Taylor
Mick Taylor
Paul Michael Taylor
Roger Taylor
Roy Taylor
Shaun Taylor
Chris Teather
Mick Teather
Helen Thickett
Charlotte Thomas
John Thomas
Mark Thomas

Steve Thomas
Adam Thompson
Howard Thompson
Ian Thompson
Noreen Thompson
Richard N.A. Thompson
Zee Thompson
David Thornhill
Lauren Thorpe
Barry Thurman
Curtis Tilt
Daniel Tinsley
Nick Tinsley
Cath & John Todd
Michael Todd
Sam Todd
Richard Tong
Denise Tracey
Richard Trehern
Stephen Tucker
Elizabeth Tunnard
Phillip Tunnard
John Turner
Joshua Turner
Eric Twigg
Lisa Twigg
Matthew Twigg
Robert Underwood
Tim Unsworth
Amy Unwin
Ray Uttley
James Valentine
Kyle Vassell
Andrew Vaughan
Hugh Vaughan
Ian Vaughan
Geoff Vause
Josh Vickers
Andy Vickery
Stephen Wadsley
Jayne & Leah Wagstaff
Ian D. Wainwright
Peter Wainwright
David Walker
Joseph Walker
Steve Walker
Nigel Waller
Glynn Wallhead
Alan Wallis
Anita Walsh
Michael Walsh
Vicky Walters
Chris Ward
Jenny Warne
Paul Warne
Andy Warrington
Kay Wassell
Margaret Watkinson
Martin Webb
Andrew West
Martin Wharin
Teala White
David Whitehouse
Chris Whittaker
Julie Whittam
Jason Wick
Annemarie Wicks
Richard Wigfield
Christopher Wild
Michelle Wild
Mike Wild
Ben Wiles
Andy Wilkes
David Wilkes
Hazel Wilkinson
Ian Wilkinson
Andrew Williams
Connor Williams
David & Joan Williams
Gwyneth & Mick Williams
Julia Williams
Mark Williams
Nat Williams
Russell Williams
Keith Williamson
Neil Wilson
Keith Winfindale
Barbara Winter
Mark Winter
John Winterbottom
Chris Wisken
Maurice Wolstenholme
Andrew Wood
Jonathan Wood
Richard Wood
Adam Woodland
James Woodland
Sophia Woodland
Gail Woods
Terry Workman
Christopher Martin Worrall
Ian Wortley
Alan Wright
David Wright
Emyrs Wright
Michael Wroe
Philip Yeardley
Matthew Young

ABOUT THE AUTHORS

John Breckin comes from a lifelong family of Rotherham United fans. His Uncle Eddie played for Rotherham County, his parents supported the Millers and John was first taken to Millmoor when he was only five, signing for the club as an apprentice professional in 1968. His total of 467 appearances leaves him third highest on the club's all-time list and his roles over the years with the Millers include: young fan, apprentice professional, full time professional, youth team captain, reserve team captain, first team captain, youth development head, youth coach, reserve team manager, caretaker manager, assistant manager, matchday hospitality host, club consultant, Millers iFollow commentary summariser, honorary Life President and veteran fan. John lives at Wickersley with his partner Gill. He has a daughter, Jess, and a large collection of Rotherham United programmes which includes one from every game he played in.

By coincidence, Les Payne's professional association with the Millers began at the same time as John. After three years in the steel-works at English Steel Corporation at Brightside, Les went to the *Rotherham Advertiser* in May 1968 as a junior reporter and fulfilled a childhood ambition of becoming a football reporter! He covered his first Rotherham United game in February 1969 and his last one at Wembley in 2014, the League One play-off final success against Leyton Orient. He was *The Advertiser*'s sports editor before moving as a sports writer at the *Sheffield Star and Green 'Un* in December 1989, spending 25 years as their Millers correspondent. Les is from Rawmarsh but now lives at Kim-berworth – in sight of both Millmoor and the New York Stadium – and has a son, Ross, daughters Olivia and Lauren and a granddaughter Alexa. He has a grandson due in 2021 and will ensure, like the rest of the family, he supports the Millers.